Salt Spring Island Cooking

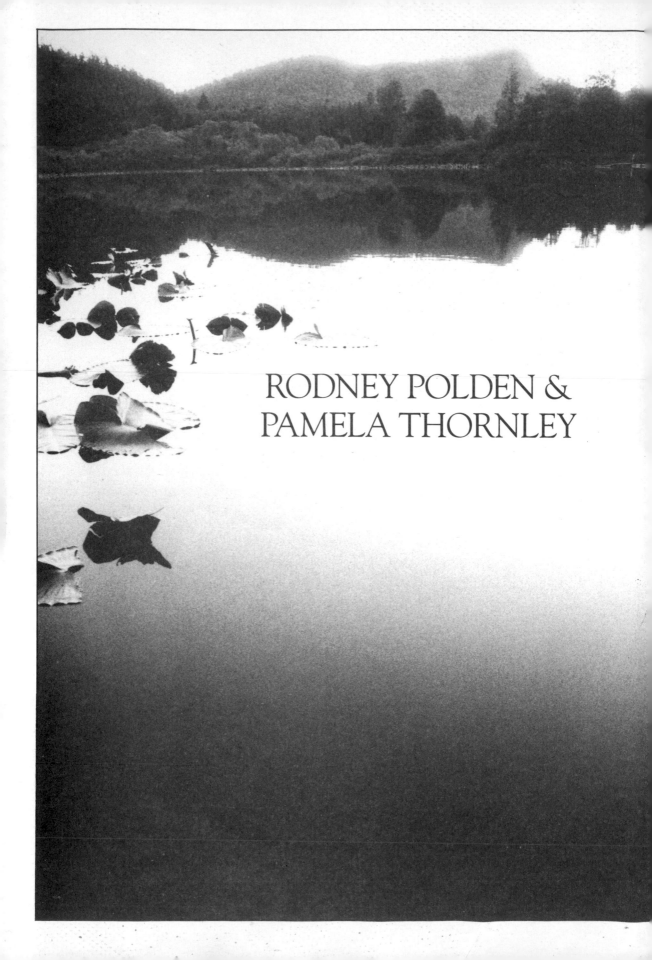

RODNEY POLDEN &
PAMELA THORNLEY

Salt Spring Island Cooking

Vegetarian Recipes from

The Salt Spring Centre

Macmillan Canada
Toronto

SALT SPRING ISLAND COOKING
Vegetarian Recipes from the Salt Spring Centre
Copyright © 1993 by Dharma Sara Satsang Society
Photographs © 1993 by Rodney Polden

Canadian Cataloguing in Publication Data

Polden, Rodney, *1948-*

Salt Spring Island Cooking : vegetarian recipes from the Salt Spring Centre

Includes index.

ISBN 0-7715-9194-2

1. Cookery, Vegetarian. I. Thornley, Pamela, *1946-* . II. Salt Spring Centre for the Creative and Healing Arts. III. Title.

TX837.P65 1993   641.5'636   C93-093001-0

2   3   4   5 MIL 97   96   95   94

Text research & development: Shirley Brown, Sid Filkow, Rodney Polden,
Ed Thornburgh and Pamela Thornley
Recipe testing: Shirley Brown, Rodney Polden, Ed Thornburgh and Pamela Thornley
Recipe testing co-ordinator: Sharada Filkow
Line drawings & calligraphy: Usha Rautenbach, Ed Thornburgh and Pamela Thornley
Mandalas: Rodney Polden and Usha Rautenbach
Design, typography and layout: Rodney Polden, Usha Rautenbach and Pamela Thornley
Photography: Rodney Polden
Cover design: Tania Craan
Front cover illustration: Laura Fernandez
Back cover illustration: Pamela Thornley and Amita Curran

Spike is a registered trademark of Modern Products, Milwaukee, Wisconsin.
Inka is a registered trademark of Krakus, Agros, Warsaw, Poland, imported by Dalimpex, Montreal.
Big Mac is a registered trademark of McDonald's Restaurants of Canada Ltd.
Diet Coke is a registered trademark of Coca-Cola Ltd., Don Mills, Ontario.

Macmillan Canada wishes to thank the Canada Council and the Ontario Ministry of Culture and Communications for supporting its publishing program. The authors wish to thank Employment and Immigration Canada for assistance in the initial stages of the project.

This book was prepared by members and friends of the Salt Spring Centre community. For further information about the activities, retreats and weekend programs of the Salt Spring Centre, please write to us at:
The Salt Spring Centre, Box 1133, Ganges, B.C., Canada, V0S 1E0,
or telephone 604-537 2326

Macmillan Canada
A Division of Canada Publishing Corporation
Toronto, Ontario, Canada

Printed in Canada

for Babaji,
with our love

Acknowledgments

This book came into being through the dedication and perseverance of a team, some of whom are residents of the Salt Spring Centre and some members of the larger community who live nearby. In addition to all those helping hands, our grateful appreciation is further due to the following friends,

for additional recipes:
Bhavani, Cinder, Ginger, Hamsa, Janaki, Julie, Maïcha, Mark, Pam, Rineke, Rajani, Sazjo, Supriti and Tangachee.

for computers, laser prints and the courage to put hands to keyboards:
Uri Cogan and Tim Collins of Tribal Drum Communications
(when the chips were down, you always came through for us)

for technical assistance with a smile, and help and guidance all along the way:
Per Rasmussen, Sheri Nielson

for invaluable advice on publishing:
Roger Coster, Marlynn Horsdal, Vic Marks, David Robinson, Gordon Soules

for photocopying, far beyond the call of duty:
Diane and Jane at KIS Office Services

for veggies and the world's widest range of beans:
Dan Jason and Zama

for the drawing of a humming-bird and morning glory:
John Beder

for help in getting the project off the ground:
Kathleen Williams of Employment and Immigration Canada

for unflagging care and attention to detail:
Denise Schon, Susan Girvan and friends at Macmillan Canada

and in recognition of extraordinary patience, support and goodwill,
our particular thanks go to our loved ones, and to the family of
the Salt Spring Centre.

Table of Contents

Worldfood... 69

Grains & Beans... 99

Vegetables... 111

Salads & Dressings... 125

Salads & Dressings, continued

Savoury Sauces... 143

Dips & Spreads... 159

Desserts & Sweet Sauces... 173

Desserts & Sweet Sauces continued....

Bread... 213

Quickbreads & Muffins... 233

Quickbreads & Muffins, continued....

Kids' Food... 247

Fast Food... 259

Drinks... 267

Introduction

Soft light filtered into the room through a huge stained-glass window, dappling the deep gloss of old fir flooring with patches of ruby, of straw yellows and leaf green. Wood panelling around the walls, mounted heads of moose and elk, and the stillness of an old house, empty but for dust, memories and a rich atmosphere. From the mullioned windows, lawns and meadows stretched over the valley bottom to the creek that runs to Blackburn Lake, and beyond, the forested slopes and mountains of Salt Spring Island. As a light wind blew down the valley, a rusted sign proclaiming 'Galleon Manor' creaked on its stanchion below the moss-covered shingles of a turret roof. Up the worn treads of a narrow stairway to the top floor, where cobwebs hung like lace at the windows.

Wherever we explored through the empty rooms, reminders of the many faces that the house had shown to the world emerged from the patina of time — once a pioneer family's grand interpretation of the Scottish manse, then working farm, chapel, school, hostel, museum.

And now...? "D'you think this could be the place?"

We had looked for so long, so many properties, so many days of travel, trips around the Lower Mainland of British Columbia, to the Interior, ferries to Vancouver Island. We always knew that somewhere..... somewhere, the place was waiting for us; we needed only the perseverance to keep looking till it appeared, keeping clear our vision of what would work, what would accommodate us all. And between the field trips to explore possible properties in all these backwaters, we met through afternoons and evenings of talk, negotiation, clarification of our individual goals, dreams and aspirations.

For ourselves, our children, our future.

"Buy land", our teacher and spiritual friend, Baba Hari Dass, had suggested to us in the first years that we had come together as a group of yoga students. It was land that would give us a focus, a base to practice our skills of co-operation together as a community; an opportunity to put our abilities and our energy together in service to the larger community around us.

So we hunted for our land. Among the Gulf Islands between Vancouver and Victoria, in a quiet wooded valley, we found it.

The owners had lived on the property as a family home, and had loved it for
its beauty and serenity for years. Now they were ready to move,
and we were the happy beneficiaries.

We had our work cut out.
As years rolled by, we cleaned and painted, cleared and planted,
built workshops and a school;
grew organic gardens for vegetables and herbs, flowers and fruit;
established a health collective to offer healing and relaxation programs;
taught evening classes in art, music, drama and dance,
in yoga and meditation.
And as those years roll by, we become a family together, sharing the work
and the play, raising our children, healing each other's hurts and celebrating
each other's joys.
It's not what we expected — it's much more than that.

We thought once that we would all live together, but the reality is a broader
community than that original idea.
While a number of us live full-time as residents of the Salt Spring Centre,
many of us live in our own homes nearby, up and down the valley,
elsewhere on the island, and in Vancouver too.

Uniting us all is our work together;
for, though we work hard, it is in some way also our play.
As we work together, whether cooking meals for a weekend program,
weeding the gardens, supervising school recess, planning staff schedules,
even typing a cookbook introduction, we are working also on ourselves:
a day-by-day path of self-discovery by creative endeavour.

We share a lot — most of us are children of a certain time,
but from the four-year-olds to the fifty-year-olds,
music, food, volleyball and zany humour over the dinner dishwashing seem
to sustain us all.

The guests who come to join us for weekend programs at the Centre
pick up on that energy among us very often.
Some return again and again, becoming familiar faces and joining us over
the dinner dishes themselves, because they found that after the massage and
the walk by the creek and the dinner, they just didn't seem to feel as
exhausted any longer as they were
when they left the city on Friday evening.
Some send their workmates to unwind here,
to try a little taste of another way of living, and find out what it is that keeps
them hopping onto that Gulf Island ferry.
In itself, that's a reward for us —

to see the faces that arrived at the beginning of the weekend,
a little tense from a job and a life that is full, sometimes just too full;
and to see some of that strain fall away, over the course of the weekend,
uncovering a lightness and a calmness that previously
had so little opportunity to surface. It shows.
When a little peace and renewal bubbles up in one of our guests,
that is to us a really fine reward for our efforts and our caring.

For our cooks, a really fine reward for
their work at chopping-board, mixing-bowl and stove,
comes when one or another guest
asks if there might be a second helping of that dessert,
and could they please have the recipe for the enchiladas.

After a time however, it came to be that we were writing out longhand, with
kitchen pencil stub on backs of envelopes,
so many recipes for soups, entrées, dressings and desserts,
that we just had to find a better way.....
Et voilà! We can lightly skip over the intervening two and a half years of
testing, tasting, tantrums and full tummies,
and proudly present to you our hopefully not-too-imperfect result.
This book brings to you
food from the Centre,
with our very sincere wishes for the health and happiness of yourself, your
family, and sentient beings everywhere.

And why vegetarian?
At the heart of what we are trying to do together, there is
an implicit goal of non-harming:
a principle that has been expressed in every religion, creed and
philosophy in one form or another, and sometimes stated as,
"Do to others as you would wish them to do to you".
For myself, I have been vegetarian for twenty years,
as is the case of many others here at the Centre.
We have found from long experience that we can live very satisfactorily,
in excellent health and clarity, without the need to take the lives of animals
for food. Since we can supply all the necessary nutrients —
vitamins, minerals, proteins and carbohydrates — from a diet of grains,
vegetables, fruits, nuts and (for some of us) milk,
this is for us a preferable path.
We hope that as you try out the recipes in this book,
you will come to discover, as we have,
that giving up eating meat is no more of a hardship
than giving up falling over was,
when you first learnt to walk.

ngredients

Most ingredients mentioned in this book will be familiar to readers but a small number may need some introduction or explanation, and hence the following:

AGAR AGAR A tasteless seaweed used as a jelling agent instead of gelatin, a slaughterhouse product. Its unique ability to absorb moisture makes agar agar beneficial to the digestive tract, supplying bulk and lubrication.

ARROWROOT FLOUR Arrowroot is so called because native Central Americans used the powdered root to absorb the poison from poison-arrow wounds. An easily digested starch often used in babyfoods and convalescent diets. Arrowroot is used for last-minute thickening when the cook wants a clear sauce with no floury aftertaste.

BAKING POWDER Combination of baking soda and cream of tartar which react together when in the presence of a liquid. The carbon dioxide produced by this reaction rises through the batter in tiny bubbles, causing the batter to swell.

BAKING SODA Used as a leavening agent in recipes containing acid ingredients — sour milk, buttermilk, molasses, honey or spices — which it neutralizes. Many recipes call for baking soda *and* baking powder.

BARLEY MALT A natural sweetener made from sprouted barley.

BREADCRUMBS Use bread that is at least a day old. Toasting slices lightly in the oven greatly assists crumbling by hand, or you can use your grater. Bread crumbs can be made for some recipes by soaking bread in water and then squeezing out excess liquid.

BROWN SUGAR Refined beet or cane sugar with molasses colouring. Sugar quickly enters the bloodstream, producing the infamous "sugar rush." Turbinado (hard to find these days) is raw, cleaned cane sugar.

BUCKWHEAT Also known as Kasha. See Grains Section, page 100. Buckwheat is a really warming grain, which makes it great for winter meals.

CAROB Believed by some to be the "manna from heaven" mentioned in the Bible. It is also called St. John's Bread. Carob powder is rich in vitamin B and minerals, low in fats. Although it is often used as a chocolate substitute, it has its own unique taste, allowing it to "stand alone" as a flavour.

EGG-REPLACER Mixture of potato starch, tapioca flour, baking-powder and methyl-cellulose. One teaspoon of egg replacer plus two tablespoons water replaces one egg in recipes, though check the instructions on the packet, since some brands vary. It can be beaten stiff, just like egg whites.

ENGEVITA YEAST A tasty condiment and seasoning, rich in Vitamin B. See also YEASTS below.

FETA CHEESE An unripened, soft, white Greek cheese that is pickled in brine or occasionally packed in olive oil.

GHEE Also known as clarified butter. For a simple method of preparation, see page 79.

GOMASIO A seasoning made from sesame seeds ground with sea salt. Sometimes ground dulse or kelp is also added.

HONEY Honey is the world's oldest sweetener. It enters our systems in a much less aggressive fashion than sucrose, needing to be assimilated and broken down by the digestive process before entering the blood stream. In baking, honey gives a moistness to cakes and cookies because it doesn't harden or crystallize during cooling. Honey contains many minerals, enzymes and some B vitamins, when unpasteurized. Store honey in a warm, dry place — it will last for years. When it hardens, just heat gently over hot water to soften it once again. Try to avoid letting raw honey get warmer than blood-heat, since over-heating, apart from destroying the beneficial enzymes, also causes it to lose flavour and fragrance and become darker.

LECITHIN An emulsifier and anti-oxidant used in baked goods, ice cream, etc. Keeps oil and water from separating. Liquid lecithin works well for greasing cookie sheets and loaf pans.

MAPLE SYRUP A sweet syrup made from the sap of the sugar maple tree. It takes 35 gallons of sap to make one gallon of syrup. Expensive, but much superior to corn syrup.

MASA HARINA For tortillas, a finely ground cornflour which has been treated with lime.

MISO Miso is made by fermenting soybeans with sea salt and rice, wheat, barley or other grains, over some two or three years. The beneficial micro-organisms which aid digestion are destroyed by boiling temperatures, so miso should always be added at the **end** of cooking. At Hiroshima in 1945, scientists discovered that those Japanese who had eaten a traditional daily breakfast of miso soup showed considerable immunity to radiation-sickness from fallout, a fact worth remembering.

MOLASSES The pungent, thick, dark syrup left over from sugar processing. Molasses contains all the minerals leached out of the sugar during refining. Blackstrap is the purest type of molasses and therefore has the most minerals. It also has the strongest flavour. (The city of Chicago suffered in the Great Molasses Flood of the late 19th century, but please don't be put off this excellent source of iron just because of that!)

NON-INSTANT MILK POWDER Retains far more of the nutrient value of milk than the instant. Available as skim and whole milk powders.

NORI A dried seaweed (Porphyra Tenera) which has been harvested in Japan for hundreds of years. It is a major foodstuff for the Japanese, who eat over 9 billion sheets of Nori each year. It can be toasted, crumpled and eaten as a snack or used to wrap steamed rice (sushi).

OILS Oils are pressed from a variety of seeds, nuts, fruits and wheat germ, and are sometimes blended. Cold pressed oils are from the very first pressing. Further pressings use solvents or heat to squeeze every tiny drop of oil from the source. By this time, it is quite viscous and needs refining, bleaching, deodorizing and watering down. All oils have a different smoking point — safflower, corn and soybean oils will smoke at a lower temperature than peanut or sesame. Using half oil, half butter can work well in many recipes.

OLIVE OIL A mono-unsaturated oil pressed or extracted by solvents from olives, retaining some of their unique flavour. The finest olive oil has only 1% acid and is from the first cold pressing of olives. It is sometimes referred to as "virgin olive oil." It is a **must** for good salad dressings, and is further recommended for having a very low cholesterol content. Pomace oil is a lower grade.

RICOTTA A cultured cheese similar to cottage cheese, but with a quite distinctive flavour.

SPIKE Spike is a commercial vegetable seasoning made from herbs and spices. There are many such preparations on the market; we use this one.

TAHINI A paste made from ground sesame seeds and their oil — much like a nut butter. Tahini goes rancid very quickly after opening, so refrigerate it immediately; better yet, make your own: grind sesame seeds with just enough sesame oil to make a paste.

TAMARI A dark, salty sauce that is a by-product of the fermentation of miso. Tamari has the same beneficial qualities as miso, but not to the same degree. Often used as a salt substitute, its character and benefits derive partly from a long fermentation period; soy sauce, its cheaper cousin, is an "instant" processed food.

TEMPEH Made from fermented soybeans, tempeh is available from healthfood stores as tasty little burgers and cutlets.

TOFU Invented in 164 B.C. by a Chinese scholar, who curdled and pressed the "milk" of cooked soybeans. High in protein, low in calories, fats and carbohydrates, and zero cholestrol.

VINEGAR (French: vin aigre — sour wine) Pungent acidic solution of fermented wine, apple cider or other substances. Vinegar results when bacteria convert the alcohol in wine or cider into acetic acid. Many kinds of delicate herb vinegars can be made by placing leafy twigs of rosemary, oregano and/or tarragon in tall glass jars full of vinegar, and standing them on a sunny windowsill for a month or two.

WASABI Powdered horseradish. Traditionally mixed with a little water and served with sushi. It's available in most specialty shops, or horseradish can be substituted. Be warned — it is potent!

WHEAT GERM The wheat seed's embryo, wheat germ is a gem of protein, minerals and vitamins. It should be stored airtight in the refrigerator; it goes rancid quickly and the process has already begun by the time the product reaches the store. Buy it from a refrigerated display, if possible, or find out when the next fresh shipment is expected. Rancid wheat germ has a decidedly bitter taste that is no enhancement to a recipe.

YEASTS (NUTRITIONAL) Vitamin B-rich yeasts without any leavening power. Engevita is grown on molasses; Brewer's is grown on hops and Torula on wood pulp. Reports indicate there is no significant nutritional difference, but there *is* a taste difference: many find Engevita's flavour almost addictive when sprinkled on grains, vegetables, etc.

YOGHURT Milk cultured by bacteria. Yoghurt is a Turkish word, but yoghurt itself dates back to the mists of antiquity. A very valuable food, it ensures a healthy population of micro-flora in the digestive tract. Fresh home-made yoghurt rivals any you can buy, and it's very simple to make.

Herbs & Spices

CARE AND FEEDING OF HERBS AND SPICES: Generally speaking, it would be good if all our herbs could be refrigerated, and all our spices could be bought whole, and ground as needed. Many of them contain volatile oils which are quickly lost if ground and stored at room temperature. Light also affects flavour. If possible, store herbs in an airtight container in a dark place. Buy from a reputable dealer, and don't buy too much at once. Those herbs or spices which lose flavour more quickly than others have been noted below in the comments. Unless otherwise mentioned, our recipes use dried herbs.

ALLSPICE Actually a distinct species, this berry receives its name from its resemblance to a combination of cinnamon, cloves and nutmeg. Used in baking pies and cakes. Allspice can be bought whole, but is most often purchased ready-ground with little flavour loss.

ANISE Anise is native to Egypt, and the ancient Egyptians and Romans used it in medicines and in ceremonial cakes. Because of its licorice flavour, anise seed is used as a flavouring for teas (and a benefit to digestion), for cookies, cakes and rolls. The seeds are best crushed before use, to release their full aroma.

BASIL Who would even think to make a tomato sauce without basil? Native to India, this annual herb has a distinctive, almost licorice scent, said to "taketh away sorrow." In some countries it was used as a test of chastity — it was supposed to wither in the hands of the impure (or those with hot, sweaty palms). It can be used fresh in pesto sauce, salads and as a garnish for cooked vegetables, and of course it is well known for its love affair with tomatoes. Because of its short growing season where we live, most of us are confined to using basil as a dried and crushed herb. Basil should be added at the beginning of cooking, so that its flavour may develop slowly.

BAY LEAF The Greeks attributed magical powers to the bay laurel tree, and crowned their athletes, poets and warriors with it. Because it's difficult to grow, even in the greenhouse, bay is usually purchased dried. Used to flavour soups and stews, bay leaves must be used sparingly and at the beginning of cooking. Scoop them out before serving, unless you want to make a game of "find the bay leaf." An unusual use for bay leaf is to add it to rice as it cooks for rice pudding.

BORAGE This little-used herb is quite hardy and will self-seed, lending blue flower accents to your garden for years to come. Leaves and flowers have the taste of fresh cucumber, making them a welcome addition to salads. Leaves can also be added to bean and pea soups. Borage is often used as an iced tea drink, with a little honey and lemon added.

CARAWAY SEEDS *Caraway* comes from the ancient Arabic *karawiya*. These pungent little seeds have been found in excavated Mesolithic hearths, indicating their use for over 5000 years. They are used in rye breads, tea cakes and, surprisingly, with cabbage and cauliflower. Caraway-seed tea is an aid to digestion.

CARDAMOM Because of its particular growing requirements, this relative of the ginger family is difficult to cultivate — and that makes it expensive. Cardamom's sweet, hard seed is available whole or ground. It has a lovely aroma and enhances the flavours of apples, pears, coffee cakes and beverages.

CAYENNE Cayenne is actually ground red cayenne pepper and it must be used with caution. Even a fat pinch of cayenne can prove to be incendiary. Avoid touching your eyes, nose and mouth after handling cayenne, or be prepared for some extremely uncomfortable results. Use it in chilis, curries, or to relieve a sore throat: just a pinch in hot lemon and honey.

CELERY SEED Celery seed comes to us from the wild celery plant, smallage, which was coaxed into cultivation by Italian gardeners many years ago. It has a very strong flavour and should be used sparingly in soups, salads and coleslaws: $1/2$ teaspoon to 4 cups of salad is fine.

CHERVIL A native of the Middle East and Russia, it has a delicate hint of anise. It makes a welcome addition to soups and salads, in which it can be used liberally because of its mild flavour. Chervil may also be sprinkled over carrots, peas and other cooked vegetables. Fresh chervil has much more flavour to it than the dried version.

CHILI These fiery little red peppers were unknown to Europe until 1494, when mentioned by Chanca, physician to Columbus, in his documentation of the West Indies. They are ground to make a hot pepper sauce. Chili powder combines ground red

chilis, cumin, garlic, oregano and other herbs, and is less intense than its parent.

CHIVES These tender onion-flavoured leaves are a boon in salads, cheeses, herb butters, cream sauces and soups. They can be dried or freeze-dried, but not frozen (they turn to slime). Chives and their cousin, garlic chives, make a pleasant addition to the herb garden, with their blue powder-puff flowers. Incidentally, those flowers make an ordinary salad take life when scattered casually over the top — and they are edible too! Chive bulbs may be pickled in white wine vinegar.

CINNAMON Cinnamon is actually the bark of the cinnamon tree, peeled and dried. Its history can be traced back to Biblical times, and it is native to Sri Lanka. It is available in stick or ground form. Cinnamon is one of the most evocative smells we know, whisking one immediately back to childhood kitchens. It is used in baking, fruit desserts, and Eastern cooking. Cinnamon sticks make great stirrers for hot drinks such as mulled wine and hot apple juice. Kids love to chew them.

CLOVES The dried flower buds of the clove tree may be purchased ground or whole. Cloves were first mentioned in the writings of the Han dynasty, 266 B.C. to 220 A.D. A clove held in the mouth before approaching the Emperor was considered *de rigueur*, to guard against bad breath. By the fourth century, cloves were widely used throughout Europe, even though until the 1800's the only source for cloves was five small islands, the Moluccas Proper in Indonesia. A clove-studded leek or onion works wonders in soups, stews and in rice as it boils. Use powdered in curries and baking.

CILANTRO Cilantro (Chinese Parsley) is the leaf of the coriander plant. It differs greatly from coriander and can't be substituted for coriander. Cilantro is used in sauces and as a salad garnish. If unavailable, a mixture of fresh parsley and a little chives makes an admirable substitute.

CORIANDER Whole coriander seeds are an essential in Middle Eastern cooking — they are best husked, which is a pain, but the pungent odor is worth it. The name *coriander* comes from the Latin *Koris*, bed-bug, as the growing plant smells of that insect. It has been cultivated for over 3000 years and is mentioned in Christian Scriptures, Ancient Greek and Sanskrit writings, and Early Egyptian papyrus writings. Ground coriander is an ingredient in curry powder. It is also used to flavour coffee, chutneys and cookies.

CUMIN Cumin, another member of the parsley family, is indigenous to the upper Nile and has been with us for some time — it was mentioned by the prophet Isaiah. Though widely used in Europe during the Middle Ages, it has lost favour over the last 300 years. This pungent spice is used in curries and to enliven grain dishes. It's best freshly ground, since it loses flavour soon after, unless kept refrigerated and tightly sealed.

CURRY POWDER A blend of various spices, depending on the manufacturer. Common spice combinations are coriander, cumin, fenugreek, cayenne, turmeric, ginger, cardamom, cinnamon and cloves. Don't restrict curry powder to curries: try it in sauces, dips and spreads.

DILL The word *Dill* is thought to come from the Saxon *dillan*, meaning to lull, for its seeds were used to coax babies to sleep. The feathery dillweed is a favourite herb among the cooks in our kitchen. Its comforting flavour is used in soups, sour cream sauces, mustard spreads,

entrées, dips and spreads. It goes well with green beans, cucumber, beet salad. Dill's flavour dissipates with long cooking, so add dillweed towards the end of your cooking time. The seed may also be used. The dried herb loses its flavour if not tightly sealed and preferably refrigerated.

FENNEL Regarded as a symbol of success in ancient Greece. A member of the parsley family with a nice licorice flavour, fennel has been used in cooking for over 2000 years, and special varieties have been developed to produce bulbous roots, thick stems or pretty foliage. It should be used sparingly or it will make food taste bitter. Fresh fennel makes a fascinating addition to salads. The seeds are sometimes used as an ingredient in curries, and as a breath sweetener and aid to digestion after a heavy meal.

FENUGREEK Fenugreek is basically a fodder crop, introduced to Europe by Benedictine monks during the ninth century. It has long been a favourite in the Middle East, where Egyptians roast the seeds for coffee and eat the leaves as a fresh green. Fenugreek seed is a curry ingredient, and makes tangy sprouts, too. The fresh leaves may also be added to curry as it cooks, giving a strong celery flavour.

GARAM MASALA A masala means a mixture of herbs and spices for curry. A simple garam masala might be, say, garlic, green cardamom seeds, cumin seeds and cinnamon, mixed in varying proportions. A standard mixture is sold at spice counters. Add garam masala to subjis, soups and raitas.

GARLIC This aggressive, pungent bulb has been both revered and despised for eons. We use it sparingly because, according to Ayurvedic medicine, garlic is a fine medicinal herb but, as with onion, it stimulates the mind, thereby hindering the yogic goal of stilling or quieting the thought processes during meditation. It enhances soups and stews if used whole and then removed before serving. Recent research suggests it has a valuable role in strengthening the immune system.

ELEPHANT GARLIC is a less assertive relative, making its presence known more and more on the West Coast. It is a member of the leek family.

Peeling garlic can be a tedious chore, so here's a method that simplifies the process: crush the garlic clove on a chopping board with a heavy knife handle; the skin will readily separate.

By the way, *never* scorch or burn garlic — it tastes just awful.

GINGER   You may buy this hot, tropical spice two ways: the fresh root, and the dried and ground stem. Fresh ginger root keeps indefinitely if frozen (you can still grate it). Ginger is used to give heat to soups, stews, curries and stir-fries, and imparts a certain friendliness to baked goods. Simmer sliced root ginger, add lemon juice and honey, and you have a great soother for sore throats and colds.

HING (Asafoetida)   Sometimes used as a garlic substitute — it has some of the same pungent qualities, but is actually a strongly flavoured brownish gum. It is used in small quantities as a condiment in East Indian cooking, and in Worcestershire Sauce. Used by Arabian physicians since the Middle Ages, as well as in 13th century Wales, it is now rarely used in the West. The Asafoetida plant is native to Persia and Afghanistan.

MARJORAM (Sweet Marjoram)   This wonderfully aromatic and compact bush will last many years in your herb garden. Marjoram was introduced into Europe from North Africa or India in the Middle Ages. It can easily be confused with its near relative, oregano, though it is much less assertive. Use marjoram in spaghetti sauces and rice dishes. This herb is one of those that must be added to a dish towards the end of the cooking time, or else you will find its flavour has dissipated.

MINT   There are many members of the mint family: applemint, peppermint, spearmint and pennyroyal, to name but a few. Mints are well known for refreshing teas, but their fresh leaves also make a good addition to green salads, fruit salads, carrots, peas, lemonade, potatoes, and tabouleh.

MUSTARD   These seeds, white or black, are used in curries and Eastern dishes, first roasted until they pop. The powder is used in dressings and mayonnaise sauces. Mustard seeds can also be sprouted for a nice hot little salad treat.

NUTMEG   The nutmeg seed, and its husk, mace, were in use by Indians and Arabs before the sixth century. They were believed to originate in the Spice Islands. To get the absolute best out of the spice, grind the nutmeg for each use — it contains a volatile oil that disappears a short time after grinding, leaving you with a brown, flavourless powder. Enhance cheese dishes, cream sauces, and vegetables with the happy flavour of fresh nutmeg.

OREGANO   Also called wild marjoram, oregano is native to Europe, Iran, the Middle East and the Himalayas. The southern variety is much more pungent than its northern counterpart. It was once used to flavour beer. Oregano should be bought in small quantities as it loses power quite quickly. Oregano is a must for spaghetti sauces, and is most compatible with tomatoes. Use it in salads, dressings and herb breads.

PANCH PURAN This mixture of spices is a favourite in dishes such as vegetable subjis. Store together the following whole spices in a jar, then grind as much as you need for the dish. Roast or fry briefly, and add the vegetables. Two parts of each of: cardamom seed, black mustard seed, anise seed, kalanji. (Kalanji is a spice available at many East Indian foodstores, and some healthfood stores.) One part of each of: fenugreek seed, bay leaves.

PARSLEY Parsley is such a pleasant experience that it deserves more attention than merely as a garnish. It complements other herbs and brings out their flavour. The flat Italian parsley is more flavourful than its curly cousin. Use parsley generously in tabouleh, soups, sauces, salads, dressings.

PEPPER Everyone is familiar with black peppercorns, but did you known they come in green, red and white as well? (White is actually black peppers with the outer covering removed.) Peppercorns were so valued they were used as rental payments in the Middle Ages. Try to use the whole peppercorns and grind them fresh with each use — ground pepper loses flavour quickly. Use whole peppercorns in soups and stews, or bruise them a little first, to release flavour. Too much pepper in a dish can result in quite a warming trend — it increases body temperature. Black pepper comes from Indonesia, South India, the West Indies, Brazil and China.

POPPY SEEDS These tiny little seeds (900,000 make up one pound!) stimulate the appetite. Use them in cakes, breads and pastry. For culinary purposes we use the seeds of the corn poppy (Flanders poppy). The rich red petals of this plant

have been used as a colouring agent since the 15th century.

ROSEMARY This delightful woody herb with its pale blue flowers grows wild on Mediterranean coasts, but can be tricky to grow in northern climates — it must be coddled along over winter. The results are well worth it. Rosemary is wonderfully aromatic — use it in soups, stews, biscuits, fruit salads, carrots, zucchini, pâtés, jams and jellies. Crush the leaves before strewing in your cooking — and err on the side of caution when using.

SAGE Sage has been cultivated for centuries, made into teas and ales, and used both medicinally and in cooking. It gets its name from the Old French word *saulje*, meaning good health. There are quite a few varieties of sage — the one with narrow leaves, pale grey-green in colour has the best flavour. Use it in stuffings and herb breads.

SAVORY Summer savory has a delicate, spicy flavour, and its relative, winter savory is stronger and more coarse. Savory has been used as a culinary herb for over 2000 years. Try chopping fresh leaves for salads, or in cheese spreads, tomato dishes and green beans.

SEA SALT Valued for thousands of years, salt was at one time worth more than gold. Wages were paid partly in salt, giving us *salary*. It is the world's oldest preservative. There is always an argument regarding how much salt is appropriate — some cooks feel insulted if their cooking is salted at the table — but people's palates differ widely regarding saltiness. Sea salt contains trace minerals as well as iodine.

SESAME SEEDS The word *sesame* can be traced back to the early Egyptian *semsemt*, a word mentioned on a papyrus around 1800 B.C. These seeds are wonderful additions to grain dishes and salads. Roast them for a few minutes to release their nutty flavour. We use the very fine grade sesame oil for massage as well as for cooking, and the paste (tahini) as a sandwich spread and ingredient in hummus.

TARRAGON Highly prized French Tarragon can be very difficult to find and grow for the herb garden, so if you do find a plant, cherish it, for the flavour is superior to Russian Tarragon. The Latin name *Artemisia* comes from the Greek goddess of the hunt, Artemis (the Roman Diana). Tarragon has a delicate, sophisticated flavour that will overpower other flavours if used indiscriminately. It marries well with dill, and it works with almost any other dish — sauces, vegetables such as asparagus, mushrooms and celery, salad dressings, entrées, soups...

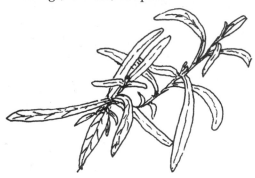

....and, oh yes, tarragon vinegar is a must for salad lovers.

THYME There are over fifty different species of thyme, but only three are considered culinary herbs. Thyme has always been associated with strength and happiness. In the Middle Ages it was a symbol of courage and was sewn into knights' clothing. Thyme will make a strong comment in your cooking, so go carefully. Use it with tomato stews, carrots, potatoes, herb cheese and stuffings.

TURMERIC Once widely used throughout Europe and the Middle East, turmeric fell into disuse during the Middle Ages. It yields a fine and intense yellow dye (as anyone who has spilt curry on their tablecloth will tell you) and it may be used, sparingly, as a food colourant as well. Turmeric is the dried, powdered root of yet another member of the ginger family, used in curries, pickles and prepared mustards. Although it appears not to be strongly flavoured, too much turmeric can ruin a dish.

VANILLA The vanilla bean, a native of Central America, was introduced to Europe in the early part of the sixteenth century. Chocolate manufacturers in France used vanilla as a flavour, and curiously enough, it was also used to flavour tobacco. Mexican vanilla is less expensive than regular vanilla. Nowadays vanilla turns up as an extract, usually with a base of alcohol, in many baked goods, drinks and confections.

Techniques, Equipment and Utensils

If you have been cooking for a while, then no doubt this glossary will contain familiar terms, but if you are not so proficient, this section may yield a few good hints for you. It's also an opportunity for us to define our terms, and make sure that we are speaking the same language.

AL DENTE Italian? Quite so. When pasta is perfectly cooked, it should be soft but still have just a tiny degree of solidity at its core, that can be felt as you bite through it, hence *al dente* — to the tooth.

BAKE To cook using dry heat in an enclosed space, such as an oven. This is an easy, painless way to cook vegetables. It works best for high-moisture root vegetables, such as potatoes and yams, and also squash. (Squash will take ages unless halved or quartered.) Remember to prick or slash the vegetables' skins first, otherwise they may explode. Baking works well if you are cooking a casserole or loaf at the same time, because everything can go into the oven for the same time (1 hour at medium heat for most potatoes) and you can sit down and finish reading *War and Peace* in peace.

BOIL "Liquid heated until large bubbles rise quickly to the surface and burst thereupon." When boiling vegetables, bring a small amount of water to the boil before adding them, then bring the water back to a boil. Simmer until tendercrisp (unless you are making mashed potatoes or yams). Don't overcook. Whenever possible, include the vegetable water into the food you are preparing, or save it for use as soup stock, since it contains many soluble vitamins, etc.

DEEP FRY Cook in hot oil deep enough to cover the pieces of food.

DICE Cut into small cubes, enabling food to cook more quickly.

DREDGE Lightly coat with a dry mixture, usually of a flour or crumb base.

DRYING GREENS When you are faced with drying a lot of salad greens, perhaps for a party, pop them into a clean pillowcase and run them through your washing machine's spin cycle. Sounds a bit brutal, but it works. Please remember though — **spin**, not wash.

FRY Cook in a small amount of fat over direct heat.

PURÉE From the French — purified, without unevenness. At one time, this meant to strain out all the impurities (lumps, bones...) leaving just a thick liquid. In this book, we usually mean to blend until quite smooth.

SAUTÉ From French — to jump! Quickly searing the food in a small amount of oil, butter and/or ghee over high heat. The pan and oil are heated first, then sliced vegetables are added and continually stirred. We generally use this term to refer to the initial quick cooking that seals the outside surface of the vegetable.

SCALD Fine for tomatoes, but please don't do it to your respected self. It's the quickest way to peel skin from tomatoes: cover them with boiling water for a few minutes and the skins will almost fall off, helped if necessary by a sharp knife.

If you should get a **minor** scald or burn while cooking, don't wait for even a moment. Get the burn area under clean cold water to cool it and get it out of the air, then it won't need to hurt much at all.

STEAM Cooking foods by suspending them over boiling water in a covered pot. Steamers come in a variety of forms — the expanding, metal "flower" type, double-boiler steamers and stackable bamboo-type baskets (These baskets are really versatile: the first box contains the longest-to-steam food; the more delicate get the top box.) When steaming vegetables together, start with the tough stuff (roots) first, then add the tenderer vegetables.

STIR-FRY Frying in butter or oil over high heat. Heat your pan or wok first, then add the oil, tipping the pan to spread the oil evenly. Add the ingredients and stir to coat with oil, then cook until tendercrisp. As with steaming, start with the roots and stem vegetables, then add their softer companions. When nearly tender, add a tiny bit of water (or tamari if you prefer), quickly cover and leave them alone for 5 minutes.

TENDERCRISP To coax the best flavour and nutrition from vegetables, cook them until they are just barely tender, but still retain their crispness.

TOAST Forget about marmalade —we're talking dry-roasting here. Many spices and some grains are much enhanced in flavour if they are briefly roasted over high heat in a dry pot or pan (not too long, and keep stirring, or they'll burn). Cumin, for instance, releases very little of its distinctive strength, aroma and pungency until it is toasted or fried.

That gives you a quick tour around the Ways and Means department, so now it's time for all the hard stuff...

Equipment & Utensils

"...WITH ALL APPLIANCES AND MEANS TO BOOT"
SHAKESPEARE: *HENRY IV*, ACT III

ALUMINUM PANS At the Salt Spring Centre, we try to avoid using pans of this metal for a couple of reasons. Since it is a relatively soft metal, a certain amount of it ends up in your food each time you cook, particularly if there is an acid ingredient. Even boiling water in an aluminum pan is enough to leach some of it into the water. The body has no need of aluminum in your food, whereas the iron that leaches into foods cooked in a cast-iron pan, for example, has a beneficial effect, since it is usable by the system. We mostly use steel, stainless steel, and cast iron cookware. Aluminum has the further drawback of being an environmentally-unfriendly substance, since it is enormously wasteful of energy in its production.

BLENDER Let's not say that machines are indispensable in the kitchen;. they are noisy, sometimes harmful, yet undeniably **quick**. Decide for yourself, but at least once in a while give yourself the satisfaction of doing it by hand — that's how body and mind stay fit. Some tasks do call (quite loudly!) for a blender or grinder, but there's much you can do with a fork, whisk, sharp knife, wooden spoon, or pestle and mortar, most of which you will be needing anyway. Work carefully if you choose to use machines, and please make sure they are well maintained — many of us have small scars from some close encounter with a "time-saver."

CHOPPING BOARD Wooden ones are fine, but get one big enough to work comfortably upon. There are also some good high-density white nylon ones available that are easy to keep clean, won't blunt your knife and don't warp when wet. Among the wooden ones, we favour a thinner (hence lighter) board which makes it easy to pick up to transfer vegetables directly into a wok.

COMPOST Every kitchen should have one — the pail, that is, not the actual heap. If you are a city-dweller and have nowhere for a compost heap, see if you can interest your local government or recycling society in starting a composting project. To many of us, composting is the key to a saner relationship with our world, our soil and our food.

FIRST AID KIT Waterproof dressings, some gentle antiseptic, comfrey ointment and your kitchen windowsill aloe vera plant (the latter both for burns) all make good friends to have in the near vicinity while you cook. We hope that the food you prepare from our recipes won't itself necessitate any first aid, but do let us know, should anything nasty happen.

FLAME-TAMER Also called a pot protector. Handy for placing underneath a simmering pot so food doesn't burn.

FOOD PROCESSOR See BLENDER above. You may or may not prefer your food processed! They do some wonderful things, and make great doorstops once they are broken or obsolete. But on the plus side, certain tasks of preparing food quickly for a large number of people *can* be facilitated by a well chosen food-processor. For small tasks, though, the clean-up takes longer than doing it by hand.

HEAVY SKILLET How many recipes include this item in the first line of the method? Find yourself a solid one, big enough for a tortilla or chapati, and make friends with it — you'll burn far less food.

KNIVES Use one you're comfortable with, and keep it sharp. A few strokes on a stone every other time you use it, and you can slice anything, without slicing you. The rectangular Japanese vegetable knife of carbon steel is superb for its balance and the edge it will hold. The whole business of cooking gets easier when the knife is sharp.

NON-STICK Steel pans and woks can be just about as non-stick as anything else, if you temper the pan first. Heat it for a short while in a moderate oven, rub vegetable oil over it, heat again for 20 minutes, re-oil, re-heat as before. The oil will be cooked into the surface, and now the pan need only be wiped clean with water (no soap) and a soft brush after each use. If the pan loses its 'non-stick' or gets burnt, just clean it thoroughly with soap and scouring, then re-temper once again by the same method.

OIL DRAINER Not always easy to find, but a much better way to deal with deep-fried food than paper towels. It fits on the side of the pan, and the inclined surface holds all the just-fried burgers etc. while the oil drains back into the pan. An alternative would be a plate set on a slope, where the food can drain briefly before going to the oven to keep warm.

OVEN THERMOMETER If you don't own one, it's worthwhile at least to borrow one to check the accuracy of your oven's settings.

PAPER PRODUCTS It takes 17 tons of trees to make 1 ton of paper. We all want our kids' kids to have trees to walk among, but the world's forests are disappearing by the hundreds of acres per minute. Meanwhile our garbage bins and dumps are overflowing. There's nothing you can do with paper products that you can't do another way — our grandmothers managed fine. So many of our problems, as well as our delights, begin in the kitchen. Let's find a better way.

PESTLE & MORTAR An easy, no-fuss way to crumble, crush or just bruise herbs and spices to release their flavour.

PLASTIC WRAP Most of the functions of plastic wrap can be handled by re-usable or recyclable containers, e.g. yoghurt pots; plastic bags slit open, with a rubber band to hold them in place; a saucepan or wok lid to cover large plates of food between preparation and mealtime. These alternatives are almost always available, free, and don't result in a garbage problem either.

SHARPENING STONE There are half as many ways to sharpen, as there are cooks. (The other half just never sharpens.) This is one way: a flat sharpening stone, a few drops of light mineral oil, and gentle, even strokes at around a 10° angle between blade and stone, alternating sides of the blade. For further help, ask a woodworking friend who has sharp chisels to show you how, or else read the instructions in *Tassajara Cooking* or a similar text, (see Bibliography).

SLOTTED SPOON A useful tool for all kinds of purposes, but particularly for fishing things out of things — a frequent task in haute cuisine.

SPATULA   If you can find a spatula made of spring-steel rather than the usual stiff ones, hang on to it. They are so much easier for manoeuvring food in and out of a frying pan, that you'll wonder why anyone ever made them any other way.

WOK   You will find whole cookbooks devoted to this estimable pan. A great many techniques are possible with just a wok, from steamed and stir-fried to bagels and bulk yoghurt, so on a tight budget, here's a good place to start equipping your first-time kitchen for vegetarian cooking.

WOODEN SPOON One indispensable item. A metal spoon will scratch your pans and wreck their coating, and if it's an aluminum pan, a metal spoon will offer up tiny particles of metal in your food as well. Wooden spoons are a whole lot more eater-friendly.

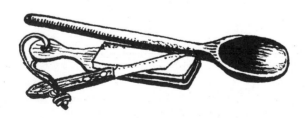

Breakfast

"The critical period in matrimony is breakfast time."
Sir A. P. Herbert: *Uncommon Law* 1935

After a night's rest, the digestive system is at its peak. Breaking the fast should raise the blood sugar level to provide energy for the day, and supply up to one third of the necessary daily nutrient requirements. Breads, cereals, fruits and vegetables provide food energy to get you going, and fibre for dietary bulk. Proteins take longer to digest, giving the slow-release energy to keep you up and running through the rest of the day.

It is an accepted fact that breakfast eaters have better concentration than those who gulp a cup of coffee and call it breakfast. They are less prone to accidents, headaches and irritability — all of which are reactions to hunger. People who start their day with a wholesome meal won't feel the need to snack to keep up their energy, and are less likely to overeat later in the day. They won't have to compensate for the empty feeling that occurs when breakfast is overlooked.

For those with no time in the mornings, smoothies will give all of the required nutrients, and a "pick-up breakfast" of a muffin, some fruit and a glass of milk (or milk substitute) can also fill the bill. Prepare cooked dishes the night before so they are ready after a quick reheat in the morning, or consider one of our overnight breakfasts.

Don't feel restricted by what has become accepted breakfast fare. The specific foods you eat are not as important as their nutritional value. If you prefer savoury foods, why not try pizza for breakfast, a bowl of last night's soup with bread, or a slice of leftover bean loaf on a sourdough muffin?

Change your approach to breakfast by combining different cooked grains to create new flavours, or add fruit (fresh or dried) while the grains are cooking for a naturally sweet cereal. Serve cooked and dry cereals with fruit juice instead of milk or milk substitutes. Replace the standard glass of fruit juice with a piece of fresh fruit.

Here are just a few menu suggestions to get you going:

muffin and fruit smoothie
slice of cornbread, piece of cheese and glass of juice
dish of oatmeal topped with fruit slices and glass of carob milk
bowl of granola topped with yoghurt and orange sections
Sid Sandwich (page 264), glass of nut milk and raw vegetable sticks
pizza muffin with a glass of juice

Apple Rings

A simple treat for breakfast. Serves two small breakfasters.

¹/₂ cup	(120 mL)	whole-wheat pastry flour
¹/₂ tsp	(2 mL)	cinnamon
2 tsp	(10 mL)	maple syrup
6 Tbsp	(90 mL)	milk, soymilk, or water
1		apple, peeled, cored, and sliced into rings
		ghee or butter for frying

Mix the flour, cinnamon, syrup, and liquid
to make a batter.
Dip the apple slices into the batter
to coat well.
Fry the slices until they are golden brown, then turn them
over and fry again until you see that familiar tawny colour
on the other side. Serve warm.

Tofu French Toast

An eggless, but protein-rich, twist to an old recipe.
Yields 3 pieces of french toast.

¹/₄ lb	(114 g)	tofu
¹/₄ cup	(60 mL)	liquid (milk, cashew or millet milk, or water)
		salt & pepper to taste
		a pinch of turmeric for colour
3		slices whole-wheat bread
		ghee or butter (for frying)

In a blender, mix the tofu, milk, salt, pepper and turmeric.
Pour the batter into a shallow dish.
Dip both sides of each slice of bread in the batter to coat them.
Fry in ghee or butter until golden brown.

Delicious with Blueberry Sauce (page 209).

Apple Muesli

This variation on the original Bircher Benner muesli makes a healthy and satisfying start to your day. Combining fibre and fruit, it gently works to keep your system regular.

Makes one serving.

1 heaping Tbsp	(20 mL)	oatmeal
¼ cup	(60 mL)	water
		juice of ½ lemon
1 Tbsp	(15 mL)	honey
1 Tbsp	(15 mL)	cream
1		large apple, grated
1 Tbsp	(15 mL)	wheat germ

IN THE EVENING:
Stir together the oatmeal, water and lemon juice. Let soak overnight.

THE NEXT MORNING:
Stir the honey and cream into the oatmeal mixture.
Add the grated apple and wheat germ.
Serve and enjoy.

Variations:
Add almonds, walnuts, sunflower seeds or coconut.
Toasted buckwheat kernels give a nutty taste, too.

For a hot breakfast on winter mornings, simply boil the quarter cup of water and pour it over all the other ingredients. Serve immediately.

OATS: "A GRAIN WHICH IN ENGLAND IS GENERALLY GIVEN TO HORSES,
BUT IN SCOTLAND SUPPORTS THE PEOPLE."
DR. SAMUEL JOHNSON (1709-1784)

Crockpot Fruited Barley

A nutritious, naturally sweet breakfast that cooks while you sleep. Add the fruit when you rise and the meal will be ready when you are!

Serves 6 - 8.

1 cup	(240 mL)	**pearl barley**
6 cups	(1.4 L)	**water**
2 cups	(480 mL)	**dried mixed fruit**
1 cup	(240 mL)	**chopped almonds** (optional)
1 cup	(240 mL)	**raisins**
½ tsp	(2 mL)	**coriander** (optional)
½ tsp	(2 mL)	**sea salt** (optional)

THE NIGHT BEFORE:

Preheat your electric crockpot to HIGH.
Place barley and half the water in a separate pot and bring to a boil.
Pour the hot barley/water mixture and remaining water into the crockpot
   and adjust the setting to LOW.
Cover and let it cook all night.
Finely chop the dried fruit, in preparation for the morning.
Toast the almonds in a dry pan over medium heat or on a baking sheet in a
   350°F (180°C) oven for 8 - 10 minutes.
Measure the rest of the ingredients and set them all aside.

IN THE MORNING:

Stir the fruit, raisins, coriander and salt into the crockpot and let it cook for
   15 minutes more.
Serve in individual dishes with almonds sprinkled on top.

*For those of us without crockpots, parboiling the barley and dried fruit before
transferring them to a wide-mouthed vacuum flask for the night achieves a similar
result.*

"GIVE ME BARLEY MEAL AND WATER, AND I WILL RIVAL JOVE HIMSELF IN HAPPINESS."
EPICURUS

Overnight Breakfast

A great breakfast for those who are too sleepy or perhaps too frenzied to prepare morning meals.

Makes 4 servings.

2¹/₂ cups	(600 mL)	rolled oats
2		medium-sized bananas
3 cups	(720 mL)	fruit juice
¹/₂ tsp	(2 mL)	sea salt
¹/₂ tsp	(2 mL)	vanilla
2 tsp	(10 mL)	maple syrup
¹/₂ cup	(120 mL)	raisins
2 cups	(480 mL)	diced fresh fruit
¹/₂ cup	(120 mL)	chopped almonds

IN THE EVENING:

Toast the rolled oats in a dry pan over medium heat, or toast them on a baking sheet for 10 minutes at 300°F (155°C). Stir the oats occasionally to keep them from burning.

Mash the bananas in a large bowl, and stir in the juice, sea salt, vanilla and maple syrup.

Add the raisins and toasted oats and stir until evenly mixed.

Cover the bowl and refrigerate overnight.

THE NEXT MORNING:

Dish up the oat mixture into individual serving bowls.

Dice the fresh fruit and divide evenly among the bowls.

Top with a sprinkle of chopped almonds and serve to your bleary-eyed breakfast companions.

Variations:
Fruit juices — apple, orange, white grape, pineapple.
Fresh fruit — apples, grape halves, peaches, pears.
Use your imagination, because there are many possibilities.

On cold days, this makes a hearty and warming breakfast
when heated for about 10 minutes over medium heat.

Granola

We know there are many granola recipes, but our guests and staff have found this one almost addictive — try it!

Makes close to 10 cups.

6 cups	(1.4 L)	small-flake rolled oats
1 cup	(240 mL)	sunflower seeds
1 cup	(240 mL)	chopped almonds
1/2 cup	(120 mL)	cashews
1 1/3 cups	(320 mL)	unsweetened grated coconut
1/2 cup	(120 mL)	oil
1/3 cup	(80 mL)	sesame seeds
3/4 cup	(180 mL)	liquid honey
1 cup	(240 mL)	raisins
1/2 cup	(120 mL)	chopped dates

In a large bowl, mix everything except the raisins, dates and oil.

Stir the granola constantly, while slowly adding first the oil and then the honey, to evenly cover the ingredients. If your honey is hard, heat it in a double boiler or add a little water and heat it gently — but please don't let it get too hot. The melted honey will blend more easily with the other ingredients.

Bake the entire quantity at 400°F (205°C) for 10 minutes, spread evenly (about 3/4 in. or 2 cm) in a lightly oiled baking tray or cookie sheet, then stir the granola thoroughly.

Continue baking for a further 15 minutes, stirring every 5 minutes, until it is golden brown.

Remove from the oven and stir in the raisins and dates. Crumble any large lumps of granola, then allow it to cool, before storing it in an airtight container.

Some milk, maybe some yoghurt, over a bowl of these nuggety little morsels and your day will unfold in ecstasy. Though we cannot actually promise this, it's not to be entirely ruled out either.

Scrambled Tofu

Serves 4 to 6 people.

1 lb	(454 g)	**tofu**
2 Tbsp	(30 mL)	**oil**
¹/₂ cup	(120 mL)	**chopped leeks**
¹/₂ cup	(120 mL)	**chopped celery**
¹/₄ cup	(60 mL)	**slivered almonds** (optional)
1 cup	(240 mL)	**sliced mushrooms** (optional)
2 tsp	(10 mL)	**tamari**
1 Tbsp	(15 mL)	**parsley**
¹/₄ tsp	(1 mL)	**sage**
¹/₄ tsp	(1 mL)	**turmeric**
		a pinch of marjoram
¹/₄ tsp	(1 mL)	**black pepper**
¹/₂ tsp	(2 mL)	**sea salt**
1 Tbsp	(15 mL)	**whole-wheat flour**

Drain the tofu in a strainer, pressing it gently to release the water, then mash it and set it aside.

Sauté the leeks, celery and almonds in oil, until the vegetables begin to soften and the almonds are slightly browned.

Add the remaining ingredients except the whole-wheat flour. Continue cooking and stirring until the mushrooms are softened and the spices are well mixed.

Sprinkle the flour over the mixture and stir until the vegetables are coated and any liquid has thickened.

Stir in the tofu, and cook over low heat for 10 to 15 minutes more.

For a breakfast that will set you up for the day, serve with
toast, pancakes, or baked beans.

For a light lunch, dress your serving plate with spinach or lettuce greens, and
mound the scrambled tofu in the middle. Garnish with fresh parsley and serve with
Crispy Fried Tomatoes (page 120)
and Scarborough Fair Biscuits (page 242).

This is also an excellent addition to the list of possible toppings for a
Sid Sandwich (page 264).

"HOPE IS A GOOD BREAKFAST, BUT IT IS A BAD SUPPER."
FRANCIS BACON: *APOTHEGMS*, 36.
(1561-1626)

Corn Hotcakes

Makes more than a dozen pancakes.

1 cup	(240 mL)	**milk, soymilk or millet milk**
1 tsp	(5 mL)	**honey** (optional)
1½ cups	(360 mL)	**cornmeal**
1 tsp	(5 mL)	**oil**
½ tsp	(2 mL)	**sea salt**
½ tsp	(2 mL)	**baking powder**
14 oz tin	(398 mL)	**creamed corn***

Scald the milk (the soy or millet milk only needs to be heated gently), and stir in the honey.

Pour the mixture into a medium-sized bowl and add the remaining ingredients.

Mix well and spoon onto an oiled griddle over medium heat.

Cook until bubbles come to the surface, then turn the hotcakes over to cook the other side until golden in colour.

Serve with applesauce, Blueberry Sauce (page 209), or maple syrup.

* And if you are using fresh or frozen corn:

1 cup	(240 mL)	**fresh or frozen corn**
2 Tbsp	(30 mL)	**cashews**
¾ cup	(180 mL)	**hot water**

Put the cashews, water and half of the corn into a blender and purée.

Stir the mixture into the pancake batter along with the rest of the corn.

"THE AGRICULTURAL POPULATION, SAYS CATO, PRODUCES... A CLASS OF CITIZENS THE LEAST GIVEN OF ALL TO EVIL DESIGNS."
PLINY THE ELDER: *NATURAL HISTORY BOOK VIII.*

Even when there is very little time for breakfast in your day, there is usually time at least for...

Good Morning, My Love !

Serves one or two recently awakened bodies.

1		**banana**
³/₄ cup	(180 mL)	**milk or plain yoghurt**
2-5 Tbsp	(30-75mL)	**wheatgerm***
¹/₄ cup	(60 mL)	**orange juice**
1 Tbsp	(15 mL)	**lemon juice**
1 Tbsp	(15 mL)	**honey**

Cut the banana in pieces, and blend it with all the other ingredients until smooth.

Experiment for yourself with ingredients like those above, and dried fruit, fresh fruit and nut milks too.

*Buy wheatgerm from a refrigerated display, if possible, and keep it refrigerated. It will quickly become bitter if kept at room temperature.

There are a million great smoothies — this has been one of them.

Soups

"JE VIS DE BONNE SOUPE ET NON
DE BEAU LANGAGE."
MOLIÈRE: *LES FEMMES SAVANTES*, ACT II, VII*

When I was first learning to cook for a family, I visited my neighbour, Leilani, mother of six, and a genius at making meals out of thin air. Leilani was just finishing cleaning and cutting vegetables for the evening meal. Onion skins, vegetable tops, bottoms, peelings, were in a plastic pail beside her. Knowing my eagerness to learn this fine art of cooking, she pointed at what I thought was the slop bucket and asked: "Know what that is?" "Garbage? Compost?" I replied hopefully. "Soup stock", she responded, with a slight note of disdain. And from that humble beginning, I learned that a good soup depends on good stock.

The soups we present to you here will stand on their own merits if made with water. But if you use your own vegetable stock ... ah! What a difference! With this in mind, keep a stock pot going on the back burner and toss in tops and bottoms of celery, potatoes, carrots, parsnips, leeks, and the skins of onion and garlic, if you use them. Stay away from brassicas — cabbage, broccoli, brussel sprouts — since they are so strongly flavoured that they will dominate all else, unless that's what you have in mind, of course. (They also smell quite foul if left for more than a few hours.) Let the stock pot putter away over low heat for an hour or so, strain it, bottle it and then freeze it or refrigerate it, until you are ready to make soup.

Our soups can be a full meal all by themselves, a delicate precursor to a main meal, or a light arpeggio on a hot day. Use them as bases for your own experiments, too!

*TRANS: "IT'S GOOD SOUP AND NOT FINE WORDS THAT KEEP ME ALIVE."

Bean Soup

A rich, hearty soup that is an all-time favourite at the Centre.

Serves 8 - 10 people.

1 cup	(240 mL)	**dry kidney beans**
1 cup	(240 mL)	**dry pinto beans**
1 cup	(240 mL)	**dry lima beans**
		(this makes 6 cups of cooked beans)
2 cups	(480 mL)	**chopped leeks**
¼ cup	(60 mL)	**olive oil**
2 cups	(480 mL)	**chopped celery**
2 cups	(480 mL)	**chopped carrots**

*(For variety, try green peppers or zucchini
to replace all or part of the celery and
carrots.)*

5 cups	(1.2 L)	**water**
1-28 oz	(796 mL)	**can whole tomatoes**
	2	**bay leaves**
1 tsp	(5 mL)	**salt**
1 tsp	(5 mL)	**pepper**
1½ tsp	(7 mL)	**basil**
1 tsp	(5 mL)	**oregano**
½ tsp	(2 mL)	**thyme**
1 tsp	(5 mL)	**chili powder**
1 Tbsp	(15 mL)	**dill weed**
2 Tbsp	(30 mL)	**butter**

Before cooking the beans, please refer to the Beans section (page 102).
Put the cooked beans in a large soup pot.
In a skillet, sauté the leeks, celery and carrots in the oil until the leeks are
   brightly coloured and a little soft.
Transfer them into the bean pot.
Add the rest of the ingredients except the dill and butter. Bring the soup to
   a boil and then simmer over medium heat for 20 minutes.
Add the dill and butter, then simmer for 10 minutes longer.

*Serve with slabs of hearty bread, and if your guests have any room,
follow with a green salad.*

hickpea Basil Soup

This is a fairly light soup that can be played with, as we have done. Have fun!

Makes 6 cups.

1 cup	(240 mL)	**dry garbanzo beans**
	1	**bay leaf**
1 cup	(240 mL)	**coarsely chopped leeks**
1 Tbsp	(15 mL)	**oil**
1 cup	(240 mL)	**chopped celery**
1 tsp	(5 mL)	**sea salt**
1 tsp	(5 mL)	**basil**
	1	**medium-sized potato, diced**

Soak the beans for two days in enough water to cover, until they begin to sprout.

Drain the beans and put them in a pot with enough fresh water to cover. Add the bay leaf, bring to the boil and simmer, covered for one hour.

In a separate pan, sauté the leeks and celery in oil until tender, then add them to the beans together with the salt and basil and potato.

If you think soup should be eaten with a fork, add a scant cup of water. If you prefer your soup thinner, add enough water or stock to get the desired consistency.

Simmer the soup for a quarter of an hour or so, until the potatoes are soft.

Serve as is, or consider one of our variations.

Dressed Up to Go to Town
A sophisticated first course.
For each cup of soup add: ¹/₂ tsp (2 mL) **dillweed,** ¹/₂ tsp (2 mL) **tarragon and 1 Tbsp (15 mL) (or less) dry red wine.**

Garbanzos Go Eastern
Ideal for any exotic occasion or a cold day.
For this version the soup should be quite thick. For each cup of soup add: ¹/₂ tsp (2 mL) **cinnamon, a pinch of ground cloves and a small handful of currants (about 1 Tbsp - 15 mL).**

Corn Chowder

Here you have the Salt Spring Centre answer to that great maritime favourite, clam chowder. The cashew milk imparts a wonderfully creamy texture to this soup.

Serves 8 to 10 people.

6 Tbsp	(90 mL)	**olive oil or butter**
2 cups	(480 mL)	**chopped leeks**
3 cups	(720 mL)	**diced potatoes**
6 cups	(1.4 L)	**water**
6 cups	(1.4 L)	**corn** (1 large package frozen corn)
1 cup	(240 mL)	**minced fresh parsley**
1½ tsp	(7 mL)	**sea salt**
½ tsp	(2 mL)	**pepper**
1 tsp	(5 mL)	**dillweed**
1 tsp	(5 mL)	**tarragon**
1 cup	(240 mL)	**cashew milk** (see page 270)

In your largest pot, sauté the leeks in olive oil or butter.
Add the potatoes and sauté for a few minutes longer.
Add the water and bring to a boil, then simmer until the potatoes are soft.
Add the corn, parsley and herbs. Continue cooking for 10 minutes.
Blend part of the soup and return it to the pot, or with a hand-held blender, blend the soup directly in the pot.
Add the cashew milk and serve as soon as the chowder is heated through.

It would seem strange to partake of these soups without a good-sized wedge of crusty bread and a dollop of butter. Perhaps it can be done if the soup, such as this one, is considered complementary to the main course. You be the judge.

Originally, maize was cultivated in the American Southwest and in Mexico thirty-five hundred years ago, but it was only one to two inches long, a far cry from today's succulent yellow giants. Nonetheless, its rich mineral and protein content helped the Indians of that time to build the most advanced culture in North America.

Cream of Broccoli Soup

An elegant and satisfying soup that is nevertheless happy to accept slightly old and stalky broccoli into its green and creamy heart. Garden-fresh is obviously preferable, but...

Makes about 7 cups.

7 cups	(1.7 L)	**coarsely chopped broccoli**
1¹/₂ tsp	(7 mL)	**sea salt**
2		**bay leaves**
		water to cover
²/₃ cup	(160 mL)	**chopped leeks**
2 Tbsp	(30 mL)	**butter or ghee**
1 cup	(240 mL)	**light cream***
¹/₄ tsp	(1 mL)	**nutmeg**
¹/₄ tsp	(1 mL)	**black pepper**
¹/₄ tsp	(1 mL)	**ground rosemary** (optional)

Cook the broccoli and bay leaves in enough salted water to cover, until tender.

Sauté the leeks in butter or ghee until soft.

Drain the broccoli and reserve the liquid. Discard the bay leaves.

Blend the leeks and broccoli with 2¹/₂ cups of the liquid until all is smooth. If you do not have this much liquid left from the broccoli, make it up with water. In a regular-size blender, you will probably need to blend all this in two or more batches — don't overfill it with nearly-boiling liquid, unless you were already planning on repainting your kitchen anyway.

Return the blended mixture to the saucepan, and add the remaining ingredients.

Heat very gently (do not allow it to boil).

Adjust the seasoning, and serve in bowls with lightly-toasted sesame seeds floating atop.

* For those who do not eat dairy products, this soup may be made with cashew milk instead.

"To be what we are,
and to become what we are capable of becoming,
is the only end of life."
Robert Louis Stevenson

Cumin Cauliflower Soup

A quick and easily prepared soup with an unusual flavour.

Serves 4.

2 cups	(480 mL)	**coarsely chopped cauliflower**
1 cup	(240 mL)	**coarsely chopped carrots**
1 cup	(240 mL)	**coarsely chopped leeks**
2 Tbsp	(30 mL)	**butter**
2 tsp	(10 mL)	**cumin seed**
2 cups	(480 mL)	**water or stock**
¼ tsp	(1 mL)	**black pepper** (or more, to taste)
1 ½ tsp	(7 mL)	**sea salt**

Steam the cauliflower and carrots until they are tender. Save the water from the steaming process and use as all or part of your stock.

Sauté the leeks in butter for a few minutes, then add cumin seeds and sauté for 1 minute more to bring out their flavour.

Transfer the ingredients to your blender or food processor (you may have to do this in two batches) and purée until smooth. Add a little stock to make the blending go more easily.

Now throw everything into your cooking pot. Add the remainder of the stock, and salt and pepper.

Heat **gently** for 15 minutes to enhance the flavours. This is a soup that does **not** improve with long cooking time.

Serve garnished with a sprig of parsley and a twist of lemon or orange.

"A HUNGRY STOMACH CANNOT HEAR."
J. DE LA FONTAINE *FABLES*

Epicurean Miso Soup

We delighted in taking this utilitarian, life-enhancing* soup and making it truly fit for a gourmet.

For 6 - 8 epicures.

2 cups	(480 mL)	thinly sliced carrots
1½ cups	(360 mL)	chopped leeks**
4 - 5 Tbsp	(60-75 mL)	oil
1 cup	(240 mL)	chopped celery
1½ Tbsp	(22 mL)	minced fresh ginger
¼ tsp	(1 mL)	cayenne
6 cups	(1.4 L)	vegetable stock or water
1 cup	(240 mL)	cooked millet or brown rice
6 Tbsp	(90 mL)	barley miso (more or less to taste)

optionally, you may add **either**:

½ tsp	(2 mL)	sea salt and
1 tsp	(5 mL)	garam masala and
1 Tbsp	(15 mL)	lemon juice...
	or	
1½ tsp	(7 mL)	dried tarragon...
	or	
1½ Tbsp	(22 mL)	finely chopped fresh tarragon

In a wok or large saucepan, sauté the carrots and leeks in oil for 4 to 5 minutes.

Add the celery, ginger and cayenne, and sauté for a further five minutes.

Add the stock and bring to a simmer. If you want a smooth homogenous soup, process three-quarters of it in a blender (best to leave some of it unblended for a little texture).

Return the soup to the wok and add the cooked grain, miso and any optional ingredients.

Heat gently for a few minutes (overheating will destroy the beneficial effects of miso) and serve hot.

Garnish with a sprinkling of paprika and a sprig of parsley.

Tarragon lends to this soup a touch of continental elegance. Garam masala produces a slightly hotter, more East Indian flavour.

**If you use garlic and onions, substitute ¾ cup (180 mL) chopped onion and 1 clove minced garlic.

*See miso in the Ingredients section (page 6).

harada's Mom's Gazpacho

A refreshing cold soup for a hot summer's day!

Makes 8 - 12 servings.

1 cup	**(240 mL)**	**finely chopped leeks**
2 cups	**(480 mL)**	**finely chopped tomatoes**
1¼ cups	**(300 mL)**	**finely chopped green peppers**
1 cup	**(240 mL)**	**finely chopped celery**
1 cup	**(240 mL)**	**finely chopped cucumber**
2 tsp	**(10 mL)**	**finely chopped chives**
1 Tbsp	**(15 mL)**	**finely chopped parsley**
1 tsp	**(5 mL)**	**freshly ground black pepper**
2 tsp	**(10 mL)**	**sea salt**
¼-½ tsp	**(1-2 mL)**	**Tabasco sauce**
1 tsp	**(5 mL)**	**Worcestershire* sauce**
½ cup	**(120 mL)**	**tarragon wine vinegar**
3 cups	**(720 mL)**	**tomato juice**

Combine all the ingredients in a large stainless steel or glass bowl.
Cover and chill for at least three hours (overnight if possible).
As an optional step, process half the soup in a blender for a smoother
texture.

**Worcestershire sauce often has anchovies in it, so check the ingredients on the
label before purchase. However, some brands omit the fishy additions without
detriment to taste, and you will no doubt be able to find such sauce in specialty
shops and, as they say, in better grocery stores everywhere.*

Potato Soup "Jerusalem"

A native plant of North America that was introduced to white settlers by Indians in the 17th century, the Jerusalem artichoke belongs to the sunflower family. It is appropriate for diabetics because of its less-complex carbohydrate content (stored as insulin rather than starch).

The flavour and texture of Jerusalem artichokes go very well with potatoes to make a slightly different potato soup. Jerusalem artichokes can vary a lot in flavour — ours are quite mild.

Serves 4 to 6.

about 2 cups	**(480 mL)**	**chopped potatoes (2 large ones)**
3 cups	**(720 mL)**	**water or vegetable stock**
1 cup	**(240 mL)**	**grated carrots** (optional)
1 cup	**(240 mL)**	**chopped celery**
3 Tbsp	**(45 mL)**	**olive oil**
4 cups	**(960 mL)**	**thinly sliced Jerusalem artichokes***
1 cup	**(240 mL)**	**finely chopped leeks**
1 Tbsp	**(15 mL)**	**grated fresh ginger OR**
³/₄ tsp	**(4 mL)**	**powdered ginger**
¹/₄ tsp	**(1 mL)**	**black pepper**
1 tsp	**(5 mL)**	**sea salt**
1 Tbsp	**(15 mL)**	**chopped parsley**
1 tsp	**(5 mL)**	**celery seed** (optional)

*Clean these knobby tubers with a stiff brush to remove the dirt — there's no need to peel them.

Wash, but do not peel, the potatoes. Cut them into ¹/₂ inch (1 cm) cubes.
Boil them in a large pot until they are just tender, and mash them
 in the pot.
Add the celery and the carrots (for colour).
In a heavy skillet, sauté the leeks and artichokes in olive oil for 3 - 5
 minutes.
Add the remaining ingredients and sauté for 2 minutes longer.
Add the mixture to the pot. Bring to a simmer, then turn off the heat and
 let the soup stand for an hour or more to develop the flavours.
Heat gently and serve. The vegetables should still have a little crispness
 left in them.

Garnish with chopped chives or green onion and a small pinch of paprika.

Salt Spring Centre Borscht

This makes a delicious, hearty soup that can serve a horde of people — or an even bigger horde if you give them small bowls.

Accompanied by a slice of crusty multigrain, rye or black bread, it becomes a meal of great substance and sustenance!

Serves 12 - 14.

½ cup	(120 mL)	vegetable oil
3 cups	(720 mL)	chopped leeks
8 cups	(1.9 L)	chopped beets
8 cups	(1.9 L)	chopped potatoes
8 cups	(1.9 L)	chopped cabbage
2 Tbsp	(30 mL)	honey
		juice of 3 medium lemons
1 tsp	(5 mL)	salt
1 tsp	(5 mL)	pepper
2 tsp	(10 mL)	dillweed
16 cups	(3.8 L)	water or soup stock

Select your largest cooking pot; add the oil and sauté the leeks, beets and potatoes in it for about 5 minutes. The cabbage can be sautéed too, or added later along with the other ingredients, since it has a shorter cooking time.

Add the honey, lemon juice, spices and liquid. Simmer, covered, for at least 30 minutes to allow the flavours to blend.

Garnish each serving with a dollop of yoghurt or sour cream, and a sprig of fennel or parsley, if you wish.

Salt Spring Centre Borscht - Family Size

Serves 4 - 6.

3 Tbsp	(45 mL)	vegetable oil
1 cup	(240 mL)	chopped leeks
2½ cups	(600 mL)	chopped beets
2½ cups	(600 mL)	chopped potatoes
2½ cups	(600 mL)	chopped cabbage
2 tsp	(10 mL)	honey
		juice of 1 lemon
½ tsp	(2 mL)	sea salt
¼ tsp	(1 mL)	black pepper
1 tsp	(5 mL)	dillweed
5 cups	(1.2 L)	water or soup stock

Method as for preceding recipe

Hot & Cold
Tomato Soup

Serve hot if the weather is frosty, or chill the soup and serve it cold during heatwaves. It's delicious either way.

The recipe makes 10 cups of soup, serving 10 to 12 people. The amounts may be halved for a family-sized quantity.

3 Tbsp	(45 mL)	olive oil
2 cups	(480 mL)	chopped leeks
2 Tbsp	(30 mL)	minced or grated ginger
2		cloves minced garlic (optional)
½ cup	(120 mL)	chopped lovage leaves
2 cups	(480 mL)	sliced carrots
2-28 oz	(796 mL)	cans tomatoes
1 tsp	(5 mL)	sea salt
		large pinch black pepper (to taste)

In a saucepan,
sauté the leeks and ginger (and garlic)
in oil, until the leeks are softened.
Add the tomatoes, lovage leaves, carrots, salt and pepper.
Simmer gently for 15 minutes,
stirring occasionally
to combine the tomatoes into the broth.

Basil and Lemon Lentil Soup

Although lentil soup is an old standby, this one has a surprisingly sophisticated appeal.

Serves 8 people.

3 Tbsp	(45 mL)	olive oil
1 cup	(240 mL)	chopped leeks
2 Tbsp	(30 mL)	basil
1 cup	(240 mL)	chopped celery
1/4 cup	(60 mL)	chopped parsnip
1 cup	(240 mL)	chopped carrots
2 cups	(480 mL)	crushed tomatoes
8 cups	(1.9 L)	water or stock
1		bay leaf
1 1/2 cups	(360 mL)	red lentils
2 1/4 tsp	(11 mL)	dill weed
1 tsp	(5 mL)	sea salt
1/2 tsp	(2 mL)	pepper
1/2 tsp	(2 mL)	lemon rind
		juice of 2 lemons

Select a large pot and sauté the leeks in olive oil until they are bright green and slightly soft.

Sauté the basil for 1 minute, along with leeks.

Add the remaining vegetables and sauté for a few minutes until they are brightly coloured.

Add the water or stock and bring to a boil.

Toss in the bay leaves.

Add the lentils and simmer for 30 minutes.

Add the salt, pepper, dill weed and lemon rind, and continue cooking for a further 30 minutes, or until the lentils are mushy.

Just before serving, stir in the lemon juice.

*Serve garnished with a slice or twist of lemon
and a sprinkling of chopped fresh parsley.*

"THEN JACOB GAVE ESAU BREAD AND POTTAGE OF LENTILS."
THE BIBLE
GENESIS CHAPTER 25

ushroom Soup

Functional fungi though they are, and subject of many a flight of fancy, mushrooms nonetheless have their own distinctive earthy flavour which we feel is successfully exploited in this recipe. The recipe can successfully be halved.

Makes 14 cups.

3 Tbsp	(45 mL)	**olive oil**
2 cups	(480 mL)	**chopped leeks**
3 cups	(720 mL)	**diced potatoes**
8 cups	(1.9 L)	**sliced mushrooms**
6 cups	(1.4 L)	**water or stock**
1 tsp	(5 mL)	**sea salt**
½ tsp	(2 mL)	**black pepper**
1½ tsp	(7 mL)	**tarragon**
2½ tsp	(12 mL)	**dill weed**
¼ cup	(60 mL)	**butter**
5 Tbsp	(75 mL)	**whole-wheat flour**
1 Tbsp	(15 mL)	**red wine** (optional)

In a good sized saucepan, sauté the leeks in olive oil.
Add the potatoes first, then the mushrooms and sauté a few minutes
  longer, stirring to keep the potatoes from sticking.
Add the water. Cover and cook until the potatoes are soft.
Stir in the salt, pepper, tarragon and dill weed.
Make a roux of the butter and flour. Stir it into the soup.
Add the wine (if using) at the end of the cooking time.

*Serve with your favourite open-faced sandwiches,
or try Sid Sandwiches on page 264.
A slice of mushroom floating on top looks rather charming.*

Non-Dairy Cream of Potato Cauliflower Soup

This is no ordinary creamed vegetable soup, believe me!

Serves 5 - 6 people.

2 Tbsp	(30 mL)	**olive oil**
1½ cups	(360 mL)	**finely chopped leeks**
4½ cups	(1.1 L)	**diced potatoes**
2½ cups	(600 mL)	**finely chopped cauliflower**
4½ cups	(1.1 L)	**water or stock**
1 cup	(240 mL)	**soy milk***
1		**bay leaf**
1 tsp	(5 mL)	**Spike or vegetable seasoning**
1½ Tbsp	(22 mL)	**tamari**
¼ tsp	(1 mL)	**black pepper**
1 tsp	(5 mL)	**basil**
1 tsp	(5 mL)	**tarragon**
1 tsp	(5 mL)	**dillweed**

In a large saucepan, sauté the leeks, potatoes and cauliflower in olive oil
until leeks are slightly soft.

Add the liquids and spices.

Simmer gently, covered, for about 30 minutes.

The soup may be blended after cooking, if you desire a creamier texture.

*Milk may be substituted for the soy milk, if you prefer a dairy cream
soup.

Garnish with a sprig of fresh dillweed, tarragon, or parsley.

"Of all the flowers in the garden,
I like the cauliflower."
Samuel Johnson
(1709-1784)

*P*ea Soup

A unique and delicious pea soup, that is slightly spicy. This recipe will size down nicely for 6 to 8 people, or you can make the large version and freeze half of it, if you are not serving it all at one sitting.

Serves 12 - 14.

2 cups	(480 mL)	green split peas
8 cups	(1.9 L)	vegetable stock or water
1/4 tsp	(1 mL)	salt
1 1/2 cups	(360 mL)	cubed potatoes
1/4 cup	(60 mL)	olive oil
1 cup	(240 mL)	finely chopped leeks
3/4 cup	(180 mL)	finely chopped carrots
3/4 cup	(180 mL)	finely chopped celery
1 tsp	(5 mL)	marjoram
1 1/2 tsp	(7 mL)	dillweed
1/2 tsp	(2 mL)	tarragon
1 1/2 Tbsp	(22 mL)	chopped fresh parsley
		pinch of cayenne pepper
1/4 tsp	(1 mL)	black pepper
1/4 tsp	(1 mL)	sea salt
3 1/2 Tbsp	(52 mL)	fresh lemon juice

In your largest pot, simmer the peas in salted water, covered, for about 30 minutes, stirring occasionally.

Add the cubed potatoes and simmer for 20 to 30 minutes more. The peas should be quite soft and beginning to break down.

Meanwhile, in a heavy skillet or wok, sauté the leeks, carrots, celery, herbs and spices in olive oil for about 5 minutes over medium heat, stirring frequently.

Add these sautéed ingredients plus the lemon juice into the soup pot and simmer for the last 10 minutes of cooking, until they are barely tender.

Turn the heat off under the soup pot, and let stand for at least one hour (preferably overnight in the fridge) to develop the flavours. Purée half of the soup in a blender if you wish, then return it to the pot. Serve hot, of course. Add more water only if you feel the soup is too thick.

Succulent Fresh Pea Soup

A quick and tastefully appealing pea soup that doesn't lose that fresh pea flavour.

Serves 4.

2¹/₂ cups	(600 mL)	water
2 cups	(480 mL)	fresh or frozen peas
1 Tbsp	(15 mL)	finely chopped leeks
¹/₂ tsp	(2 mL)	fresh mint
¹/₂ tsp	(2 mL)	sea salt
1¹/₂ cups	(360 mL)	additional water

Bring 1 cup (240 mL) of water to a boil.

Add the peas, bring the water to a boil again, and cook for two minutes.

Liquefy the peas with the cooking water in a blender.

Pour the soup back into the pot and gradually add the remaining water.

Stir in the leeks, mint and sea salt. Do not reheat the soup at this point, or use hot water rather than warm, because further cooking will destroy the fresh flavour of the peas.

Serve immediately, or chill it to serve on a hot summer's day.

Simply Squash Soup

Here's a sweet, delicate something you can do with all the winter squash you saved from the garden last autumn.

Serves 4 - 6.

2 cups	(480 mL)	coarsely chopped leeks
2 Tbsp	(30 mL)	butter
7 cups	(1.6 L)	coarsely chopped and peeled yellow squash
1 tsp	(5 mL)	salt
		water to cover

Sauté the leeks in butter in a large pot until softened.

Add the squash, salt and water.

Cook until the squash is tender.

Purée half of the soup and return it to the soup pot.

Mix, warm up if necessary, and serve.

ia's Greek Lentil Soup

*Inspired by the wonderful lentil soup
served at Periklis Restaurant in Victoria, this recipe
was the gift of Sia, their cook.*

2 cups	(480 mL)	**brown lentils**
3 cups	(720 mL)	**chopped leeks**
6		**bay leaves**
1 or 2		**cloves garlic, minced** (optional)
1½ tsp	(7 mL)	**oregano**
½ cup	(120 mL)	**olive oil**
10 cups	(2.4 L)	**water**
1 - 2 tsp	(5 - 10 mL)	**sea salt**
5 Tbsp	(75 mL)	**tomato paste**
1 Tbsp	(15 mL)	**vinegar**

Pick over the lentils and remove any tiny twigs or stones.

Wash the lentils, then place them in a large pan with the leeks, bay leaves,
   garlic (if using), oregano, oil and water.

Bring to the boil and simmer over low heat for about 2 hours.

Add the salt, tomato paste and vinegar, and serve.

*A blob of thick yoghurt or sour cream, and a few toasted sesame seeds scattered
over the surface make a very appealing garnish for this soup.*

GARLIC, LEEKS AND ONIONS:

At the Salt Spring Centre, we are blessed with both soil and climate that are conducive to growing leeks. We enjoy their mild, almost sweet flavour, and consequently use them in many recipes that might otherwise specify onions, garlic or both. You may find, however, that in other parts of the country leeks are sometimes either hard to obtain or discouragingly expensive. Please do not be deterred from any of our recipes on this account though, since in many cases mild onions may be substituted for the leeks by using (for example) three quarters of a medium, mild onion in place of one and a half cups (360 mL) chopped leeks. For more about garlic and onions, see pages 11 and 12.

Entrées

"KISSING DON'T LAST;
COOKERY DO!"
G. MEREDITH
ORDEAL OF RICHARD FEVEREL

These main meal suggestions are of a more generic nature than the exotica in the Worldfood section. They are meant to please, to nourish and make replete. These are good family meals, not too long in preparation for working parents, and not so complex that children cannot help.

We hope that your mealtimes, shared with family or with friends, are calm and loving times. Eat unhurriedly; discuss pleasantly; listen carefully; rest a little after your meal so that your poor body can digest for you without interruption.

Bean Burgers

Were you wondering what to do with some extra cooked beans? Put them to good use in this satisfying recipe, and become an instant success in your own home.

Makes 8 patties, ¹/₂" (12 mm) thick.

2 Tbsp	(30 mL)	chopped green onions
¹/₄ cup	(60 mL)	finely diced celery
3 Tbsp	(45 mL)	oil
1 cup	(240 mL)	cooked pinto beans, or other similar beans
1 cup	(240 mL)	cooked brown rice
1 cup	(240 mL)	ground sunflower seeds
¹/₂ cup	(120 mL)	grated cheese (or UnCheese, see recipe page 168)
¹/₄ cup	(60 mL)	whole wheat flour
2 tsp	(10 mL)	sweet pickle relish
2 Tbsp	(30 mL)	ketchup (see recipe page 147)
2 tsp	(10 mL)	tamari
		pinch of black pepper
¹/₂ tsp	(2 mL)	sea salt
¹/₂ tsp	(2 mL)	mustard powder
¹/₄ tsp	(1 mL)	oregano
¹/₂ tsp	(2 mL)	chili powder
		Engevita yeast to coat the patties

Sauté the green onions and celery in 1 Tbsp (15 mL) of the oil until tender.
Mash the beans in a large bowl, and stir in the rest of the ingredients.
Mix until well blended.
Shape the mixture into 8 patties, coat them with yeast, and fry them over medium heat in the remaining 2 Tbsp (30 mL) oil. They should be cooked slowly, and turned once only.
When they are well browned, remove them from the pan and serve with chili sauce, ketchup, sliced pickles, relishes, and big, big buns.

This recipe also works well as a loaf:
Place the mixture into a greased loaf tin and bake it for 40 minutes at 350°F (180°C).

Serve the burgers with Uma's Barbeque Sauce (page 155), for a piquant addition.

unflower Millet Burgers

*These burgers were **so good**, we had great difficulty keeping them away from wandering food testers (which included the cooks!)*

Makes about twelve 3 1/2" (9 cm) patties.

1 lb	(454 g)	tofu
1 cup	(240 mL)	sunflower seeds
1 cup	(240 mL)	cooked millet (about 1/3 cup dry)
1 cup	(240 mL)	grated carrots
1/2 cup	(120 mL)	finely chopped leeks
1 cup	(240 mL)	coarse breadcrumbs
1 Tbsp	(15 mL)	engevita yeast
2 Tbsp	(30 mL)	tamari
1 tsp	(5 mL)	thyme
1 tsp	(5 mL)	sage
1 1/2 tsp	(7 mL)	sea salt
1/2 tsp	(2 mL)	pepper
2 tsp	(10 mL)	dillweed
1 Tbsp	(15 mL)	freshly squeezed lemon juice
1/4 cup	(60 mL)	oil

Drain excess water from the block of tofu by squeezing it gently in a sieve or colander.

Toast the sunflower seeds and grind them coarsely.

Place all of the ingredients in a large bowl, and mash them together until they are well mixed.

Form into 3 1/2 in. (9 cm) patties.

Fry in a lightly oiled pan until browned and crispy — this will allow the inside to cook.

You can treat these as traditional burgers — you know, served in a bun with condiments — or they can share your plate with steamed vegetables or a salad.

"WE ARE ALL IN THE GUTTER, BUT SOME OF US ARE LOOKING AT THE STARS."
OSCAR WILDE (1854-1900)

# *T ofu Burgers*

And here's another look at burgers — very quick and protein rich.

Makes about ten 3" (8 cm) burgers.

1 cup	(240 mL)	**fine whole-wheat or rye breadcrumbs**
¹/₂ cup	(120 mL)	**finely chopped leeks**
1 lb	(454 g)	**tofu, blended or mashed**
1 Tbsp	(15 mL)	**tamari**
¹/₄ tsp	(1 mL)	**sea salt**
¹/₄ tsp	(1 mL)	**pepper**
¹/₂ tsp	(2 mL)	**sage**
1 cup	(240 mL)	**engevita yeast, for coating the burgers**
		olive oil or ghee for frying

In a bowl, mix all the ingredients except the engevita yeast.
Moisten your hands and form the mixture into patties.
Dip them in the engevita yeast, coating both sides.
Fry them in olive oil or ghee until browned.

Serve these burgers traditional-style, or turn them into a complete meal with stir-fried or steamed vegetables and a salad.
One might also consider a tasty sauce to complement them.

> *Celtic tribes believed the houseleek to be a sign of good luck, protecting the building from fire, lightning, witches and evil spirits. Perhaps there is a connection between this belief and the fact that Charlemagne passed a law requiring that these plants be grown on the roof of every dwelling.*

Kasha Tofu Burgers

Kasha, also known as buckwheat groats, adds a nice texture to this burger recipe. This can also make a decent loaf: liberally grease the loafpan, cover the loaftop with ketchup or a ketchup look-alike and cook in a moderate oven for half an hour.

Makes about 8 - 10 burgers.

6 Tbsp	(90 mL)	**very finely chopped leeks**
3 cups	(720 mL)	**cooked kasha**
		(refer to Grains Section, page 100)
1 lb	(454 g)	**mashed tofu**
¼ cup	(60 mL)	**engevita yeast**
2 Tbsp	(30 mL)	**tamari**
1 tsp	(5 mL)	**Spike, vegetable seasoning or salt**
1 tsp	(5 mL)	**chili powder**
1 tsp	(5 mL)	**basil**
1 tsp	(5 mL)	**dillweed**
½ tsp	(2 mL)	**thyme**
3 Tbsp	(45 mL)	**olive oil**
¾ cup	(180 mL)	**dry breadcrumbs**
		pinch cayenne (optional)

Purée the chopped leeks in a food processor or blender.
Combine leeks, kasha and tofu in a large bowl, mashing the ingredients
   with a fork.
Add the yeast, tamari, seasonings, herbs and olive oil.
Fold in the breadcrumbs and mix thoroughly.
Now wet your hands and form the mixture into patties about ½" thick.
   You will need to moisten your hands quite often as you make them.
Choose your largest frying-pan, so that you will be able to fry several
   patties at a time.
Fry the burgers in olive oil or ghee, for 5 - 7 minutes each side.

*If you don't want to use a blender or food processor, chop the leeks as finely as you
can before mashing together the remaining ingredients. Your burgers will be a
little coarser, but your kitchen will be quieter.*

Outrageous Cabbage Rolls

A sweet and savoury taste treat that proves cabbage rolls need not be an all day project. It's quite simple — try it! These rolls will keep quite well in the refrigerator for a day or two.

Serves 6 - 8.

1		large head of cabbage
3¹/₂ cups	(840 mL)	cooked brown rice
		(about 2 cups [480 mL] **uncooked**)
1¹/₂ cups	(360 mL)	chopped leeks
³/₄ cup	(180 mL)	raisins
³/₄ cup	(180 mL)	chopped almonds
1¹/₂ Tbsp	(22 mL)	olive oil
¹/₂ tsp	(2 mL)	Spike or vegetable seasoning
2 tsp	(10 mL)	dillweed
2 tsp	(10 mL)	basil
2 tsp	(10 mL)	oregano
1¹/₂ tsp	(7 mL)	chili powder
¹/₂ tsp	(2 mL)	pepper
5¹/₄ cups	(1.3 L)	puréed tomatoes (1¹/₂ large cans)

Steam the head of cabbage until it is just tender, then carefully separate the leaves.

Combine all the other ingredients in a large bowl.

Place 2 Tbsp (30 mL) of the mixture on a cabbage leaf and roll it up. Tuck the ends under, as if you are making little parcels. Repeat for the remainder of the mixture.

Place them fold-side down in an oiled 12" x 18" (5 L) baking dish.

THE SAUCE :

1¹/₂ cups	(360 mL)	tomato paste (2 small 5¹/₂ oz cans)
1¹/₂ cups	(360 mL)	water
2 Tbsp	(30 mL)	lemon juice (about 1 lemon)
3 Tbsp	(45 mL)	honey

Combine the ingredients in a bowl and mix well.

Pour the sauce over the cabbage rolls in the baking dish.

Bake at 375°F (190°C) for 30 to 45 minutes.

The stuffing can also be used to fill squash (cut them in half lengthwise and clean out the seeds and pulp); green peppers; or tomatoes (for tomatoes use inside pulp in place of some or all of the puréed tomatoes).

Sharada's Cashew-Carrot Loaf

At the Salt Spring Centre, we celebrate a number of different festivals through the course of the year, reflecting the diversity of our backgrounds. This recipe was created ten years ago especially for Passover (using matzo-meal instead of flour), and we have served it at the Centre every year since then. It is a delicious item for everyday as much as for feast-day.

6 cups	(1.4 L)	**chopped carrots**
2 cups	(480 mL)	**ground cashews**
3 Tbsp	(45 mL)	**oil**
1 cup	(240 mL)	**finely chopped leeks**
1 cup	(240 mL)	**finely chopped celery**
½ cup	(120 mL)	**whole-wheat flour**
1 tsp	(5 mL)	**sea salt**
½ tsp	(2 mL)	**black pepper**
2 tsp	(10 mL)	**crushed sage**
½ tsp	(2 mL)	**thyme**
1 tsp	(5 mL)	**basil**

Steam the carrots until tender, then mash them using a fork, potato-masher, blender or food-processor. Six cups of chopped raw carrots make about 3 cups of mashed.

Grind the cashews in a food processor or blender until they are quite fine. Add the oil to the blender, if necessary to help with the grinding.

Mix all the ingredients together and place in an oiled loaf-tin.

Bake at 350°F (180°C) for 35 - 45 minutes, or until the top edges begin to look dry.

"TIS AN ILL COOK THAT CANNOT LICK HER OWN FINGERS."
WILLIAM SHAKESPEARE: *ROMEO AND JULIET*

Nut Roast

Serve this loaf to your carnivorous acquaintances, and show them what they are missing! With one of the sauces suggested below, it makes a delicious centrepiece to a meal. Although the cooking time is lengthy, you will find that preparation is surprisingly quick...and consumption time even shorter!

Makes 1 loaf, serving 4 - 6.

1¹/₂ cups	(360 mL)	finely chopped leeks
¹/₄ cup	(60 mL)	butter or oil
	6	medium mushrooms, finely chopped
	4	large tomatoes, peeled and chopped
1 cup	(240 mL)	almonds, ground
1 cup	(240 mL)	cashews, ground
1 cup	(240 mL)	filberts or hazelnuts, ground
	1	large green apple, cored and grated
1¹/₂ cups	(360 mL)	fine breadcrumbs
3 Tbsp	(45 mL)	chopped fresh parsley
¹/₄ tsp	(1 mL)	paprika
1 tsp	(5 mL)	basil
1 tsp	(5 mL)	thyme
¹/₂ tsp	(2 mL)	crushed sage
3 tsp	(15 mL)	egg-replacer PLUS
3 Tbsp	(45 mL)	water
3 Tbsp	(45 mL)	tamari

Gently sauté the leeks in butter or oil until soft but not browned.

Put them into a large bowl and add all the remaining ingredients except the tamari and egg-replacer mixture.

Mix well.

Blend the egg-replacer and water until creamy and lumpless.

Add the egg-replacer mixture and tamari to other ingredients, stir well, and allow to stand for 10 minutes.

Firmly pack the mixture into an oiled 9" x 5" (23 x 13 cm) loaf pan.

Stand the loaf pan in a baking dish, and add water to halfway up the loaf pan. (You may need to replenish the water bath, so keep an eye on it.)

Bake at 400°F (205°C) for one hour, then reduce heat to 350°F (180°C) for another 1¹/₂ hours. The top should be dark brown, but not black.

Allow the nut roast to cool for 5 minutes before turning it out onto a dish. (You will need to loosen around the sides thoroughly with a knife first.)

Serve with yeast gravy (page 157), tamari sauce (page 154), or mushroom sauce (page 150).

kara Loaf

If you have ever wondered what you were going to do with all that material (called okara) left over from making soy milk, here's your answer.

1 cup	(240 mL)	ground walnuts
1 cup	(240 mL)	ground sunflower seeds
1 Tbsp	(15 mL)	butter or ghee
2 cups	(480 mL)	finely chopped leeks
2 Tbsp	(30 mL)	oil
2 cups	(480 mL)	okara (see page 279)
2 cups	(480 mL)	grated carrot
1 Tbsp	(15 mL)	tamari
1 Tbsp	(15 mL)	engevita yeast
3 Tbsp	(45 mL)	soy flour or white flour (as a binder)
1 Tbsp	(15 mL)	oregano

Sauté the walnuts and sunflower seeds in butter or ghee until they are
   slightly browned and a nice toasty aroma fills the air.
Set them aside in a bowl, and sauté the leeks in the leftover oil until they
   turn bright green.
Mix all the ingredients thoroughly and pour into an oiled *glass* loaf pan.
   (A glass pan is recommended because metal reacts with some of these
   ingredients to cause an unsightly blackening on the loaf.)
Bake at 350°F (180°C) for 40 to 50 minutes, then serve with one of our
   savoury sauces and perhaps some steamed greens.

This mix works well for burgers too.

"OPPORTUNITY IS MISSED BY MOST PEOPLE
BECAUSE IT IS DRESSED IN OVERALLS AND LOOKS LIKE WORK."
THOMAS EDISON (1847-1931)

Taking the lowly red kidney bean to undreamed of culinary heights, we present for you:

Vegetarian Chili

This amount will serve a horde of 10 or so.

8 cups	(1.9 L)	cooked red kidney beans
		(approx. 5 cups raw)
1 tsp	(5 mL)	baking soda
1 cup	(240 mL)	sunflower seeds
2 cups	(480 mL)	coarsely chopped leeks
1 cup	(240 mL)	coarsely chopped carrots
1½ cups	(360 mL)	chopped celery
1½ tsp	(7 mL)	oregano
1½ tsp	(7 mL)	freshly grated ginger
2 tsp	(10 mL)	ground cumin
1 tsp	(5 mL)	crushed red chili peppers
2 Tbsp	(30 mL)	chili powder
1 - 28 oz. tin	(796 mL)	crushed tomatoes
	2	green peppers
2 Tbsp	(30 mL)	tamari

Begin by soaking the beans overnight. Next day, discard the bean liquid and cover beans with fresh water.

Bring to a boil with 1 tsp baking soda then simmer, covered, for about 2½ hours — until the skins break when blown upon.

Drain off the bean liquid, but please save it! You may need it if your beans are too dry.

Now toss in all the other ingredients except the green pepper and tamari.

Adjust the beans for dryness by adding the bean liquid, if needed.

About half an hour before serving, chop the green peppers coarsely and add them with the tamari. Continue to simmer over low heat.

Serve with a side salad and thick slices of bread for a filling and nutritious meal.

"BETTER IS A DINNER OF HERBS WHERE LOVE IS,
THAN A STALLED OX AND HATRED THEREIN."
THE BIBLE : *PROVERBS*

Garden Pasta

This pasta is versatile as well as pretty and will happily accept whatever you have on hand. Try carrots, peas and green beans.

Serves 6 - 8 people.

2 cups	(480 mL)	chopped fresh tomatoes
3 cups	(720 mL)	cooked noodles or macaroni
1 cup	(240 mL)	chopped leeks
3 Tbsp	(45 mL)	olive oil
3 cups	(720 mL)	chopped broccoli
2 cups	(480 mL)	chopped cauliflower
2 cups	(480 mL)	chopped celery
2 cups	(480 mL)	thinly sliced cabbage
½ cup	(120 mL)	chopped green peppers
1½ cups	(360 mL)	cubed tofu
2 tsp	(10 mL)	basil
2 tsp	(10 mL)	oregano (optional)
1 tsp	(5 mL)	dillweed
1½ tsp	(7 mL)	chili powder
¼ tsp	(1 mL)	black pepper
1½ Tbsp	(22 mL)	tamari

Cook the noodles or macaroni according to package directions. (It's difficult to estimate a dry measure, because pastas differ from one to the next, but dry macaroni usually doubles in volume.)

Drain the noodles and set aside.

While the noodles cook, sauté the leeks in olive oil in a large frying pan or wok for about 3 minutes.

Add the vegetables, starting with the broccoli and cauliflower. Stir until coated with oil and heated through. Next stir in the celery, cabbage and green peppers. Keep stirring the vegetables until they begin to soften.

Mix in the tofu, tomatoes and seasonings. Stir-fry until the vegetables are tendercrisp.

Quickly stir in the noodles and cook until the noodles are heated through. Serve immediately.

Have crusty rolls on hand, so your guests can clean their plates of all the juices. Extra freshly grated pepper, tamari, nutritional yeast and grated parmesan do well as condiments for this meal.

easant Pie

Place this tasty winter-vegetable pie before your serfs and enjoy their eternal devotion.

Makes one 8 inch (23 cm) double-crust pie.

THE CRUST:

1¼ cups	(300 mL)	**whole-wheat pastry flour**
1 tsp	(5 mL)	**sea salt** (optional)
½ cup	(120 mL)	**cream cheese**
3 Tbsp	(45 mL)	**butter**
1 Tbsp	(15 mL)	**grated parmesan cheese**
⅓ cup	(80 mL)	**ice-water**

Toss the flour, salt, and parmesan together in a large bowl.

Rub or cut the softened cream cheese and butter into the flour mixture, until it looks like coarse meal.

Mix the ice-water into the above mixture. It may still look a little crumbly, but don't despair.

Gather the dough into a ball, and cut it in half.

Roll out one half, and use it to line the pie-plate for the bottom crust.

Set the pie-plate aside in the fridge, along with the remainder of the dough, while you make the filling.

"WHAT A UNIQUE SENSATION! WHAT A MARVELOUS SENSORY EXPERIENCE IS HUNGER! IT IS NOT PRECISELY A KIND OF PAIN, BUT A FEELING THAT STARTS OUT AS A SLIGHT TICKLE."
CHEVALIER DE JAUCOURT, CA. 1765
DICTIONNAIRE ENCYCLOPÉDIE, S.V. "HUNGER"

THE FILLING:

1 Tbsp	(15 mL)	**prepared Dijon mustard**
4 cups	(960 mL)	**not too finely chopped leeks**
3 cups	(720 mL)	**shredded cabbage**
5 Tbsp	(75 mL)	**butter**
1 tsp	(5 mL)	**basil**
1 tsp	(5 mL)	**tarragon**
1 tsp	(5 mL)	**marjoram**
2 cups	(480 mL)	**chopped mushrooms**
½ tsp	(2 mL)	**sea salt**
1 tsp	(5 mL)	**dill**

Spread the mustard on the piecrust.

Sauté the leeks and cabbage in **3 Tbsp** (45 mL) butter until softened. Sprinkle herbs over them and set aside.

Sauté the mushrooms in **2 Tbsp** (30 mL) butter until nicely softened.

Pour the leeks and cabbage into the pie-plate; sprinkle with salt, then add the mushrooms and mushroom juice.

Sprinkle with dill.

Roll out the other half of the dough and cover the pie. Press the top and bottom crusts together with a fork and trim the edges.

Cut a slit or two in the top crust, to allow steam to escape while the pie cooks.

Bake at 400°F (205°C) for 15 minutes, then 350°F (180°C) for 20 minutes.

Got some leftover pie-crust? Roll it out, pat in some sesame seeds, cut it into strips, twist them and bake on a cookie sheet for 15 minutes along with the pie at 400°F (205°C).

Serve this substantial pie with a green salad glistening with a simple oil and vinegar dressing, or for the more hearty appetites, some green vegetables, such as broccoli or chard.

Shepherd's ie

*A filling, nourishing meal, albeit
a far cry from the traditional
meat 'n' potatoes version —
and kids love it.*

Serves 8 - 10 people.

THE LOWER LAYER:

2 Tbsp	(30 mL)	vegetable oil
2 cups	(480 mL)	chopped leeks
1⅓ cups	(320 mL)	small flake oats
⅔ cup	(160 mL)	ground sunflower seeds
⅔ cup	(160 mL)	whole-wheat breadcrumbs
1 tsp	(5 mL)	sea salt
½ tsp	(2 mL)	thyme
¼ tsp	(1 mL)	sage
1 tsp	(5 mL)	basil
3 Tbsp	(45 mL)	engevita yeast
¼ cup	(60 mL)	vegetable oil
⅔ cup	(160 mL)	water
		paprika (to taste)

Sauté the leeks in oil.
Transfer to a bowl and add the remaining ingredients. Mix well.
Pat the mixture into the bottom of an oiled 8" x 10" (2.5 L) baking pan.

THE UPPER LAYER:

5 cups	(1.2 L)	mixed vegetables, including frozen (or fresh) corn, peas, yellow or green beans
2 Tbsp	(30 mL)	tamari
¼ cup	(60 mL)	milk or soymilk

Mix the vegetables, tamari and milk together, then pat into an even layer
on top of the first one.

THE TOPPING:

6 cups	(1.4 L)	**cubed potatoes**
⅓ cup	(80 mL)	**milk or soymilk**
3 Tbsp	(45 mL)	**butter**
1 tsp	(5 mL)	**sea salt**
½ tsp	(2 mL)	**pepper**

Steam the potatoes until they are quite soft, then mash them and mix with
   the milk, butter, salt and pepper.
Spread the mashed potatoes over the vegetable filling.
Garnish the pie with a sprinkle of paprika, then bake it at 450°F (235°C)
   for 45 minutes.

*Creamy Curry Sauce (see page 146) makes a delicious accompaniment to this pie,
as does Tamari Cream Sauce (page 154).*

Tofu Quiche

Where would we be without our beloved tofu? Tofu can shamelssly assume whatever flavour may seize the whim of the cook, but we still respect it for the unpretentious invention that it is.

Makes one 8 inch (23 cm) pie.

1 lb	(454 g)	**tofu**
2 Tbsp	(30 mL)	**tamari**
¹/₄ tsp	(1 mL)	**black pepper**
¹/₄ tsp	(1 mL)	**nutmeg**
1 Tbsp	(15 mL)	**mustard powder**
		pinch of sea salt
2 cups	(480 mL)	**finely chopped leeks**
3 Tbsp	(45 mL)	**olive oil**
¹/₃ cup	(80 mL)	**sesame seeds**
1¹/₂ tsp	(7 mL)	**tahini**
		whole-wheat pie crust (half the recipe on page 58, or your own recipe) pre-baked for 10 minutes at 400°F (205°C)

OPTIONAL:

2 cups	(480 mL)	**cubed eggplant**
3 Tbsp	(45 mL)	**oil**
2 Tbsp	(30 mL)	**lemon juice**

In a bowl, mash the tofu with the tamari, pepper, nutmeg, mustard and salt, and set aside.

Sauté the leeks in oil until soft and bright green.

In a separate frying pan (do not oil), toast the sesame seeds until lightly browned. Stir constantly to keep them from burning.

Add the leeks and the toasted sesame seeds to the tofu mixture. Stir until well blended.

If you are using eggplant, sauté it in the oil until browned and soft, then remove it from the pan and sprinkle with lemon juice. Spread over the bottom of the pie shell before adding the rest of the filling.

Fill the pie shell with the tofu mixture, pressing it lightly into place.

Garnish with a sprinkling of nutmeg or arrange red pepper slices attractively on the top.

Bake at 350°F (180°C) for 30 minutes.

Sharada's Vege-Pie

Another Salt Spring Centre classic, a favourite of residents and visitors alike.

Makes 2 terrific 8 inch (20 cm) pies.

THE CRUST:

Prepare two pie-shells, using the pie crust recipe on page 198 or any
favourite recipe of your own. Prebake for 10 minutes.

THE FILLING:

1½ cups	(360 mL)	**chopped leeks**
10 cups	(2.4 L)	**chopped cauliflower**
2 cups	(480 mL)	**chopped red and yellow peppers**
4 tsp	(20 mL)	**dillweed**
2 tsp	(10 mL)	**basil**
¼ cup	(60 mL)	**tamari**
5 tsp	(25 mL)	**chili powder**
¼ tsp	(1 mL)	**pepper**
3 Tbsp	(45 mL)	**olive oil**
⅓ cup	(80 mL)	**flour** (for thickening)
		pinch of cayenne
⅔ cup	(160 mL)	**water**
2-4 cups	(480-960 mL)	**grated cheese**

Sauté the vegetables and herbs in olive oil until just soft.
Mix the flour and cayenne together, and sprinkle over the vegetables.
Stir in the water and cook until thickened.
Fill the pie shells.
Sprinkle 1 - 2 cups (240 - 480 mL) grated cheese over each pie.
Bake at 350°F (180°C) for 30-40 minutes.

Serve with a crisp salad and steamed greens.

"THE MURALS IN RESTAURANTS ARE ON A PAR WITH THE FOOD IN MUSEUMS."
PETER DE VRIES (1910 -)

Sazjo's Sweet Rice Dumplings

This is a fun, quick recipe that lends itself well to experimentation. Try adding a teaspoon or two (5 mL+) of an herb (maybe dillweed) to the dumplings.

Serves 4.

THE SAUCE		
3 cups	(720 mL)	**water**
¹/₂ cup	(120 mL)	**whole-wheat or brown rice flour**
1 Tbsp	(15 mL)	**oil**
2 cups	(480 mL)	**sliced mushrooms**
2 Tbsp	(30 mL)	**tamari**
1 Tbsp	(15 mL)	**tahini or almond butter**

First, put 1 cup (240 mL) water in the fridge to cool.

In a cast iron frying pan, dry roast the flour over medium to high heat for 2 - 3 minutes. Stir just to keep the flour from burning. Once the flour smells nice and nutty and has darkened a little, transfer to a bowl.

In a lightly oiled saucepan, sauté the mushrooms until golden brown. Turn off the heat, add the other 2 cups (480 mL) water and stir it in.

Mix the cupful (240 mL) of cold water with the roasted flour. Stir to make a paste, then add to the mushrooms and combine.

Still stirring, bring the sauce to a gentle boil. Stir the tamari and tahini into the sauce. Let simmer over gentle heat for 10 - 15 minutes, while you make:

THE DUMPLINGS		
2 cups	(480 mL)	**sweet brown rice flour***
4 tsp	(20 mL)	**baking powder**
¹/₂ tsp	(2 mL)	**salt**
2 tsp	(10 mL)	**oil**
³/₄ cup	(180 mL)	**hot water**

Sift together the dry ingredients and rub in the oil. Stir the hot water into the mix and blend it until it forms a dough. Knead it until smooth, with an ear lobe consistency.

Roll out the dough on a floured surface to about ¹/₂" thick (12 mm) and cut it into stars or circles, say an inch or two (3 - 5 cm) in diameter.

Pop the dumplings into a big potful of just-below-boiling water, over low heat. Cover the pot with a glass plate or pie-dish, so you can check that they are not crowded, while they steam for 10 minutes.

*If you can't find sweet brown rice flour, 1 cup (240 mL) ordinary brown rice flour plus 1 cup (240 mL) whole-wheat flour will do.

Serve the dumplings in the sauce, sprinkled with minced parsley on the top. Accompany them with lots of steamed vegetables and rice or quinoa.

Ratatouille

This recipe relies on the eggplant, also known as the aubergine, originally native to South Asia. The Chinese were using it by the 3rd Century A.D., albeit rather tentatively, since it didn't really become a culinary hit until the 6th Century.

Makes 6 to 8 servings.

1		large eggplant
1½ cups	(360 mL)	chopped celery (2-3 stalks)
1½ cups	(360 mL)	chopped green pepper
1½ cups	(360 mL)	chopped zucchini
2 cups	(480 mL)	chopped leeks
3-4 Tbsp	(45-60 mL)	olive oil
1 tsp	(5 mL)	Spike or vegetable seasoning
1-2 tsp	(5-10 mL)	dillweed
¾ tsp	(3 mL)	sea salt
2 tsp	(10 mL)	basil
1 - 28 oz	(796 mL)	can tomatoes (drained)
½ cup	(120 mL)	tomato paste (almost a small tin)

TOPPING:

1 cup	(240 mL)	bread, cracker or corn flake crumbs
1 tsp	(5 mL)	Spike or vegetable seasoning
1 tsp	(5 mL)	dill weed
		pinch black pepper
¾ cup	(180 mL)	grated mild cheese (optional)

Cube the eggplant and sprinkle it generously with salt. Let it stand for at least 15 minutes to draw out the excess moisture.

Pat the eggplant dry with a paper towel and steam it until it is soft.

Meanwhile, sauté the celery, green pepper, zucchini and leeks until just tender. Remove from heat and add the spices and herbs, the drained tomatoes and the tomato paste. Save the tomato juice to make soup.

Add the eggplant and combine thoroughly, then pour everything into an oiled 8" x 12" (20 x 30 cm) baking pan.

Preheat the oven while you put the topping mix together by mixing bread crumbs and seasonings. Sprinkle evenly over the ratatouille and top with cheese.

Bake at 350°F (180°C) for 30 minutes.

Serve with a cool green or spinach salad and buttered basmati rice topped with a lemon wedge and a squeeze of lemon juice.

Stir-Fried Vegetables

Sure, anyone can come up with some stir-fry medley. But try this combination just for fun.

Serves 5 - 6 people.

2 Tbsp	(30 mL)	oil
2 Tbsp	(30 mL)	grated ginger
1½ cups	(360 mL)	chopped leeks
¼ cup	(60 mL)	slivered nuts (cashews or almonds)
1 cup	(240 mL)	chopped carrots
3 cups	(720 mL)	chopped cauliflower
3 cups	(720 mL)	chopped broccoli
2 cups	(480 mL)	chopped zucchini
1½ cups	(360 mL)	frozen peas
1 cup	(240 mL)	sliced green peppers
2 cups	(480 mL)	cubed tofu
		juice of ½ lemon
⅓ cup	(80 mL)	tamari

Heat the oil in a wok over fairly high heat.

Sauté the ginger, leeks and nuts.

Add the carrots, cauliflower and broccoli. Remember — the key to successful stir-frying is high heat and almost constant stirring.

Add the zucchini, frozen peas and peppers last.

Stir in the tofu, lemon and tamari. Keep stirring!

Cover for a few minutes until the vegetables are just tender, not soft — the broccoli should still be bright green.

You can vary the vegetables as you like. Some suggestions are to add celery, bean-sprouts, bok choy or sui choy. When adding the vegetables, the ones that take the longest to cook should go in first, the softer vegetables later.

Stuffed Vine Leaves

Before beginning, please check the section on Beans, page 102, regarding cooking times for Black Soy Beans. And if you like an incendiary taste, increase the chili peppers.

Serves 4.

1 cup	(240 mL)	sunflower seeds
1½ tsp	(7 mL)	butter
2 cups	(480 mL)	finely chopped leeks
2 Tbsp	(30 mL)	oil
1 Tbsp	(15 mL)	ground coriander
5 cups	(1.2 L)	cooked black soybeans
1½ cups	(360 mL)	breadcrumbs (preferably rye)
1 tsp	(5 mL)	crushed chili peppers
2 Tbsp	(30 mL)	dillweed
½ tsp	(2 mL)	sea salt
		grape leaves for wrapping

Roast the sunflower seeds in a large skillet in butter to bring out the flavour.

Sauté the leeks in oil until they are bright green and just tender.

Add the coriander to the leeks and stir while cooking for 2 minutes more.

Transfer the leek mixture to a blender and add sunflower seeds, soybeans, breadcrumbs, chili peppers, dill and salt, processing them together (in batches if necessary), until thoroughly mixed.

Spoon **2 Tbsp** (30 mL) of the mixture onto the middle of a grape leaf. Fold the bottom edge partly over the filling.

Fold the sides in towards the middle, then roll from the bottom towards the top edge.

Place seam-side down in an oiled 12" x 18" (4 L) baking dish.

Bake for 30 minutes at 375°F (190°C).

If you wish to serve these as a warm dish, use the Tomato Sauce from the Outrageous Cabbage Rolls recipe (page 52).
They are often served chilled as an entrée,
or as an hors d'oeuvre with Raita (page 70).

GRAPE LEAVES

Canned or bottled grape leaves can be purchased from food specialty shops. They are packed in brine which you may wish to wash off before using. Either way, they will need to be drained before use. If you use fresh grape leaves, choose young ones, about 4" (10 cm) across. Snip off the stems and plunge into boiling water for 2-3 minutes.

Worldfood

Big Macs in Moscow, hot dogs in Kuala Lumpur, and pizza, French fries and Diet Coke just about everywhere. As eating becomes a trans-national industry, we see the rapid spread of packaged and convenience food throughout the countries of the world, and the progressive homogenization of both the diet and the culture associated with it. In the past decade, the "global village" that many of us eagerly awaited seems to have arrived; we just never realised that it might turn out to look like Los Angeles.

But all is not yet lost. As young people gain access to realms of travel that were unthinkable to their parents' generation, so they return home with a more cosmopolitan, more multi-cultural notion of what food is, and what it can be. When you have sat on a tiny beach beside the Aegean eating crusty bread, olives, briny Feta cheese, tomatoes and fresh figs, all washed down with Retsina, then you may never again find such relish in a tired old Humungusburger and plastic milkshake.

Ethiopian spiced bread, baked eggplant, fresh pine-nuts by the Adriatic, a street corner falafel in Luxor on the Nile, even simple but perfect baked potatoes rolled out of the campfire embers while Pacific breakers thunder onto the evening sands of Carmanah. It's not only the place that brings magic to meals of this kind; a difference of attitude toward the whole notion of food comes from the change in mental setting when you travel, and the discovery of previously untried ingredients.

One starts to question why mainstream North American food must rely on such a limited a range of notes, techniques that bludgeon the food rather than cultivate its inherent qualities. For answer, one need look no further than the menu of every small café, the kind of weekday lunch venues that have defined the eating expectations of North America for generations: typically, no more than one or two items will be free of meat. Because of this pre-occupation, every other form of food, from the salad to the bread roll, will likely have suffered in its preparation. All are mere garnishes to the *real* point of the business, namely the steak, the burger, the roast.

Elsewhere around the world, the focus is somewhat different; in fact, the whole construction of a meal is different, with sometimes one particular dish taking a central place, but more often a selection of grain, vegetable, and other dishes, complementing each other and providing a balanced whole.

As more and more people turn to a vegetarian diet, both for reasons of health and out of a desire no longer to be involved in the mechanized killing of the meat industry, so the shape and balance of mealtimes is coming to include many more traditional dishes from other, less meat-based cultures.

Our aim in presenting the recipes in this chapter was to share with you some of those dishes that we ourselves have come to enjoy and regard as standbys, peppered with a few less well known ones that may pique your palate. That wasn't always an easy task, for all kinds of reasons: is

Tabouleh a salad, or an ethnic dish? Is spaghetti still Italian? Much of the discussion revolved around semantics such as these, but sometimes one cook would dismiss Guacamole as being too well known to be included at all, while another insisted most people would never have heard of it.

In contrast to the growing uniformity of bland, characterless commercial food stuffed with fats and salt that seems to be sweeping the cities of the globe, it is cheering to see a counterpoint of so many new recipes and themes in food emerging from a wider familiarity with the cooking of other cultures. As example, you should see the range of delicacies offered by vendors at the Saturday morning Salt Spring 'farmers' market' — jars of wonderful freshly-made herb pesto among them. Even our supermarket now carries items that would once have necessitated a trip to the city, many of them, such as the dairy-fresh tofu, produced on the island by our inventive and industrious neighbours.

We have lots to learn from the cooking of other cultures, and some to offer, too. Perhaps the most hopeful note to end on, lies in all the permutations and cross-fertilisations that are developing between one country's cooking and another; sometimes that gives us tofu wieners, but once in a while it can result in a quite splendid notion.

Cucumber Raita

India

Cool and refreshing, raita is the fire brigade of East Indian cooking. After a bite of searingly hot curry, it puts out the fire in your mouth in a way that water never could. Please don't think, however, that this is the limit of raita's repertoire, for it makes a pleasing condiment or "moistener" to accompany many kinds of drier or more spicy main dishes.

Makes about 3½ cups (840 mL).

1½ cups	(360 mL)	peeled, minced cucumber
2 cups	(480 mL)	thick, whole milk yoghurt
		pinch sea salt
1 tsp	(5 mL)	fresh lemon juice
2½ tsp	(12 mL)	ground cumin

Peel and mince the cucumber, then mash it with a fork in the bowl you're going to make the raita in. The idea is to extract a bit of juice, but not to turn it into a shapeless green blob.

Add the yoghurt, salt and lemon juice.

Toast the cumin in a skillet over medium heat for a minute to bring out the flavour, then mix it thoroughly with the yoghurt.

Serve slightly chilled.

Tamale Pie

Mexico

This unusual pie, crowned by a cornbread crust, can be served with a little yoghurt or sour cream, a green salad and a slice of melon for a colourful and tasty dinner.

Makes one 12" pie, serving 4 - 6 people.

1 cup	(240 mL)	chopped leeks
½ cup	(120 mL)	chopped celery
1 cup	(240 mL)	chopped green pepper
3 Tbsp	(45 mL)	vegetable oil
1 cup	(240 mL)	frozen corn, or cooked fresh corn
2 cups	(480 mL)	crushed tomatoes
¼ cup	(60 mL)	chopped pimento or red pepper
1½ tsp	(7 mL)	honey
2½ Tbsp	(37 mL)	chili powder
¼ tsp	(1 mL)	cayenne (more or less, to taste)
		fat pinch of black pepper
1 tsp	(5 mL)	sea salt
1 Tbsp	(15 mL)	lime or lemon juice (optional)
2½ cups	(600 mL)	cooked kidney beans
		cornbread topping
		(use recipe page 238)
1 tsp	(5 mL)	anise or fennel seed

In a large skillet, sauté the leeks, celery and green pepper in the oil until they are just tender.

Add the remaining ingredients and cook gently until they are heated through.

Adjust the seasoning of the pie-filling to your taste.

Now oil a deep-sided 12" pie-dish and fill with the beans and vegetables.

Make the cornbread according to the recipe and spread the mixture on top of the pie, no more than half an inch thick.

Sprinkle the anise or fennel seed over the topping, and bake at 400°F (205°C) for 40 minutes, or until the top is browned and crispy.

Allow the pie to cool for 5 minutes or so before serving.

This pie is moderately spicy,
so children may prefer it with less chili powder and cayenne.
On the other hand, for a real kick, use an extra 1 Tbsp (15 mL) chili powder
and one crushed red chili pepper in the vegetable/bean mixture.

Chapatis

India

Delicious and quick, chapatis are a staple of the diet of millions of Indians, and their elephants. They are at their best straight off the top of the stove, with a little butter and whatever you choose. Learn them — you will love them, and so will your kids. When the shops are closed and you are out of bread, there are still chapatis lurking in your sack of flour.

Makes about one dozen chapatis.

2 cups	(480 mL)	**whole-wheat flour**
1 tsp	(5 mL)	**sea salt**
¾ cup	(180 mL)	**water (more or less)**

Sift the flour and salt together, into a bowl.

Pour the water little by little into a well in the middle of the flour, mixing it into the liquid to form a soft dough.

Turn the dough onto a floured board, and knead until it is smooth and stretchy (5-10 minutes). Now cover it with a damp cloth and leave it for a half hour or more, before cooking. (If really necessary, this step may be omitted.)

At this point, the dough can be refrigerated (or frozen) in a plastic bag, if you do not wish to use it right away, and the remaining steps will take only a few minutes.

Divide your dough into about a dozen pieces, then form each one into a little ball. Flatten each ball with your fingers, then roll it out on a lightly-floured board, turning it a quarter turn after each pass of the rolling pin to make a neat disc.

Heat a large, heavy skillet over a moderate flame, and toast the chapati, turning it once, until the "damp" patches disappear. Pressing it lightly against the skillet wherever it puffs, will help it to cook evenly.

Take it from the pan when it is just starting to brown, and flip it onto another burner (on medium heat), so that it is directly over the flame or electric coil. Keep it moving for a few moments, so that the steam trying to escape from the interior of the chapati will make it puff up like a balloon.

When it is toasty and puffed, transfer the chapati quickly to a plate (tongs? fingers?), spread it with a little butter if you wish and enjoy it while it's still hot.

You can keep chapatis hot and almost in peak condition by wrapping them interleaved in a tea towel, stored on a plate in a 200°F (95°C) oven for a short while.

Curried Cous-Cous

India

    All over India, but particularly in the north, where the Himalayas climb white-capped into the sky bordering Nepal and Tibet, you may encounter sadhus, renunciate holy-men who have given up all but a few possessions and lead simple lives often in remote places, in their search for enlightenment.

    This recipe is for a dish often eaten by sadhus, having the advantages of cooking quite quickly, and requiring just one pan. It uses cous-cous, a wheat-grain that you will probably find in many health-food stores and delicatessens.

Serves 2 friendly sadhus.

1 cup	(240 mL)	**finely chopped leeks**
3 Tbsp	(45 mL)	**ghee or oil**
		1" piece of fresh ginger, finely chopped
	1	**finely chopped green pepper curry power and/or garam masala**
	1 or 2	**chopped tomatoes**
1 cup	(240 mL)	**cous-cous**
2 cups	(480 mL)	**boiling water**

Other similar vegetables may substitute for green pepper and the tomatoes, according to what you have available.

Optional ingredients to add include:

cilantro	**parsley**
mushrooms	**black pepper**
turmeric	**garlic**

In a wok, fry the chopped leeks in ghee or oil for a few minutes.

Add the ginger, green pepper (if you have it) herbs, spices and any additional ingredients of your choice. Cook for two minutes longer.

Add the chopped tomatoes and the cous-cous. Continue stirring for one minute, before pouring on the boiling water.

Add a little salt if you wish, and simmer, covered, for 5 to 10 minutes.

    Serve with yoghurt or tamari, preferably at dusk beside a small campfire in the bend of a river rushing among forests and high mountains. Watch the moon rise. Drink chai. Find peace in the stillness of this beautiful world.

Currying Flavour

India

Spicy, sweet and colourful, a favourite curry. Other comparable vegetables may replace the celery and cauliflower, if these are not available.

Serves 4 - 6.

9		medium carrots
4		sticks of celery
1		small cauliflower
1 tsp	(5 mL)	mustard seed
2 tsp	(10 mL)	cumin seed
2 tsp	(10 mL)	turmeric
½ tsp	(2 mL)	cayenne
½ tsp	(2 mL)	fenugreek seed
1 tsp	(5 mL)	cardamom seed
3"	(75 mm)	stick of cinnamon
½ tsp	(2 mL)	ground ginger
4 Tbsp	(60 mL)	butter or ghee
2 Tbsp	(30 mL)	finely chopped leeks
		juice of 3 large oranges—just under ¾ cup (180 mL)
1½ cups	(360 mL)	water
1 tsp	(5 mL)	sea salt
1 cup	(240 mL)	raisins
2		large tomatoes
3		bananas
1 cup	(240 mL)	yoghurt

Cut the carrots into thin flat strips, about ¼" (6 mm) thick by 3" (75 mm) long.

Chop the celery in ½" (12 mm) sections.

Separate the cauliflower into small florets, then thinly slice the remaining heart.

Measure the spices out into a bowl.

Heat the butter or ghee gently in a wok or similar large pan, and fry the spices for a few minutes.

Add the leeks, and stir.

Add the carrots and continue frying, turning them well to coat them with the butter or ghee and spices.

Now add the celery and cauliflower, and do the same.

After all the ingredients are coated with spices and beginning to soften, pour on the orange juice, some water, and the salt.

Scatter the raisins over the curry, and simmer, covered, at a gentle bubble until the vegetables are cooked through but not soft. Add more of the water as necessary, so the curry does not get too dry.

Scald the tomatoes in boiling water, then peel and dice them before adding to the pan, to continue cooking for a few minutes.

Peel the bananas and cut them in long diagonal slices ½" thick, then combine them gently into the curry, so that they soften among the vegetables.

Pour the yoghurt in a big circle over the curry a minute or two before you take it to the table, accompanied by rice or chapatis, or both.

Serve hot!

The dancing form of Shiva, the Nataraja, represents the eternal, whirling, dancing energy of the universe that materialises, endures, then is once again danced out of existence in a never-ending cycle of change throughout the natural world.

Enchiladas

Mexico.........   Can't afford a trip south this winter?
Ah well, treat yourself to enchiladas instead.

Serves 4 - 6.

1½ cups	(360 mL)	finely chopped leeks
1 cup	(240 mL)	finely chopped green pepper
3 Tbsp	(45 mL)	vegetable or olive oil
1 tsp	(5 mL)	sea salt
3 Tbsp	(45 mL)	chili powder
1 Tbsp	(15 mL)	minced jalapeño pepper
OR 1 tsp	(5 mL)	cayenne pepper (but not both!)
¼ cup	(60 mL)	fresh lemon juice
		(about 1 large lemon)
1½ tsp	(7 mL)	ground cumin
3 cups	(720 mL)	pinto or kidney beans, cooked
4 - 6 Tbsp	(60-90mL)	liquid from cooking the beans

OR: omit the beans and cumin, and use:

3 cups	(720 mL)	Frijoles Refritos
		(See recipe on page 88)

12 corn tortillas*
vegetable oil or water to cook
 the tortillas
Enchilada Sauce
  (recipe on page 78)

Optional:

		2 mashed, ripe avocados
½ cup	(120 mL)	**sour cream or plain yoghurt**
		chopped black olives
½ lb	(227 g)	**mild, white cheese**

In a large, heavy skillet, sauté the leeks and green pepper in oil until they are just tender.

Combine the remaining ingredients in a large bowl and add the sauteéd vegetables. Mix everything thoroughly.

Pour ¼" of oil into a small skillet.

Heat the oil and dip the tortillas into it, one by one, to soften and moisten them. Allow the excess oil to drain off. (You could substitute hot water for oil if you're worried about your waistline.)

Put 2 to 3 Tbsp (30-45 mL) of filling in a line across the middle of each tortilla. Roll them up and then place them, seam-side down, in an oiled 8"x12" (2.5 L) baking pan.

Cover generously with Enchilada Sauce, and top with grated mild cheese if desired. Bake for 20 minutes at 350°F (180°C).

Garnishes: sour cream or yoghurt, fresh melon slices,
Guacamole (page 163), and Salsa! (page 152).

* Homemade tortillas are wonderful, but they do take time to make.
Substitute store-bought tortillas if you must,
but make sure you treat yourself to the real thing someday.
You'll find our own recipe for them on page 89.

Enchilada Sauce

Mexico

An invention to moisten the already flavourful enchiladas — not intended to mask their flavour. We suggest that this sauce might also be used over Outrageous Cabbage Rolls, Stuffed Vine Leaves, and other similar recipes.

Makes about 3 ½ cups (840 mL).

3 Tbsp	(45 mL)	**chili powder**
¹/₂ tsp	(2 mL)	**sea salt**
¹/₄ cup	(60 mL)	**cornmeal**
6 Tbsp	(90 mL)	**whole wheat flour**
¹/₂ cup	(120 mL)	**vegetable oil**
28-oz tin	(796 mL)	**crushed tomatoes**

Optional:
3 Tbsp	(45 mL)	**lemon juice**
		cayenne pepper to taste

In a saucepan, sauté the chili powder, salt, cornmeal, and flour in the oil for a minute or two. Then add the tomatoes and any optional ingredients and simmer the sauce for about 10 minutes, stirring occasionally.

If necessary, thin the sauce with water or vegetable stock to achieve the desired consistency. The sauce should not be too thin and runny, but it should pour easily over the enchiladas.

This is a fairly spicy sauce — you may want to start with a smaller quantity of chili powder and taste-test, before you decide to add any more.

hee

Ghee is wonderful to cook with — it imparts a special "sweetness" to vegetables, grains and spices, and doesn't burn as quickly as butter. Ghee is a staple of East Indian cooking. Westerners call it "clarified butter".

Since ghee will keep for many months at room temperature, there is no need to refrigerate it — part of the reason for its use in India, of course.

1 lb   (454 g)   **butter**

Heat the butter over a low flame so that it doesn't brown.

When it's all melted, let it sit, preferably in a cool spot, and then skim off all the white-ish milk solids that accumulate on top. You may wish to pour it through a strainer as well, to remove the last specks of solid matter.

A lovely golden liquid is left, and that's what you're after.

Store it in a wide-mouthed jar, since at cooler temperatures it may thicken enough to need spooning rather than pouring.

Falafels

One of the most satisfying eat-from-
your-hand meals you could hope to
find, and a traditional favourite
throughout the Middle East. This
variation strays
tofu-wards from the classic.

Middle East
Serves 6 - 8.

2 cups	(480 mL)	**dry garbanzo beans** (about 4 cups cooked beans)
1 cup	(240 mL)	**leftover bean cooking water**
	½	**loaf whole-wheat bread**
1 lb	(454 g)	**tofu, mashed**
½ cup	(120 mL)	**finely chopped leeks**
¼ cup	(60 mL)	**tamari**
1 tsp	(5 mL)	**ground cumin**
1 tsp	(5 mL)	**dillweed**
1 tsp	(5 mL)	**sea salt**
¼ tsp	(1 mL)	**black pepper**
	3	**cloves garlic, minced** (optional)
		cornmeal, for coating
		oil for frying
	12 - 15	**pita breads**
		shredded lettuce
		chopped tomato

Soak beans overnight and discard the soaking water. Add 6 cups (1.4 L) water and bring to a boil. Cook the garbanzos 40 minutes or until tender. Reserve 1 cup (240 mL) of the cooking water.

Process the beans with just enough of the cooking water to keep things moving in the blender.

Make bread-crumbs from the half loaf, either by crumbling dry bread, or by soaking the bread in water then squeezing out as much moisture as possible.

Combine all the ingredients in a large bowl.

Shape the mixture into 1½" (4 cm) balls, then roll them in cornmeal until well coated.

Heat ½" (12 mm) of oil in a saucepan (but don't let it smoke) and fry the balls, turning them in the oil until browned all over.

Lift them from the oil with a slotted spoon, and drain briefly before transferring them to a plate in a 225°F (105°C) oven.

While the last batch is frying, wrap the pita breads in a tea-towel and warm them for a short while in the oven.

Cut the pita breads in half and open them. Put several balls in the pocket, pour Falafel Sauce over them (recipe below), and top with the lettuce and tomato.

Falafel Sauce

½ **cup**	(120 mL)	**oil** (olive oil, sunflower oil or a combination)
½ **cup**	(120 mL)	**tahini**
¼ **cup**	(60 mL)	**lemon juice** (or more!)
2 Tbsp	(30 mL)	**tamari**
2		**cloves garlic, minced** (optional)

Blend all the ingredients until smooth.

This sauce makes a fine salad dressing, too. In fact it has proven so popular among falafel-eaters around these parts, that we often increase the amounts given in this recipe, so that we can all ladle it on to our hearts' content. Any extra remaining at the end of the meal doesn't usually last too long.

Bitterness and Joy on the Road to Kweilin

China

*The recipe serves six, making about thirty or so crisply savoury balls
in a sweet and sour sauce.*

1½ lbs	(675 g)	**tofu**
2½ Tbsp	(37 mL)	**tahini (or peanut butter)**
2½ Tbsp	(37 mL)	**tamari**
½ cup	(120 mL)	**finely chopped parsley**
½ cup	(120 mL)	**finely chopped chives**
½ cup	(120 mL)	**finely chopped leeks**
1 cup	(240 mL)	**finely chopped Jerusalem artichokes (or water-chestnuts)**
1½ cups	(360 mL)	**finely chopped mushrooms**
1½ cups	(360 mL)	**finely chopped celery**
1½ tsp	(7 mL)	**ground cumin**
¼ tsp	(1 mL)	**ground black pepper**
1 cup	(240 mL)	**coarse cornmeal**
		oil for frying

Mash the tofu in a bowl, and mix in all the other ingredients, except the
cornmeal and oil, until a uniform consistency is reached.

Form the mixture into 2" (5 cm) balls and roll them in cornmeal to cover
well.

In a large heavy skillet, fry the balls in ½" (12 mm) of oil (but don't let it
smoke), until they are brown and crispy all over. Lift them from the oil
with a slotted spoon, drain briefly and transfer to a plate in a warm oven
while you prepare...

THE SAUCE:	1½ cups	(360 mL)	**canned crushed pineapple**
	2 Tbsp	(30 mL)	**arrowroot flour**
	¼ cup	(60 mL)	**tamari**
	¼ tsp	(1 mL)	**paprika**
	½ cup	(120 mL)	**brown sugar**
	½ cup	(120 mL)	**apple cider vinegar**

Toss the crushed pineapple into the blender and process till smooth.

Mix the arrowroot with a little of the pineapple liquid until smooth.

Combine all the sauce ingredients in a small saucepan and simmer over
low heat until thickened to the desired slurpiness.

*These little delights are best presented hot on a bed of basmati rice, with fresh,
lightly-steamed kale, chard, spinach or broccoli.*

Potato Cauliflower Subji

Northern India

Mark Twain remarked that the cauliflower was just a "cabbage with a college education." Perhaps if we could have presented him with this curry, he might have thought more highly of this versatile vegetable.

Serves 6 - 8 hungry people.

5 tsp	(25 mL)	ground cumin
1 Tbsp	(15 mL)	ground coriander
1 Tbsp	(15 mL)	turmeric
1 Tbsp	(15 mL)	chili powder
4 tsp	(20 mL)	garam masala
½ tsp	(2 mL)	sea salt
¾ cup	(180 mL)	ghee or butter
2 cups	(480 mL)	chopped leeks
2 Tbsp	(30 mL)	grated fresh ginger
4 cups	(960 mL)	chopped potatoes
8 cups	(1.9 L)	chopped cauliflower
2 cups	(480 mL)	canned tomatoes, puréed
2 Tbsp	(30 mL)	lemon juice
2 - 2½ cups	(480 - 600mL)	water

Sauté the spices in ghee for about one minute.
Add the leeks and ginger and stir while cooking for a couple of minutes.
Add the potatoes. (You may need to add a little water at this point.)
Cook until the potatoes are getting close to being tender, adding more
  water as needed.
Add the cauliflower and continue cooking.
When the potatoes and cauliflower are soft, add the tomatoes and the
  lemon juice, and serve hot.

*To reduce the cooking time, you can steam the potatoes beforehand,
until they just begin to soften.
If you like a hotter curry, add more chili powder or a pinch of cayenne.*

*Chapatis and perhaps some raita would make fine accompaniments
to this meal; you will find the recipes on pages 72 and 70.*

"BETWEEN LIVING AND DREAMING, THERE IS A THIRD THING.
GUESS IT."

ANTONIO MACHADO (1875 - 1939)

Lasagna al Tofu

Somewhere in vegetarian Italy.

A lasagna that needs no cheese, yet tastes every bit as good as the traditional version.

THE SAUCE:

½ cup	(120 mL)	minced celery
1¼ cups	(300 mL)	chopped leeks
½ cup	(120 mL)	chopped green pepper
2 Tbsp	(30 mL)	oil
⅓ cup	(80 mL)	tomato paste (half of a small tin)
2 tsp	(10 mL)	oregano
2½ tsp	(12 mL)	basil
2		bay leaves
28-oz tin	(796 mL)	crushed tomatoes
1 tsp	(5 mL)	blackstrap molasses
2 tsp	(10 mL)	tamari

Sauté the celery, leeks and green pepper in oil, until the leeks are soft.
Add all the remaining ingredients, and leave to simmer gently for about an
  hour, with an occasional stir.

THE FILLING:

1 lb	(454 g)	tofu
2 cups	(480 mL)	finely chopped leeks
2 Tbsp	(30 mL)	olive oil
2 tsp	(10 mL)	dillweed
1 tsp	(5 mL)	basil
4 cups	(960 mL)	torn spinach* or young nettle leaves
10		lasagna noodles
1 cup	(240 mL)	grated Cashew UnCheese (see recipe page 168), or regular cheese if you prefer.

* Use more if you really like spinach.

Mash the tofu, and sauté it with the leeks in oil.

Sprinkle the dillweed over the mixture, and continue cooking.

Boil the noodles in plenty of salted water with a dash of oil, until they are cooked al dente (check package directions — pastas vary in cooking times).

If you are using more than 4 cups (960 mL) spinach, steam it first for a few minutes. Otherwise combine it raw with the tofu, leeks and herbs.

Arrange layers of the ingredients in a 9"x 12" (3 L) baking dish in the following order: half the sauce, half the noodles, tofu mixture, Cashew UnCheese (or cheese), remainder of the noodles, and sauce on top.

Bake the lasagna at 350°F (180°C) for 30 - 45 minutes.

Other variations for cheese-lovers include topping the lasagna with Parmesan, and putting a layer of Ricotta or cottage cheese in the middle.

"ONE MAY LIVE WITHOUT LOVE — WHAT IS PASSION BUT PINING?
BUT WHERE IS THE MAN WHO CAN LIVE WITHOUT DINING?"
OWEN MEREDITH: *LUCILE*
(1831-1891)

Panir

In India, the combination of tropical climate and a plentiful supply
of milk has given rise to many ways for preserving the nutritional value
that might otherwise be wasted. In an Indian household, excess milk is sometimes
turned into a batch of panir, a light-tasting cheese often cooked with vegetables.
The process takes a little time, but not much effort.

5 cups   (1.2 L)   **milk, whole or homogenized**
juice of 2 lemons

Heat the milk over a moderate flame, until it just begins to boil.
Pour in the lemon juice and stir, then immediately remove the pan from the
   heat and leave it to sit undisturbed while the curds form.
Line a strainer with several thicknesses of cheesecloth or muslin, and pour
   the curds and whey through, gently pressing the curds to remove most
   of the liquid. (The whey may be used in cooking.)
Gather the edges of the cloth together, pressing the curds inside into a little
   ball, then tie the neck of the bag with string and hang it to drip
   somewhere out of your way overnight. (A good spot would be under
   your tap perhaps.)
The next day, flatten the panir into a little, um, can I say hockey puck, and
   press it, still wrapped in its cloth, on a solid plate or board, under a
   heavy object. Suitable weights might include a large, clean, smooth rock,
   a heavy saucepan filled with water or something similar. The panir will
   need from several hours to half a day to reach the right, dense and
   slightly 'bouncy' consistency, and will be about $\frac{1}{2}$" to $\frac{3}{4}$" (12 - 18 mm)
   thick.
Now unwrap the cheese, and cut it with a sharp knife into cubes or
   rectangles, ready to be used in your vegetable dish.

Panir alone has little flavour, though it does have a lot of protein; however, when
fried, it imparts a satisfying texture to the other softer ingredients in the dish,
   adopting their blend of flavours for an unusual effect that justifies the
time it took you to prepare it.

In the following recipe for Muttar Panir, you may
substitute tofu for the panir, should your time be short,
or if you do not include dairy products in your diet.

Muttar Panir

This will serve six people as a side dish, poured over a bed of rice or bulgur.
Though it does take time to prepare the whole recipe starting from scratch,
we think you will find it worthwhile.

Serves 6.

½ cup	(120 mL)	sliced leeks
1"		(or more) piece of fresh ginger
½ cup	(120 mL)	water
7 Tbsp	(105 mL)	oil
		panir, cubed (amount made from recipe on previous page)
¼ tsp	(1 mL)	crushed dried chili pepper
1 Tbsp	(15 mL)	ground coriander
¼ tsp	(1 mL)	turmeric
7 Tbsp	(105 mL)	canned crushed tomatoes
	OR	2 large tomatoes, peeled & crushed
2 cups	(480 mL)	whey from the panir, or water
1 tsp	(5 mL)	sea salt
		ground black pepper
5 cups	(1.2 L)	fresh or defrosted frozen peas

Put the sliced leeks in a blender with the ginger and water, and purée to
make a smooth paste.

Heat the oil in a large saucepan and fry the cubed panir until it has
browned on all sides. Using your most "non-stick" saucepan or cast iron
pan will help with this, and so will keeping those little cubes of panir on
the move when they first go into the hot oil.

When the panir has been lightly browned, lift the cubes out with a slotted
spoon, drain briefly and set them aside on a plate.

Over low heat, fry the chili for a minute in the same pan, then add the leek
and ginger paste, and cook for 10 minutes, stirring frequently.

Add the coriander and turmeric and stir.

Add the tomatoes and fry the mixture for several minutes more, as it turns
to a rich, deep-red colour.

Now add the whey, or water, salt and a little freshly ground black pepper.

Stir to give an even sauce. Bring to a boil, then lower heat and simmer,
covered, for 10 more minutes.

Now you can add the cubes of panir and the peas. Continue simmering,
covered, for just a few more minutes — until the peas are cooked.

Frijoles Refritos

Mexico

These refried beans can also be used as a filling for burritos, or even as a splendid breakfast for the adventurous soul who is unfettered by mundane convention.

2 cups	(480 mL)	**finely chopped leeks**
¹/₃ cup	(80 mL)	**oil**
4 cups	(960 mL)	**cooked pinto or red kidney beans**
		(about 2 cups dry)
2 Tbsp	(30 mL)	**tamari**
1¹/₂ tsp	(7 mL)	**ground cumin***

* If you eat garlic, you may wish to replace the cumin with 3 small cloves of garlic, minced or finely chopped.

In a large, heavy skillet, sauté the leeks in 3 Tbsp (30 mL) oil until they are bright green and tender.
Mix all the ingredients with the remaining oil, then fry in the pan until thoroughly heated.

As an option, you can also add diced green pepper or jalapeño peppers sprinkled on top.

Serve topped with grated cheese as a side dish, accompanied by Guacamole (page 163), sour cream or yoghurt, hot Salsa! (page 152), corn tortillas (opposite), slices of cantaloupe and a fresh green salad. Fiesta!

Lonestar Tortillas

Mexico

Making tortillas is not a quick process, but the flavour is so far superior to store-bought that you will probably find them well worth the effort.

Makes twelve 6" tortillas.

2 cups	(480 mL)	**masa harina***
¹/₂ tsp	(2 mL)	**sea salt**
1 cup	(240 mL)	**water**
1¹/₂ Tbsp	(22 mL)	**lemon juice**

> *Masa harina is a finely-ground cornmeal treated with lime water, available at many health-food stores and delicatessens. Regular cornmeal will **not** work.

In a mixing-bowl, combine the masa harina and sea salt.

Add the lemon juice to the water, and stir it into the dry ingredients.

Knead this dough for a few minutes, then roll it into a "log" about two inches thick. Cut it in half; then cut each half in half, and cut each of these four sections into three, to give a dozen equal pieces.

In Mexico, women shape the tortillas by patting them between their hands. However, for those of us not trained since birth to do this, the easiest method is to place each piece between small sheets of wax paper and roll it out with a rolling-pin. Or roll them out on a floured, smooth surface such as an arborite countertop. The tortilla should be between ¹/₁₆" and ¹/₈" (2-3 mm) thick.

Remove the wax paper, and trim the tortilla with a knife, if you prefer a neat circle.

Lightly oil a heavy skillet, using a small piece of towel soaked in oil, or a pastry brush. Repeat this after each tortilla has been cooked.

Start on high heat, then reduce it to medium, and fry the tortilla on each side for 3 to 5 minutes or until lightly browned. The second side may puff up when you cook it. The tortilla should still be fairly pliable after cooking.

Keep the cooked tortillas wrapped in a slightly moistened towel until you're ready to fill them, but don't keep them waiting too long — they lose that fresh, just-made flavour.

Spiced Dal

India

This spicy and protein-rich dish often becomes a favourite for adults at first taste. Children may prefer it minus the spices and with a dab of butter melting on top, so cook a certain amount extra for them. Great served with rice and vegetable curries.

Serves 4 - 6 people, as a side dish.

2 cups	(480 mL)	yellow split peas
5½ cups	(1.3 L)	water
1 tsp	(5 mL)	sea salt
¼ cup	(60 mL)	ghee or butter
2½ tsp	(12 mL)	cumin seed
1½ tsp	(7 mL)	ground turmeric
2" piece	(5 cm)	of stick cinnamon, broken
½ tsp	(2 mL)	cayenne
½ tsp	(2 mL)	ground ginger
½ tsp	(2 mL)	coriander seed
1 tsp	(5 mL)	mustard seed
9		whole cloves
1 tsp	(5 mL)	garam masala
½ tsp	(2 mL)	curry powder

Wash the split peas thoroughly in several changes of water, and drain them.

Bring them to a boil in the salted water, then simmer until very soft, about 45 minutes, stirring often to prevent them from sticking as they cook.

Fry the spices in ghee or butter over medium heat (don't let it smoke!), until the mustard seeds pop.

Pour the spice mixture into the split peas and stir thoroughly to mix.

Cook for a few minutes longer, but do not allow it to stick to the pan. Add more water if necessary to achieve the consistency you desire.

Remove the pieces of cinnamon, if you wish, or leave them in for rustic texture and a sweet surprise.

Serve <u>hot</u>.

You may wish to increase, or double, the given quantity of cayenne and ginger, depending on how hot you like your food, and what other dishes you are serving with the dal.

This dal improves with a little time to sit, covered, and contemplate itself over very low heat. Spice flavours blend and mature, character builds.....ah!

Yam and Parsnip Subji

India

This popular curry has a sweet but spicy ambience. The quantities below make an ideal basis for a party menu.

Serves 12.

²/₃ cup	(160 mL)	ghee or butter
1 Tbsp	(15 mL)	turmeric
2 Tbsp	(30 mL)	ground coriander
2 Tbsp	(30 mL)	ground cumin
2 Tbsp	(30 mL)	chili powder
3 Tbsp	(45 mL)	garam masala
1 tsp	(5 mL)	sea salt
3 cups	(720 mL)	chopped leeks
¹/₂ cup	(120 mL)	grated fresh ginger
8 cups	(1.9 L)	thinly sliced parsnips
10 cups	(2.4 L)	thinly sliced yams
3 cups	(720 mL)	water

In a large pot, sauté the spices in ghee for just one minute over
  medium heat.
Add the leeks and ginger and sauté them for a few minutes, stirring
  often.
Add the parsnips, yams, and water and cover the pot.
Cook until the vegetables are tender, stirring occasionally.

*Serve over rice, with Cucumber Raita (page 70), slices of cold melon,
toasted cashews and peanuts, and chutney.*

"THE PRESENT IS A GIFT."
ANON.

Torta Rustica

Italy

This "country pie" looks and tastes so great that it gives even a novice the air of a master chef. Spontaneous applause greeted the first test to emerge from our oven! Makes one 9" (23 cm) deep-dish pie (or use an 8"x 8" [1.5 L] baking dish).

THE DOUGH:

½ cup	(120 mL)	**warm water**
1 tsp	(5 mL)	**honey or sugar**
1 Tbsp	(15 mL)	**active dry yeast**
1 cup	(240 mL)	**warm milk or soy milk**
1 Tbsp	(15 mL)	**olive oil**
1 Tbsp	(15 mL)	**honey** (optional)
1½ tsp	(7 mL)	**Spike or vegetable seasoning**
3 cups	(720 mL)	**unbleached white flour**

In a bowl, combine the warm water, honey, and yeast. Let stand for 10 minutes or until the yeast bubbles up.

Now mix in the milk, oil, Spike, and extra sweetener, if using.

Stir in 2 cups (480 mL) of flour. Beat until gluten forms (dough becomes sticky and forms strands — about 300 strokes). Work in the remaining flour and knead on a floured board for 5 minutes but don't add too much more!

Instead, pour a little oil onto the kneading board, and some on your hands, and continue kneading for another 5 minutes.

Set the dough aside in a warm, draft-free place until it has doubled in bulk (45 minutes to 1 hour).

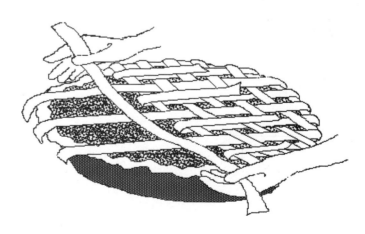

THE FILLING:

2 cups	(480 mL)	**finely chopped leeks**
¼ cup	(60 mL)	**olive oil or butter**
6 cups	(1.4 L)	**coarsely chopped washed spinach** (about two bunches) **OR young nettle leaves**
¼ tsp	(1 mL)	**nutmeg**
¼ tsp	(1 mL)	**black pepper**
2 tsp	(10 mL)	**basil**
1 Tbsp	(15 mL)	**egg replacer** (optional) **with appropriate amount of water**
1 cup	(240 mL)	**grated parmesan cheese**
1 cup	(240 mL)	**crumbled ricotta cheese** **(or use cottage cheese)**

Sauté the leeks in oil until they are softened, and then toss in the spinach and briefly sauté so that it reduces in bulk.

In a large bowl, combine the sautéed leeks and spinach with the nutmeg and pepper.

Add the remaining ingredients and mix well.

Oil a 9-inch (23 cm) pie dish or an 8-inch (1.5 L) baking dish.

Punch down the risen dough, remove it from the bowl and cut it in half.

Roll out one half quite thinly on a lightly oiled surface, until it is several inches bigger in diameter than your pie dish or baking dish.

Press it into the dish and bring it up the sides. Trim around the edge.

Pour in the filling and pat it down. Don't worry if it looks like too much — it will cook down.

Roll out the remaining dough and cut it into strips.

Weave them, lattice-fashion, over the top of the pie (see illustration opposite). Where each strip joins the edge of the bottom-crust, moisten the pastry and pinch the two pieces together, so that they seal the edges and stay attached when baked.

Bake at 350°F (180°C) for 30 minutes.

"IS IT SO SMALL A THING
TO HAVE ENJOYED THE SUN
TO HAVE LIV'D LIGHT IN THE SPRING
TO HAVE LOV'D, TO HAVE THOUGHT, TO HAVE DONE."
MATTHEW ARNOLD (1822-1888)

SunMoon  ushrooms

China

Serves 4 - 8 as a side dish or appetizer.

Add rice and steamed greens to these hot-and-sour, crispy and succulent little morsels, shimmering in their tangy sauce, and you have an unforgettable main course.

THE BATTER:

2 tsp	(10 mL)	**egg-replacer, with appropriate amount of water**
6 Tbsp	(90 mL)	**arrowroot flour**
6 Tbsp	(90 mL)	**sweet rice flour** (or unbleached white flour)
½ cup	(120 mL)	**water**
1½ lbs	(680 g)	**fresh mushrooms**
1 cup	(240 mL)	**fine dry breadcrumbs** **vegetable oil for frying**

Select well-formed mushrooms that are in good condition — some large and some small makes for an interesting variety.

Wipe them clean, and trim the bottom off the stems.

Combine the batter ingredients, adding the water a little at a time so that all the lumps can be stirred out as you go.

Dip each mushroom in the batter, then roll it in breadcrumbs.

Heat a couple of inches of oil in a deep saucepan until it is hot but not smoking, 350 - 375°F (180 - 190°C).

Fry the mushrooms until they are golden brown and crisp. Lift them from the oil with a slotted spoon, and drain briefly before transferring to a plate in a warm oven.

(Let the oil cool, strain it and then store it in the refrigerator until the next time you need to deep-fry something.)

THE SAUCE:

1 Tbsp	(15 mL)	oil
1 tsp	(5 mL)	crushed chili peppers (use a little less if you are sensitive to hot food)
	1	medium carrot
	1	medium leek, sliced thin
$^2/_3$ cup	(160 mL)	water
$^1/_3$ cup	(80 mL)	apple cider vinegar
$^1/_3$ cup	(80 mL)	brown sugar
$^1/_3$ cup	(80 mL)	pineapple juice or syrup from can of pineapple
1 Tbsp	(15 mL)	arrowroot flour or cornstarch
$^3/_4$ cup	(180 mL)	pineapple chunks, well-drained

Scrub the carrot and cut it into fat slivers about $^1/_2$" (12 mm) thick.

In a large frying pan or wok over high heat, sauté the carrot, leek and chili in oil for a couple of minutes.

Add $^1/_3$ cup (80 mL) water, the vinegar, sugar and juice and bring to a boil.

Mix the arrowroot flour with the remaining $^1/_3$ cup (80 mL) water, and add it to the sauce, stirring constantly until it thickens and bubbles — then remove from heat. An arrowroot-thickened sauce will thin out if overcooked.

Add the pineapple chunks and fried mushrooms to the pan, turning them in the sauce so that they are well coated.

Serve instantly, so the mushrooms arrive still crisp and marvellous in the mouths of your eager guests!

"O NIGHTS AND SUPPERS OF THE GODS!"
HORACE: *SATIRES*

Sushi

Japan

This recipe may seem somewhat long and daunting, but in fact it is suprisingly simple. In Japan, making sushi is an art; would-be sushi chefs spend two years just learning how to cook rice perfectly. Using this recipe, you can learn how to make the entire sushi in just about one hour. So you see? You're getting off lightly.

1 cup	(240 mL)	**short grain brown rice***
2¼ cups	(540 mL)	**water**
		pinch of salt
5 Tbsp	(75 mL)	**brown rice vinegar**
4		**sheets of nori seaweed**
½		**lemon**
		(for sticking nori rolls together)

* Short grain brown rice is recommended because it has more gluten in it, and therefore holds together better.

Cook the rice for about 40 minutes (see Grains section, page 100).
When it is done, allow it to cool by fluffing up with a fork occasionally, then stir in the vinegar.
Toast each sheet of nori by holding it over a low flame or electric burner for a short while.

THE FILLING:

1		**carrot**
1		**avocado**
2 tsp	(10 mL)	**wasabi** (see Ingredients page 7)
1½ tsp	(7 mL)	**water**
4 Tbsp	(60 mL)	**toasted sesame seeds**
		tamari
		alfalfa or mung bean sprouts

Optional:	**cucumber strips**
	pickled daikon radish
	chives or green onions
	tofu strips marinated in tamari

Peel the carrot, then cut it lengthwise into long, very thin strips. Steam them with a little water in a wide pan until they are just tender.
Cut the avocado into thin slices.

Mix the wasabi powder with the water to make a paste.

Toast the sesame seeds in a heavy skillet, stirring frequently until they are lightly browned.

FORMING THE SUSHI — STEP ONE:

Have a bowl of water available to wet your hands periodically while handling the rice, to keep it from sticking to your hands.

Divide the rice into four equal amounts, then put one quarter of it onto the first sheet of nori.

With your hands, press the rice out thinly, about ¼" (6 mm) thick, leaving a ½" (12 mm) strip of nori showing at the bottom of the sheet, and ¾" (2 cm) at the top.

Lightly sprinkle the rice with tamari and sesame seeds.

Place two or three carrot strips on top of the rice, across the width of the sheet and about 2" (5 cm) from the bottom.

Place 3 pieces of avocado on top of the carrots, then put the sprouts on top of the avocado.

With your finger, spread a line of wasabi onto the rice next to the carrots.

Now you're ready to roll!

STEP TWO:

Starting from the bottom, roll up the nori, making sure you tuck in the leading edge firmly as you roll.

When you get to the top, squeeze a little lemon juice onto the exposed edge of the nori sheet. This will help the roll stick together.

Place the roll seam-side down on the table, then give it a squeeze with your hands to make it firm. Allow the roll to stand for five minutes. This will further firm the roll.

Cut into one inch (2.5 cm) pieces with a large, sharp knife. Dipping the blade in water lessens the tendency of the rice to stick to the knife.

To avoid ejecting the filling like toothpaste from a tube, make a little incision with a gentle sawing motion of the knife. Once the nori "skin" is broken, finish the cut with one quick, firm, downward slice. You may need to "saw" the bottom skin of nori.

Serve with a bowl of tamari, mixed with a little wasabi, in which to dip the sushi. Arrange the sushi attractively on a plate garnished with paper-thin slices of cucumber and radishes (layered like fallen dominoes), 2 or 3 tomato or lemon wedges, perhaps a few chives (with their edible flowers).

Grains

Grains made it possible for humankind to change from being foragers to a way of life as agrarians, sowing and harvesting the foods that best supplied them with the calories and protein they needed. Grains are still the principal food of human beings, whether as a bowl of rice in Indonesia, barley *tsampa* in Nepal, a long baguette at breakfast in Marseilles, or cornmeal tortillas in Baja California.

In the past generation, an increased emphasis on meat in the North American diet has meant that now most meals are structured around the meat content. This has led to a waste of the available nutrients found in grains, since very little of the minerals and vitamins that they contain are passed on to the consumer of the grain-fed meat. Twenty-one pounds of grains, mostly fit for human consumption, are fed to an animal to result in one pound of meat protein. This degree of waste is only made possible by depleting the poorer nations of nutrients and concentrating them in the wealthiest nations as animal fodder. Meanwhile, one third of mankind starves or is under-nourished. There is a strong case to be made for using grains well, understanding their history, and their value to the whole of our human family. We have sufficient grain, that no-one need go hungry.

Grains must be stored in a cool dry place, in a protective container; this way they last unimpaired virtually forever. Grains are quite wonderful, really — you can use them in soups and main dishes, or as complements to curries and sauces (see our Sauces chapter); add something spicy or herby to the cooking water; or use them cold in desserts...... the only limit is your imagination.

On the following pages you will find a brief description of the different types, cooking instructions and a few clues as to how to use grains. Nutritional information is available from a number of books (see bibliography). Remember that most grains are low in lysine, one of the amino acids that make up a complete protein, and beans contain lysine in abundance. Combining the two gives a more balanced protein.

The cooking method for all of the grains except rice is basically the same. First bring the measured amount of water to a boil, then add the grain. Cover the pot and lower the heat to keep the liquid simmering until the grain is cooked.

Rice is cooked a little differently, because you start with cold water, rice and a pinch of salt. Bring this to a boil and let it boil for 5 minutes. (The 5 minutes is included in the cooking time on our chart.) Then lower the heat to keep the rice barely simmering. Now **don't peek**..... it has to steam undisturbed. When the cooking time is finished, remove the pot from the heat and let it stand for a few minutes (see the chart). O.K., *now* you can look. We bet you will see perfect rice every time.

BARLEY The principal grain used for bread-making in Europe during the Middle Ages, barley was subsequently brought to North America by colonists in the 1700's, where it was valued, among other things, for brewing beer. This is a very hardy and ancient grain, usually grown with little or no pesticide or fungicide. Barley flour is an excellent subsitute grain for those with wheat allergies. It gives a sweet, moist taste to baked goods. If you're using whole barley in soups, it can be pre-soaked to shorten cooking time. Barley can also be sprouted for use in breads and soups.

BULGUR Bulgur is partly-cooked cracked wheat. Often, bulgur is sautéed before cooking, giving it a nice, nutty flavour. As an alternative to cooking, you can just soak this grain for 30 minutes before use — you won't need to cook it again. A great recipe using bulgur is Tabouleh (page 134).

BUCKWHEAT GROATS (also known as Kasha, when toasted.) Buckwheat has been cultivated in Europe since the Middle Ages. These three-cornered seeds can be used as a cereal or rice substitute. Roasting them in a little oil (1 cup buckwheat to 2 Tbsp butter or oil) brings out their naturally nutty flavour.

CRACKED WHEAT Similar to bulgur, but not pre-cooked, so **you** have to cook it. Dry-roast cracked wheat in a skillet until it just begins to pop. Then cook it. Bring water to a boil before adding the grain gradually so that the boiling never stops. Turn the heat down to a simmer and cook slowly.

WHOLE WHEAT BERRIES Whole kernels of wheat provide a nice change from rice or bulgur. Because they are hard, they keep well and hold their nutritional value. Be sure to buy organic kernels, though, to be free of pesticides. They have a delicate flavour, and it doesn't take many wheat berries to fill you up! They're good with just butter and tamari sauce. Wheat berries are often sprouted for a day and used in breads.

CORNMEAL Coarsely ground corn — there are various grinds, the finer ones being used in baking. Cornmeal is full of polyunsaturated oil and quickly goes rancid after grinding. The best course is to grind one's own cornmeal in order to avoid that slightly bitter taste (from rancidity) that can come through in cooking. If this is not possible, ask your merchant about freshness; store it in a cool, dry place.

MILLET Millet is an ancient and very nutritious grain. Because of its sweetness, it is often used as a breakfast grain (see the breakfast recipes in the Kids' Food section). Dry-roasting before cooking brings out the natural flavour of the millet; some people prefer to roast it in ghee. If you are making millet milk, you will need another cup of water to produce a softer grain for blending.

RICE Rice in its many forms is as old as time itself, and a staple for many diets. Long-grain rice tends to separate into fluffy grains, whereas short grain rice tends to cling together — making it useful for puddings or molded dishes. Rinse and drain rice before cooking but don't soak it! Some folks like to briefly toast their rice in a little oil before cooking, to keep the rice kernels from sticking together. (You can also add a tablespoon of oil to the cooking water to achieve the same result.)
Brown: husked but not polished, brown rice contains 25% more protein than white, and is higher in minerals and B vitamins. It is also lower in cholesterol.
Basmati: This is a sweeter, East Indian rice, and comes in both brown and white.

White or Polished: Rice without its skin.

QUINOA (pronouced 'keenwah'). Although thousands of years old, this South American seed is making new strides into North American markets because of its high protein and mineral content — highest in fact, of all grains and seeds. Because of its hardiness and the resin-like coating on the seeds (washed off before marketing), quinoa needs no pesticides. It is claimed that quinoa comes closer than any other food to supplying all the essential life-sustaining nutrients. Unlike other grains, Quinoa is high in the amino acid lysine. We should mention that a little of the bitter coating sometimes remains on the seeds — rinsing will ensure sweetness.

Type of Grain	Grain/Water Ratio	Cooking Time (min.)	Yield (cups)
Barley	1:2½	60	3
Bulgur	1:2	15	2½
Buckwheat	1:1¾	30	2
Cracked Wheat	1:3	20	2½
Wheat Berries	1:5	90	3
Cornmeal	1:4	30	3½
Millet	1:2	40	3½
Quinoa	1:2	15	3
Basmati Rice	1:2	25	2 (let stand 5 min.)
Brown Rice	1:2½	50	2 (let stand 10 min.)
White Rice	1:2	25	1½ (let stand 5 min.)

Beans!

The wild ancestor of most of the commonly-used beans in North America originated in South America, but beans of one kind or another have been cultivated for thousands and thousands of years: native agrarian Indians planted beans in hillocks along with the corn. Beans have twice the protein of grains, are low in fats and carbohydrates and a good source of B vitamins and iron.

Many beans lend themselves to sprouting, which produces a "living" food, rich in vitamins, minerals and enzymes. Here's a simple way to sprout beans or grains: use only a small amount of seeds, say one or two tablespoons. Place them in a glass jar and cover them with water. Fasten a square of cheesecloth or flexible window-screening over the jar-mouth and secure it with a rubber band. Next day, pour off the water and rinse the seeds thoroughly with fresh water, before draining. After this, rinse them twice each successive day, draining thoroughly then leaving the jar mouth-down so no water can accumulate around the seeds. In three to five days, you'll have a crop of brand-new sprouts, full of vitality.

To remove the gas-producing effect from any kind of beans, soak them at least overnight, or preferably for 24 hours. Drain the water off — it is rich in minerals and can be used for your house plants. Soaking usually reduces the cooking time by half (more energy efficient!) Use fresh water for cooking, making sure the beans are well covered, then cook for the recommended time. Thorough chewing, of course, is the necessary last step for beans to be well assimilated without digestive problems. Using these methods has ensured us of happy bean eating, and, unless your digestion is quite unusual, it is likely to work for you too.

Odd though it may seem, for many people beans are best eaten in the morning, when digestion is at optimum performance. The recipe for Frijoles Refritos (page 88) lends itself well to breakfasts.

Now let's take a look at each bean variety and its corresponding merits:

ADUKI (also Azuki/Adzuki) This small red Japanese bean is considered the most easily digested of all beans. Use them instead of mung beans in Khichari, page 108.

BLACK BEANS Black beans are a staple of Latin America, Mexico and Southwestern North America. They make a great soup. Like black soybeans, these beans will also dye any other bean they are soaked with — so cook them separately, unless you find the appearance attractive.

BLACK TURTLE BEANS Especially rich in minerals (calcium, phosphorus, potassium and iron) and B vitamins, these beans also have a great protein content — almost one quarter of their weight. A rich, savoury taste makes them popular in all kinds of bean dishes. Buy them organically grown by the bag, if your local supplier is able to get them, and the price for *amazing* beans will be no more than for any other. Our kids love them in Speedy Burritos (page 262).

GARBANZOS (or Chickpeas) are high in protein, a source of calcium, iron, potassium and B vitamins. A common and well-loved item in Middle Eastern cooking, garbanzos are slowly gaining favour in the West. One look at this little bean will quickly tell you why its nickname is "chickpea." See our recipes for Hummus on page 164, and Chickpea Basil Soup on page 31.

KIDNEY BEANS These are the "quick cookers" among the big beans. They retain their shape and colour after cooking, making them useful for salads.

LENTILS Lentils are one of the earliest cultivars, going back to at least 7000 B.C. They come in brown, red, yellow and green. All lentils cook quickly, particularly the reds. The commonly-available brown lentils are rather stronger in terms of nutrients. We've used lentils in Basil & Lemon Lentil Soup (page 40), and Sia's Greek Lentil Soup (page 45). A good source of protein, iron and B vitamins.

MUNG BEANS Probably familiar to most people as the bean in bean sprouts, used in Chinese cooking and salads. They are also an easily digestible bean when cooked. (see Khichari, page 108).

LIMA BEANS (Baby and Large — also called Butter Beans). Another of the world's oldest cultivated vegetables, having been found in Incan tombs dating back to 6000 B.C. It is thought that South American Indians traded these beans throughout the New World. Limas got their name from Lima, Peru, around the time of the California Gold Rush in the mid-1800's, when the United States was flooded with them. Both the baby and large varieties cook up quite quickly and are underestimated here in the West for flavour and versatility. See Fassoulia p. 105.

NAVY BEANS These small white beans are a good addition to soups and stews. They can be cooked with lots of water to make a smooth broth.

PINTO BEANS This very pretty bean is quite popular for chilis and salads, as well as soups and stews. They are similar to kidney beans in flavour, but, being smaller, they cook a little faster.

SOYBEANS Soybeans have been feeding the Chinese population for over 5,000 years; North Americans, though, were largely unaware of this protein-rich bean until the 1950's. The common soybean varieties are basically boring and require long cooking, but they are of such high nutritive value that many ingenious recipes have been developed to improve on their blandness. Soy beans are our source of tofu, the vegetarian's friend; miso, fermented soy bean paste, which we use in many soups; and tempeh, fermented whole soy beans. A couple of useful recipes using soybeans are Soy Milk, page 279 and Okara Loaf, page 55. Remember, while soybeans are soaking they should be kept in a cool place since they tend to ferment rather quickly. It should be noted that if the soy beans are old, both their cooking time and the amount of water will have to be increased.

SOYBEANS, BLACK These soybeans are a variety called "Black Jet," especially suited to mild coastal summers. They have a sweet nutty flavour and are easily digested. Black soybeans are attractive, not only because they are delicious, but because they do not require long cooking.

At present, they are available by mail order through Dan Jason of Salt Spring Seeds (or via the Centre). They can be substituted in any soybean recipe (except soymilk), or used as any other bean. They make an attractive addition to bean salads. Remember when soaking black soy beans that they will ferment quickly in warm weather, like other soybeans. Also, you may find that they will dye other beans if soaked together.

SPLIT PEAS Yellow splits are a particularly useful and quick-cooking legume, that provide an easy source of protein for a meal. Try them in Spiced Dal, page 90, or serve them plain with a little butter, a favourite with children. Green splits go well in soups, such as Pea Soup (surprise!) on page 43.

Type of Bean	Ratio of Soaked Beans to Water	Cooking Time (minutes)	Yield (1 cup dry)
Aduki	1:4	40	3
Black Soybeans	1:2½	90	2
Black Beans	1:1½	40	2⅓
Black Turtle	1:2	45	2½
Garbanzos	1:3	40	2½
Kidney	1:2	35	3
Brown Lentils*	1:2	45	2½
Red Lentils*	1:2	10	2
Limas (small)	1:2	35	2
Limas (big)	1:2½	40	2
Navy Beans	1:2	30	2⅔
Mung Beans*	1:4	35	2½
Pintos	1:4	45	2½
Split Peas*	1:3	45	3
Soy Beans	1:4	2 - 4 hrs	2½

*do not require soaking

NB: Cooking times also depend on the freshness of the beans — older ones will take longer; the amount of water required will depend on whether your cooking pot is wide-based (requiring more water). If you would like more broth with your finished product (for soups, perhaps), you must add more liquid. Generally speaking, beans are adequately cooked when you can mash them against the roof of your mouth with your tongue, or when the skin of the bean splits when you blow on it.

Fassoulia

This simple and absolutely delicious recipe comes from the island of Crete, where it is served around Eastertime as a protein substitute for meat.

Serves 4 to 6 as a side dish.

4 cups	(960 mL)	**fresh broad beans** (shelled)
OR:		
2 cups	(480 mL)	**dry large lima beans**
2 cups	(480 mL)	**coarsely chopped leeks**
2 Tbsp	(30 mL)	**olive oil**
3½ Tbsp	(52 mL)	**lemon juice** (1 large lemon)
1 tsp	(5 mL)	**sea salt**
½ cup	(120 mL)	**additional olive oil**

Cook the broad beans or limas until tender in a large pot. (See previous pages for cooking instructions for dry limas.)

Sauté the leeks in the olive oil for a few minutes, until they are softened.

Drain off any excess liquid from the beans, then add the leeks, lemon juice, salt and additional olive oil to the pot.

Mix well and serve immediately.

Garnish with a wedge of tomato and a sprinkling of chopped parsley or mint.

*Fassoulia is often served drenched in olive oil,
with a Greek salad and crusty white bread.
The bread is used to soak up the olive oil from the beans and the salad. Delicious!
However, this dish is also excellent served with
cooked spinach, rice and tomatoes,
or any vegetable dish.*

Five Minute Fried Rice

Plan ahead for this quick re-heat recipe — cook twice the amount of rice you need and refrigerate the extra until needed.

Serves 4.

2 Tbsp	(30 mL)	**vegetable oil**
½ cup	(120 mL)	**chopped leeks**
¼ cup	(60 mL)	**chopped green pepper**
2 Tbsp	(30 mL)	**coarsely grated carrot**
3 cups	(720 mL)	**cooked brown rice**
1 Tbsp	(15 mL)	**tamari**

Heat the oil in a frying pan and sauté the vegetables until slightly softened.
Add the cooked rice and stir constantly to keep it from sticking.
When the rice is heated through, stir in the tamari until it is evenly mixed.
Keep over moderate heat, still stirring, until piping hot.
Serve immediately.

Serve with roasted, slivered almonds or toasted sunflower seeds sprinkled on top.

Ginger Noodles

This quick, unique pasta dish fits well with any steamed or stir-fried vegetable.
If you make the recipe with Chinese rice noodles, you can serve it chilled.

This recipe is for 6 people.

		noodles for 6 people
		(spaghetti, chinese rice noodles or other long noodles)
2 cups	(480 mL)	**thinly sliced leeks** (long, thin slices)
½ cup	(120 mL)	**thinly sliced root ginger** (long, very thin matchsticks)
3 Tbsp	(45 mL)	**vegetable oil**
¼ cup	(60 mL)	**tamari**

Cook and drain the noodles according to package directions.
Sauté the leeks and ginger in the oil in a wok.
Add the cooked noodles and tamari.
Heat and stir briefly, then serve.

Ginger lovers — increase sliced ginger by ⅓ cup (80 mL).
Tamari lovers — increase tamari to ⅓ cup (80 mL).

"WORK HONESTLY
MEDITATE EVERY DAY
MEET PEOPLE WITHOUT FEAR
AND PLAY."

BABA HARI DASS

Khichari

Pronounced 'kitcheree.' This is nourishing and "balancing" — perhaps one of the most easily digested foods we know.

If you wish, you may double the spices for more of a tweak to your taste buds. Adding half a teaspoon (2 mL) or more of miso to each soup bowl full of khichari gives a nice fullness to the flavour too.

Makes four modest servings.

1 cup	(240 mL)	mung beans
1 cup	(240 mL)	brown rice
1 tsp	(5 mL)	ground cumin
	15	black peppercorns
¼ tsp	(1 mL)	mustard seeds
2 Tbsp	(30 mL)	ghee or butter
1 tsp	(5 mL)	turmeric
½ tsp	(2 mL)	garam masala
		big pinch of ground cardamom
1 cup	(240 mL)	finely chopped leeks
1 Tbsp	(15 mL)	ghee or oil
4 cups	(960 mL)	water or stock, or more
½ tsp	(2 mL)	sea salt

Cook the mung beans in a saucepan with plenty of water to cover. They'll take about 30 minutes (if split) to 45 minutes (if whole) to become soft.

Cook the brown rice in 2½ cups (600 mL) water for 50 minutes.

In a large frying pan, sauté the cumin, peppercorns and mustard seeds in ghee until the mustard seeds pop.

Mix the turmeric and garam masala into the spicy ghee and spices until well blended.

Now sauté the beans and rice in the ghee for about 2 minutes, then transfer the mixture to your saucepan.

Sauté the leeks in a tablespoon (15 mL) of ghee until soft, then tip them into the saucepan and add the water and salt.

The longer you cook the khichari, the thicker it gets, so you may need more water. Best cooking time is about 20 minutes at a simmer.

Serve with a dollop of yoghurt and a ring of tamari soy sauce (if you're not using miso). Remember too, you can substitute red lentils for mung beans. And you can substitute a finely chopped garlic clove for the leeks.

Lemon Rice

A simple recipe that gives rice a fragrant and flavourful twist.

Serves 4 people.

¹/₂ **cup**	(120 mL)	**chopped celery**
¹/₄ **cup**	(60 mL)	**chopped chives or green onions**
2 Tbsp	(30 mL)	**butter**
3 cups	(720 mL)	**cooked basmati rice**
¹/₂ **tsp**	(2 mL)	**thyme**
¹/₄ **tsp**	(1 mL)	**black pepper**
¹/₄ **tsp**	(1 mL)	**sea salt**
2 - 4 Tbsp	(30-60 mL)	**lemon juice**
1 Tbsp	(15 mL)	**grated lemon rind**

Sauté the celery and chives in butter until softened.
Stir in the rice and the remaining ingredients.
Cook over low heat for a few minutes, stirring all the time, to let the
   flavours blend.
Serve hot and steamy.

*Serve with stir-fried vegetables, tofu cutlets or just
as a different treatment for rice.*

Lentil Rice Salad

*A Hindu proverb runs "Rice is good, but lentils are my life." This complete-meal-
salad lets you enjoy the good life!*

Serves 4 to 6 salad lovers.

2 cups	(480 mL)	**cooked lentils**
2 cups	(480 mL)	**cooked basmati rice**
1 cup	(240 mL)	**grated carrot**
³/₄ **cup**	(180 mL)	**chopped leeks**

Simply mix everything in a bowl and toss with Raghunath's Ginger
   Paprika Dressing (page 140) until the ingredients are evenly coated.

*Serve at room temperature, to bring out the fullest flavour, on a bed of lettuce or
spinach greens for an attractive and spicy little salad.*

Vegetables

We humans would be in a sorry mess indeed if suddenly we were robbed of our vegetables. Not only are they pleasing to the eye and palate, but vegetables also supply us with many vital minerals and vitamins. Peoples or animals who are strict carnivores must eat the entrails of their victims for the flora contained therein for these life supporting nutrients, otherwise denied them by an environment that doesn't always support vegetation.

BUYING:
We've been trained to select the brightest, crispest, firmest vegetables — but is that correct? Do they really contain more nutritional value than the more dowdy veggies, or have they been artifically plumped and primped to just look good? The best vegetables, of course, are those that come from your own garden. If you must buy them, try to buy them from a grocer who has a local supplier, so there is less risk of the trickery of chemical use to enhance the vegetable's fresh appearance. Buying vegetables in season will also mean a local source with the added bonus of reasonable prices for a plentiful supply. Don't be afraid to dig beneath the surface display — gently, of course — sometimes the best vegetables are hidden beneath their aging counterparts in the hopes that the older ones will be chosen first. Remember, too, that wilting leaves on the outside can be hiding a perfectly good heart.

STORAGE:
Vegetables crave cold storage because cold air retards the breakdown of the enzymes inherent in all food. Plastic bags or any sealed container stop the moisture loss which causes wilting. Except for mushrooms of course: store them in paper bags to absorb moisture or in the open, as they sweat and spoil quickly. They will dry out over time; the good news is that they are still usable (some people even buy them that way!).

Tomatoes breathe and ought not be stored in plastic. Carrots and parsnips should have their tops cut off before storage. With the tops still attached, the sap will keep running from the root to the leaves, robbing the root of nutrients and moisture. This method also prevents your refrigerator from becoming a science project if vegetables are kept overlong. An exception to this is beets — leave the root and at least one inch of the stem intact, so when cooking, the "beet blood" and nutrients will be contained. Potatoes should be stored in a cool, dry, dark place with good air circulation, (starches turn to sugar in the fridge). Don't store them with the onions or the apples (which also need this type of storage — at least until cut), since onions and apples emit a gas that ages potatoes very quickly. When light and potato meet, the potato skin turns green and poisonous, so be careful.

In any event, we do recommend buying in smaller quantities (or sharing larger ones) so that storage time is minimized. Vitamins disappear over time, and unless you grew them yourself, you really have very little idea of where the vegetables have been and for how long.

Preparation:

Now it's time to wash your produce in preparation for cooking. A scrub brush works well and removes very little of the valuable outer skin. Use cold or lukewarm water so as not to destroy vitamins near the surface. Be quick about it, too, as many vitamins and minerals are water soluble — no long luxurious soaks for our veggies. If for some reason you must prepare produce well in advance of cooking, tuck the peeled veggies away in the refrigerator in a plastic bag or container.

Cooking Methods:

For vegetables absolutely bursting with flavour, vitamins and minerals, cook them until just barely tender: when they reach their brightest colour. Pieces should be as uniform in size as possible so that they will cook evenly.

Of the many ways to cook your vegetables, steaming is the preferred method.

There is minimal vitamin loss during the cooking process and the brilliant colours of the vegetables are retained. Have a look through the Techniques Section (pp 15-16) for other ideas on vegetable cookery.

If steamed or boiled vegetables are not served immediately after cooking, or if they are to be eaten cold, dunk them in cold water, drain and place in a storage or serving dish. This stops the cooking process and sets the bright colour. The flavour and texture will be preserved, and further loss of Vitamin C will be prevented. To reheat for the table, quickly warm the dish of vegetables in a saucepan of hot water, or pour hot melted butter over the top.

Vegetable Tricks:

White vegetables such as turnips and cauliflower will stay white for you if you add a pinch of cream of tartar to the cooking water. Red vegetables will stay red if you add a bit of lemon juice to the cooking water. It will also give other vegetables a bit of a lift.

When cooking over a campfire, a delightful and easy way to do vegetables is to wrap them in foil and place them directly on the embers. Turn the packet over often to prevent severe blackening of the outermost pieces. The vegetables will have a subtle smoked flavour.

Seasoning:

Try this! Instead of relying on salt, perk up your vegetables with a pinch of herbs (see the chart on the next page), chopped leek or green pepper, or chopped nuts or seeds. And a dab of honey can do wonders for a pot of green beans!

Here are a few suggestions for agreeable combinations:

Beets	basil, bay leaf, cardamom, dill, lemon, tarragon
Broccoli	marjoram, oregano, tarragon
Brussels sprouts	basil, dill, caraway, savory, thyme
Carrots	basil, dill, marjoram, parsley, thyme
Cauliflower	dill, rosemary, savory, tarragon
Cabbage	caraway, celery seed, dill, savory, tarragon
Cucumber	basil, savory, tarragon
Green beans	basil, dill, marjoram, oregano, rosemary, savory, thyme
Onions	basil, oregano, thyme
Peas	basil, dill, mint, oregano, savory
Potatoes	basil, chives, dill, marjoram, mint, parsley, savory
Squash	basil, dill, oregano, savory
Spinach	oregano, rosemary, tarragon, thyme
Tomatoes	basil, bay leaf, dill, parsley, oregano

"YOU MUST CHEW YOUR DRINKS, AND DRINK YOUR FOOD."
MAHATMA GANDHI (1869-1948)

Broccoli with Lemon and Dill

Tired of serving boring old broccoli? This version brings it back to life.

Serves 4 - 6.

1¹/₂ Tbsp	(22 mL)	olive oil
¹/₂ cup	(120 mL)	chopped leeks
5 cups	(1.2 L)	chopped broccoli
1¹/₂ tsp	(7 mL)	dillweed
		juice of ¹/₂ lemon
2 Tbsp	(30 mL)	tamari
¹/₄ cup	(60 mL)	water

Sauté the leeks in a skillet for a few minutes.
Add the broccoli and then the remaining ingredients.
Cook just until the broccoli is tender and still bright green.

Tomato Broccoli

..... and one more way to dress up broccoli.

Serves 4 - 6 broccoli fans.

¹/₂ cup	(120 mL)	chopped leeks
2 Tbsp	(30 mL)	olive oil
5 cups	(1.2 L)	chopped broccoli
2 cups	(480 mL)	whole peeled tomatoes
¹/₂ tsp	(2 mL)	basil
¹/₂ tsp	(2 mL)	oregano
		pinch of pepper
2 tsp	(10 mL)	lemon juice

Sauté the leeks in 2 Tbsp (30 mL) olive oil in a large, heavy skillet or wok.
Add the broccoli, then tomatoes, seasonings and lemon.
Cover and simmer until the broccoli is tender, but still bright green.

Serve as a side dish, spooning the sauce over individual portions of cooked grain, such as rice, bulgur, quinoa....

Broccoli and Mushroom Casserole

Serves 4 - 6 people.

5 - 6		broccoli florets and peeled stems
1		coarsely chopped large onion
2 cups	(480 mL)	sliced mushrooms
2 Tbsp	(30 mL)	butter or oil
¼ cup	(60 mL)	chopped almonds
1 cup	(240 mL)	bread crumbs
1 cup	(240 mL)	grated cheese

THE SAUCE:

¼ cup	(60 mL)	butter
¼ cup	(60 mL)	flour
2 cups	(480 mL)	milk

Steam the broccoli florets and stems until tendercrisp.

In a large pan, sauté the onions and mushrooms in a knob of butter (2 Tbsp or 30 mL) until softened.

In a separate pan, melt ¼ cup (60 mL) butter over low heat and gradually add the flour.

Slowly stir in the milk. Keep stirring over low heat until the mixture is smooth and thickened (if lumps form, take a whisk to them and beat them smooth!)

Add this white sauce to the onion/mushroom pan.

Add ½ cup (120 mL) of the cheese, 2 Tbsp (30 mL) almonds and 2 Tbsp (30 mL) of the bread crumbs. Stir until evenly mixed.

Gently stir in the steamed broccoli.

Spread the mixture in an oiled 8"x 8" (2 L) baking dish.

Sprinkle the remaining bread crumbs, almonds and cheese over the top.

Bake at 350°F (180°C) for 30 minutes.

The topping should be browned and crispy when done.

For a non-dairy version, substitute Cashew UnCheese (page 168) for the cheese and use the following white sauce:

1½ cups	(360 mL)	hot water
½ cup	(120 mL)	cashews
2 Tbsp	(30 mL)	engevita yeast
2 Tbsp	(30 mL)	flour
½ tsp	(2 mL)	salt

Put all of the ingredients in a blender and process until creamy.
Use as directed in the recipe.

acrificial Eggplant

*A great appetizer for company, an excellent dish to complement a curry (and the only time you're **supposed** to burn the food).*

One small eggplant makes 1¹/₂ cups (360 mL).

1		**small eggplant**
1 cup	(240 mL)	**finely chopped leeks**
2 Tbsp	(30 mL)	**butter**
¹/₄ tsp	(1 mL)	**sea salt** (or more)
1 Tbsp	(15 mL)	**lemon juice**

Place the eggplant over an open flame and turn it frequently, cooking until the skin is charred all over and the insides are soft. The best place to do this is over an open fire or a gas flame. If neither is available, place the eggplant under the grill in an electric oven. Warning — your smoke detector might go off, so open those windows.

Peel away the charred skin once it has cooled enough to handle, and cut the insides of the eggplant into small pieces.

Sauté the leeks in butter until they are just softened, then add the salt and lemon juice.

Simmer gently for 10 minutes, stirring constantly.

Remove from the heat, then stir in the eggplant, sprinkle all over with more lemon juice to taste and serve.

"As for the Princesse, she still lingers at the gate, all wystfullie, and sends him, by her attendants, woven baskets of great dry'd egg-plants...."

The Privie Journall of Sir Henry Burlingame
March 1608.
(via John Barth[1])

Colcannon

From Ireland, basic, tasty fare — a way to make the most of some simple,
inexpensive vegetables.

Serves 4 - 6.

6		**medium potatoes**
¼ cup	(60 mL)	**butter or oil**
1 tsp	(5 mL)	**sea salt**
¼ tsp	(1 mL)	**black pepper**
¼ cup	(60 mL)	**milk**
1½ cups	(360 mL)	**shredded cabbage**
1 cup	(240 mL)	**finely chopped leeks**
¼ cup	(60 mL)	**fine dry breadcrumbs**

Scrub the potatoes, quarter them and cook in water to cover, until tender.

Drain the potatoes (but save the water), mash them by hand, then add 1
Tbsp (15 mL) of the butter, salt, pepper and milk and mash again.
Please, use a fork or a potato masher. Food processors turn mashed
potatoes into woodworking glue.

Cook the cabbage in the water you used for the potatoes, for about 10
minutes or less, then drain.

While the cabbage is cooking, sauté the leeks in a tablespoon (15 mL) of the
butter or oil until soft, but not browned.

Thoroughly mix the potatoes, cabbage and leeks in a large bowl.

Butter a 1½ quart (1.5 L) baking dish, and scatter one tablespoon of the
breadcrumbs around to coat the dish.

Put the mixture into the dish, smooth the top with a fork (in a long spiral, if
you wish!) and sprinkle the remaining breadcrumbs over the top. Take
the last 2 tablespoons (30 mL) butter in little dabs, and dot them all over
the surface.

Bake your Colcannon at 400°F (205°C) for about 20 minutes, then serve it
good and hot, to be sure.

Curried Cabbage

Cabbage is sometimes maligned. However, cabbage has saved many a family's budget from near disaster during the winter months because of its availability year round and its inexpensiveness. Here is one more thing you can do with it.

Serves 4 - 6.

1 Tbsp	(15 mL)	**chili powder**
½ tsp	(2 mL)	**sea salt**
1 tsp	(5 mL)	**turmeric**
½ cup	(120 mL)	**ghee or butter**
2 Tbsp	(30 mL)	**grated ginger**
2 cups	(480 mL)	**chopped leeks**
	1	**medium cabbage, thinly sliced**

Sauté the spices in ghee or butter for a minute or two.
Add the leeks and ginger and cook until the leeks turn bright green.
Add the cabbage and stir so that all the ingredients are coated with spices.
Cover and cook over medium-low heat until the cabbage is soft.

A good accompaniment to serve with Tofu Cutlets (page 265), kasha burgers, and various grain dishes.

Roasted Parsnips

A simple yet splendidly munchy way to serve this often neglected species.

parsnips
oil
salt (optional)

Scrub the parsnips, and remove tops and tails.
Cut them in half lengthways, or quarters if big. Skinnies stay whole.
Pour a little oil onto a baking sheet, and roll the parsnips in it until they are
  well coated.
Scatter a very little salt over them, and roast at about 350°F (180°C),
  turning once, until they are crisp at the tips and soft at the thick end.
  This will take about 20 minutes.
When you turn them, roll them in the oil once again, to re-coat.

Lemon Feta Beets

Perhaps beets, feta and dillweed seem unlikely partners to some, but we found the combination quite titillating. Try it!

Serves 6 - 7 people.

5 cups	(1.2 L)	**diced beets**
½ cup	(120 mL)	**crumbled feta**
1 Tbsp	(15 mL)	**dillweed**
	juice of	**1 lemon**

This is simple! Just steam the beets until tender; toss everything
together and serve. Naturally, everything will turn pink.

Leftovers make a terrific salad.

Mustard Glazed Carrots

This novel method of serving carrots lends a bold new accent to grains and steamed vegetables.

2 lbs	(1 kg)	**carrots** (about 8 medium)
1½ Tbsp	(22 mL)	**butter**
1½ Tbsp	(22 mL)	**prepared hot mustard**
1 Tbsp	(15 mL)	**brown sugar**

Scrub the carrots and slice them into not-too-small chunks. Steam until
almost soft. This will make about 2½ cups.
Mix the remaining ingredients together in a saucepan and cook over low
heat until the sugar is melted.
Add the carrots, and stir so that they are evenly glaze-coated.
Serve immediately.

Crispy Fried Tomatoes

This colourful side dish   *is great served with or without the sauce.*

Makes 4 servings.

		4 fresh tomatoes
1 cup	(240 mL)	**bread crumbs**
½ tsp	(2 mL)	**sea salt**
¼ tsp	(1 mL)	**black pepper**
¼ cup	(60 mL)	**Parmesan cheese**
2 Tbsp	(30 mL)	**chopped parsley**
2 Tbsp	(30 mL)	**butter**

THE SAUCE:

¼ tsp	(1 mL)	**paprika**
1 Tbsp	(15 mL)	**flour**
1 Tbsp	(15 mL)	**butter**
½ cup	(120 mL)	**tomato juice**
½ cup	(120 mL)	**milk, cream, or water**
¼ tsp	(1 mL)	**black pepper**
¼ tsp	(1 mL)	**sea salt**
		remaining bread crumbs (optional)

Cut the tomatoes into ½" slices.

Add the seasonings to the bread crumbs and dredge the tomato slices in the crumbs. Save leftover crumbs for the serving plate or for the sauce.

Heat the butter until foamy but not browned. Lower the heat slightly and fry the tomatoes on both sides until browned and crispy.

Meanwhile, line a serving plate with bread crumbs, shredded lettuce or spinach greens.

Just before removing them from the pan, sprinkle the tomato slices with a little parmesan and parsley, if you wish.

Arrange the slices on the serving plate.

To make the sauce, lower the heat under the frying pan and add the paprika, butter and flour, whisking it quickly to keep the mixture smooth. Add the tomato juice, pepper and salt and stir until thickened. Gradually add the milk (if using) and heat through.

Drizzle the sauce over the tomatoes and serve, or you can serve the sauce on the side, if you wish.

The Lowly Cauliflower

Serves 4.

1		**medium head of cauliflower**
2 Tbsp	(30 mL)	**butter or olive oil**
¼ cup	(60 mL)	**chopped parsley**
1 Tbsp	(15 mL)	**lemon juice**
¼ tsp	(1 mL)	**sea salt**
¼ tsp	(1 mL)	**dillweed**

Break up the cauliflower head into florets and steam them until softened, about 15 minutes.

Sauté the rest of the ingredients in a medium-sized saucepan until the parsley turns bright green.

Toss the cauliflower into the sauce to coat it and serve immediately.

VARIATIONS:

Replace the dillweed with anise, garlic, basil, tarragon or whatever strikes your fancy.

Sweet Potato Crisp

Instead of just baking or boiling sweet potatoes, why not combine both cooking methods like this:

Feeds a family of 4 quite nicely.

4		**sweet potatoes**
1 cup	(240 mL)	**bread crumbs**
2 Tbsp	(15 mL)	**butter**
½ cup	(120 mL)	**finely chopped almonds**

Scrub the sweet potatoes, then, steam or boil them until soft (about 20 minutes). When soft enough, mash them.

While the potatoes are cooking, toast the bread crumbs and almonds in the butter and sauté till toasty.

Spread the mashed potatoes in a baking dish and sprinkle the bread crumbs and almonds over the top.

Bake at 350°F (180°C) for 20 minutes or until the topping is nicely browned.

Greek Zucchini

A simple and elegant way to dress up the humble zucchini.

Serves 6 - 8.

2 Tbsp	(30 mL)	**olive oil**
1 cup	(240 mL)	**chopped leeks**
6 cups	(1.4 L)	**thinly sliced zucchini**
1½ tsp	(7 mL)	**basil**
1½ tsp	(7 mL)	**oregano**
1½ Tbsp	(22 mL)	**tamari**
1½ Tbsp	(22 mL)	**lemon juice**
¼ tsp	(1 mL)	**pepper**
1 cup	(240 mL)	**crushed canned tomatoes**

In a large pan or skillet, sauté the leeks in olive oil for 5-10 minutes, until they are a little soft.

Add the zucchini and sauté briefly.

Add the seasonings and canned tomatoes.

Cover and simmer until the zucchini is tender but not soft.

This recipe will halve quite easily. Remember that when faced with halving 1½ teaspoons or Tablespoons, a scant measure will do.

"WE ARE THE MIRROR AS WELL AS THE FACE IN IT.
WE ARE TASTING THE TASTE THIS MINUTE OF ETERNITY.
WE ARE THE PAIN AND WHAT CURES PAIN, BOTH.
WE ARE THE SWEET, COLD WATER AND THE JAR THAT POURS."

RUMI, 13TH CENTURY SUFI POET
FROM *OPEN SECRET*, TRANSLATION OF RUMI, BY COLEMAN BARKS

Wedgies

A deliciously addictive, low calorie replacement for french fries. You can enjoy these without any guilty feelings.

Serves 6.

1 cup	(240 mL)	**cornmeal**
1 Tbsp	(15 mL)	**finely minced leek**
1 tsp	(5 mL)	**engevita yeast**
1 Tbsp	(15 mL)	**parsley**
1 tsp	(5 mL)	**oregano**
1 tsp	(5 mL)	**celery seed**
1 tsp	(5 mL)	**basil**
		a fat pinch of pepper
½ tsp	(2 mL)	**salt**
	6 - 8	**potatoes**

Scrub the potatoes, peeling them only if you wish to.

Combine all the ingredients except potatoes in a bowl and mix well.

Cut the potatoes into wedges, about 6 or 8 per potato, then dredge them in the cornmeal mixture.

Lay them out on a lightly-oiled cookie sheet.

Bake at 375°F (190°C) for 25 minutes, then turn them over to brown the other sides. Bake for another 15 to 20 minutes, until done.

Try these crispy little treats with Eden's Ketchup (page 147), and you'll never go back to fries and brand name ketchup again.

"SINCE WARS BEGIN IN THE MINDS OF MEN, IT IS IN THE
MINDS OF MEN THAT THE DEFENCES OF PEACE MUST BE
CONSTRUCTED."
CONSTITUTION OF UNESCO

Sautéed Vegetables

This is a speedy way to "dress up" a vegetable.

Serves 4.

3 cups	(720 mL)	**sliced or chopped vegetable**
2 Tbsp	(30 mL)	**oil or butter**
¼ cup	(60 mL)	**chopped leeks**
¼ cup	(60 mL)	**chopped celery** (optional)
¼ cup	(60 mL)	**chopped red or green pepper** (optional)
1 Tbsp	(30 mL)	**sesame or sunflower seeds**

Thinly slice or chop any firm fresh vegetable — squash, carrots, parsnips,
broccoli or cauliflower are all good contenders for this dish.
Sauté the leeks, celery and pepper in oil for a minute or two.
Add the chopped vegetable.
Keep stirring while frying until the vegetable is tendercrisp.
Arrange on a serving plate and sprinkle the seeds over the top.

"The vegetable world presents an almost infinite variety
of objects, calculated not only to gratify the senses,
but to delight the most refined taste, and to elevate
the mind to the God of Nature."
H. Phillips: *Cultivated Vegetables*
19th century

Salads & Dressings

"My salad days,
when I was green
in judgment."

Shakespeare: *Antony & Cleopatra*, Act I

Long ago, a cook was considered highly desirable if she arranged her "sallet" (as it was called then), as an artful centrepiece: one that would please the eye as well as the palate. Consider, for example, *Salamagundi* — a salad arranged on a round dish, with an endive or chicory representing the sun in the middle, that radiated herring strips, sections of chopped eggs, parsley, perhaps some other vegetable, and then watercress neatly arranged outside all. Radishes, capers, olives and tiny white onions were then cleverly inserted throughout. No dressing was used; just salt, from whence the word "sallet"

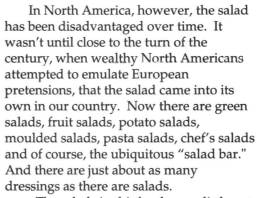

derives.

In North America, however, the salad has been disadvantaged over time. It wasn't until close to the turn of the century, when wealthy North Americans attempted to emulate European pretensions, that the salad came into its own in our country. Now there are green salads, fruit salads, potato salads, moulded salads, pasta salads, chef's salads and of course, the ubiquitous "salad bar." And there are just about as many dressings as there are salads.

The salads in this book are a little out of the ordinary, and are designed to tickle your imagination into producing your own "*salamagundis*." Change the vegetables; change the spices; add a little more of this, a little less of that; use beets instead of carrots; use lentils instead of kidney beans; throw in some lettuce, parsley, fresh dill. Vary the dressings on the salads; and vary the dressings themselves — now here's where you can really have some fun: use vinegar instead of lemon juice or vice versa; use cream instead of cashew milk; basil instead of dill; and on and on and on.

Ambika's Bean Salad

A truly superb bean salad that uses no sugar.

You can use any dry beans you fancy, but we like the rich colour mixture of equal parts kidney beans, garbanzos, and black soy beans* (substitute black beans or black turtle beans if necessary). Whichever beans you use, this salad will get rave reviews.

Serves 4 - 6.

4 cups	(960 mL)	**cooked beans** (about 1^1/$_2$ cups (360 mL) dry beans — see p. 102 for bean cooking instructions)
^{1}/$_2$ **cup**	(120 mL)	**minced leeks, shallots, or chives**
6 Tbsp	(90 mL)	**olive oil**
2 Tbsp	(30 mL)	**fresh lemon juice**
2 Tbsp	(30 mL)	**dillweed or basil**
^{1}/$_2$ **tsp**	(2 mL)	**sea salt** (to taste)
^{1}/$_2$ **tsp**	(2 mL)	**tamari**
		pinch cayenne pepper

In a bowl, combine warm cooked beans, leeks, oil, lemon juice, dill, salt, tamari and pepper. Gently mix to make sure beans are well coated.

Now chill for an hour or two to allow the flavours to mingle.

Make individual servings by putting a half cup or more of the mixture onto a deep green leaf of romaine, or other leaf lettuce.

Garnish with a lemon wedge, a sprig of parsley, fresh dill, chervil, or chive flowers.

Exquisite!

*Black soy beans, though not widely available, are worth hunting for. Their flavour is excellent — far superior to regular soy beans, and they cook faster, too. We found out about them from Dan Jason, one of the gardeners here at the Centre, whose company, Salt Spring Seeds, supplies by mail a wider range of bean varieties than almost any other seed company in North America.

Marinated Bean Salad

There are many effective bean salads — this is our stunningly delicious version, that makes enough bean salad for a crowd of people — and you can freeze it!

Feeds 12 - 15.

2 cups	(480 mL)	**cooked lima beans**
2 cups	(480 mL)	**cooked kidney beans**
2 cups	(480 mL)	**cooked pinto beans**
2 cups	(480 mL)	**cooked garbanzo beans**
1 lb	(454 g)	**green beans** (fresh if you can get them, or frozen, OR 1 tin of canned beans)
1 lb	(454 g)	**wax beans** (fresh, or frozen, OR 1 tin of canned beans)
1¹/₂ cup	(360 mL)	**finely chopped leeks**
1		**green pepper, diced** (or red pepper, or both!)
³/₄ cup	(180 mL)	**vegetable oil**
³/₄ cup	(180 mL)	**apple cider vinegar**
³/₄ cup	(180 mL)	**brown sugar**

If you don't have cooked beans on hand, then we recommend reading the Beans section (page 102) for cooking and soaking instructions.

Drain the cooked beans, add green beans, wax beans, leeks and green pepper.

For the dressing, mix oil, vinegar and sugar thoroughly and toss into the beans until they are nicely drenched.

Mix all the ingredients and let stand one or two days in the fridge.

This colourful salad looks quite wonderful on a lettuce leaf or two. Serve with a chunk of whole wheat or sourdough bread. What more could one want?

ab Caraway Salad

If this title seems a little strange to you, then I'm sure you're not alone. The salad itself reads a little strange too, but it is so quick to prepare and such a novel taste, that you may overcome your reservations and try it. Actually, Genghis Khan took a very similar salad with him and his hordes as they invaded Europe. The idea stayed with the Europeans after Genghis disappeared into the dust. "Hated him; loved the cabbage."

1		**medium-sized green cabbage**
1¹/₂ **tsp**	(7 mL)	**sea salt**
1¹/₂ **tsp**	(7 mL)	**caraway seeds**

Shred the cabbage with a sharp knife, then check it over for any remaining large pieces of the "ribs" of the cabbage leaves, and cut them small too.

Put the cabbage into a large bowl, and sprinkle the salt all over it, followed by the caraway seeds.

Now take a small handful of the mixture and rub it between your fingertips, to gently bruise it and further separate the shredded slices of cabbage. This draws out a natural liquor from the cabbage, and marinades the salad.

When all of the cabbage has been rubbed in this way, leave it to sit for a little while (half an hour to half a day) somewhere chilly before serving.

The cabbage is indigenous to Europe and Western Asia — in fact, it is one of the oldest cultivars. The Romans claimed cabbages were "tears of repentance" of one of their gods, and so looked upon them much more favourably than we do today.

Carrot Beet Salad

Rumour has it that carrots are indigenous to Afghanistan and were purple when first discovered to be edible. However, the purple was bred out in favour of the familiar yellow-orange of today. One can imagine what this simple, beautiful and unique salad might have looked like hundreds of years ago.

Serves at least 4.

2¹/₂ cups	(600 mL)	grated carrots
1 cup	(240 mL)	grated beets
1 cup	(240 mL)	crumbled feta cheese
¹/₂ tsp	(2 mL)	Spike or vegetable seasoning
2 tsp	(10 mL)	nutritional yeast
1¹/₂ tsp	(7 mL)	dillweed
2 Tbsp	(30 mL)	vinegar
2 Tbsp	(30 mL)	olive oil

All you do is just combine everything into one delicious salad! Of course, you can vary the combination of carrots and beets, or you can just use carrots.

Shirley's Bean Sprout Salad

We thought this to be such a novel way to use bean sprouts that we really should share it. The dressing is unusual and easily adapted to other salads — try it!

Serves 4.

¹/₄ cup	(60 mL)	oil
2 Tbsp	(30 mL)	lemon juice or cider vinegar
2 Tbsp	(30 mL)	tamari
¹/₃ cup	(80 mL)	thinly chopped leeks
¹/₄ tsp	(1 mL)	sea salt
2 Tbsp	(30 mL)	sesame seeds
2 Tbsp	(30 mL)	chopped parsley
¹/₄ tsp	(1 mL)	grated ginger
3 cups	(720 mL)	mung bean sprouts

Mix the marinade ingredients, pour over the sprouts and toss lightly. Let the sprouts rest for at least one hour at room temperature. Chill before serving.

This recipe will easily accept one more cupful of sprouts if you have them.

ushroom Radish Salad

An unusual combination of vegetables which quickly became a Salt Spring Centre favourite.

Serves 4.

THE SALAD:

2 cups	(480 mL)	sliced fresh mushrooms
2 cups	(480 mL)	thinly sliced radishes
3/4 cup	(180 mL)	thinly sliced green onions
1/2 cup	(120 mL)	chopped parsley
1/2 cup	(120 mL)	grated white cheese
		pinch black pepper
2 Tbsp	(30 mL)	chopped tarragon or fennel

THE DRESSING:

2 tsp	(10 mL)	Dijon mustard
1/4 cup	(60 mL)	cider vinegar
1/2 tsp	(2 mL)	sea salt
		fat pinch black pepper
3/4 cup	(180 mL)	olive oil

Mix the salad ingredients in a large bowl.

Mix the dressing ingredients in a separate bowl.

Pour 1/2 cup (120 mL) of the dressing over the salad and mix gently until the salad is evenly coated.

Chill before serving.

Serve the rest of the dressing at the side.

"THE MAN PULLING RADISHES
POINTED THE WAY
WITH A RADISH."
ISSA (1763-1827)

Potato Salad

Native to South America, the potato struggled for acceptance in many parts of an uncompromising world. Here is Salt Spring Centre's own, traditional, and outstandingly tasty potato salad, heralding the potato's arrival into vegetable society.

Serves 6.

6 cups	(1.4 L)	**cubed potatoes**
1 cup	(240 mL)	**finely chopped carrots**
1 cup	(240 mL)	**finely chopped leeks**
1 cup	(240 mL)	**finely chopped celery**
1 cup	(240 mL)	**finely chopped red pepper**
¼ cup	(60 mL)	**finely chopped parsley**
½ cup	(120 mL)	**chopped dill pickles**
2 cups	(480 mL)	**Tofu Mayonnaise** (recipe on page 141)

Steam the potatoes until they are cooked but not soft, and leave them to cool.

Add the other vegetable ingredients to the potatoes.

Pour the mayonnaise over the mixed vegetables and stir lightly until they are all well coated.

Garnish your salad with parsley and a sprinkle of paprika before serving.

If you are a pickle fun, increase the quantity to one cup.

By the late 17th century, the Irish were cultivating potatoes to the tune of 252 lbs. per week for the average (at the time) family with six children, leading the English to believe the potato was, indeed, an aphrodisiac.

Summer Supper Salad

Perfect for warm summer evenings; a light cool meal with good protein.

Serves 4 - 6.

4 cups	(960 mL)	**cooked kidney beans**
4 cups	(960 mL)	**cooked macaroni or rotini**
1 cup	(240 mL)	**chopped green pepper**
		(may be part red pepper)
	2	**celery sticks, chopped**
1 cup	(240 mL)	**chopped leeks**
4 tsp	(20 mL)	**chili powder**
2 Tbsp	(30 mL)	**lemon juice**
1 Tbsp	(15 mL)	**dillweed**
1 tsp	(5 mL)	**chopped cilantro**
1¹/₂ tsp	(7 mL)	**sea salt**

Raghunath's Ginger Paprika Dressing (page 140)
OR Chili Vinaigrette (page 136)

Toss all the ingredients together.
Add enough salad dressing to make the salad moist without drowning it.
Let the salad stand for several hours in a cool spot before serving, if
   possible, to allow the flavours to blossom.

*If you use colourful pasta (tomato or spinach), your salad will be doubly pleasing,
to the eye as well as the palate.*

*Serve with iced herbal tea,
garden fresh tomato slices, fresh
cucumber with lemon juice and
nasturtium flowers, or a cool
fruit salad.*

S on of Tuna Salad

So alarmingly like tuna fish, you will need to offer reassurance to your family and guests!

(It will take 1-2 days to sprout the sunflower seeds, depending on how warm it is in your kitchen.)

Makes 3 cups of un-fishy salad.

4 cups	(960 mL)	**sprouted sunflower seeds**
1 cup	(240 mL)	**finely chopped leeks**
1½ cups	(360 mL)	**finely chopped celery**
4 Tbsp	(60 mL)	**olive oil**
4 Tbsp	(60 mL)	**tamari**
4 Tbsp	(60 mL)	**mayonnaise (tofu mayo or any other)**

To sprout the sunflower seeds, soak 2 cups (480 mL) raw sunflower seeds in water (1 cup [240 mL] of seeds in each of two quart-size jars with water to cover).

Cover the jars with a small piece of window screen material, cheesecloth or nylon mesh, secured with an elastic band. Let stand overnight.

The next morning drain the water and rinse the seeds with fresh water, pouring it through the screen. Pour the water out and lay the jars on their sides, at an angle so they drain completely.

Rinse morning and evening until the seeds have tails about ¼" long. The seeds double in size, so you'll end up with the required amount of 4 cups (960 mL) of sprouts.

Grind the sunflower seed sprouts together with the leeks and celery.

Add the olive oil and tamari, then stir in the mayonnaise.

This makes a great salad served on a bed of lettuce and garnished with tomato wedges, or spread on whole grain bread with lettuce or alfalfa sprouts.

Tabouleh

This version of Middle Eastern Tabouleh sucessfully converted a notorious Tabouleh-hater to a Tabouleh-fanatic with one tiny mouthful. He was also delighted when we used quinoa instead of bulgur. Gave it a distinctly New World feel, he said.

Serves at least 4 as a main dish.

3¹/₂ cups	(840 mL)	**water**
³/₄ cup	(180 mL)	**bulgur or 1 cup (240 mL) cooked quinoa***
2 cups	(480 mL)	**finely chopped parsley**
¹/₂ cup	(120 mL)	**minced leeks**
2 Tbsp	(30 mL)	**finely chopped fresh mint or 2 tsp (10 mL) dried mint**
	2	**medium tomatoes**
4 Tbsp	(60 mL)	**fresh lemon juice**
4 Tbsp	(60 mL)	**olive oil**
		salt to taste
		one head of romaine lettuce

Soak the bulgur in water for about 45 minutes.

Cut the tomatoes in half, core them, dice them fairly small, then set them aside until the bulgur is ready.

Pour off any excess liquid from the bulgur. Line a colander with a tea towel, then put in the bulgur and gather the edges of the towel together to make a bag. Squeeze out any remaining water.

Drain the tomatoes, then combine them with the other ingredients in a large bowl, and mix thoroughly.

Adjust the amount of salt, oil, and lemon juice to your taste. The mint should tickle the taste buds, but not overpower the salad.

Tabouleh is traditionally eaten with the fingers, using the firm inner leaves of romaine lettuce as an edible bowl.
Serve it on a plate garnished with lettuce leaves.

*Please refer to the Grains section (page 101) for the successful cooking of mineral-rich quinoa.

Tropical Coleslaw

Put on a pair of shorts, your most colourful shirt and sunglasses, then make this salad, and teleport yourself South.

Serves 4 - 6.

2 cups	(480 mL)	**finely shredded green cabbage**
¹⁄₂ cup	(120 mL)	**shredded red cabbage**
1 cup	(240 mL)	**coarsely grated carrots**
¹⁄₂ cup	(120 mL)	**sunflower seeds**
1 cup	(240 mL)	**tinned pineapple chunks**
¹⁄₄ cup	(60 mL)	**chopped walnuts**
¹⁄₂ cup	(120 mL)	**avocado pieces**
1¹⁄₂ cups	(360 mL)	**Pineapple Dressing** (page 139)

Drain the pineapple chunks and save the juice for the dressing.
Toss the pineapple with the rest of the coleslaw ingredients.
Pour over enough pineapple dressing to moisten the coleslaw.
Chill before serving.

An attractive way to serve this would be to layer the ingredients in a clear glass bowl in the order given, with avocado slices as a decorative garnish. Pour the dressing over just before serving.

Nice additions are papaya or mango chunks, fresh grape halves or raisins.

"THE MOST BEAUTIFUL THING
WE CAN EXPERIENCE IS THE MYSTERIOUS.
IT IS THE SOURCE OF ALL TRUE ART AND SCIENCE."
ALBERT EINSTEIN

Chili Vinaigrette

Makes 2 cups (480 mL) of zesty dressing.

1 cup	(240 mL)	**olive oil**
½ cup	(120 mL)	**apple cider vinegar or malt vinegar**
2 tsp	(10 mL)	**dill weed**
½ tsp	(2 mL)	**celery seed**
1 tsp	(5 mL)	**Spike or vegetable seasoning**
2 Tbsp	(30 mL)	**chili powder**
1-5½ oz	(156 mL)	**tin tomato paste**

Blend all the ingredients until creamy. Use a whisk or a blender, whatever suits your fancy.

Cream 'n' Cream Dressing

A good cream dressing for green salad that accepts variations to suit other uses and personal preference.

Makes 2 cups (480 mL).

⅓ cup	(80 mL)	**olive oil**
⅓ cup	(80 mL)	**light cream**
¼ cup	(60 mL)	**apple cider vinegar**
1 cup	(240 mL)	**sour cream**
1 Tbsp	(15 mL)	**lemon juice**
¼ tsp	(1 mL)	**black pepper**
¼ - ½ tsp	(1-2 mL)	**sea salt**
1 - 4		**cloves garlic, finely minced**
		(optional)

Beat all the ingredients together in a bowl with a hand whisk.
This dressing is best if given a few hours to chill and blend flavours.

Some people like this dressing with a dab of honey added.

ucumber Salad Dressing

A fresh tasting, delicate dressing that could almost double as a drink.

Makes 1½ cups (360 mL).

1		**cucumber, carefully peeled**
2 Tbsp	(30 mL)	**freshly squeezed lemon juice**
1 Tbsp	(15 mL)	**chopped leek**
½ cup	(120 mL)	**cashews**
½ tsp	(2 mL)	**ground coriander**
		pinch of sea salt
2 tsp	(10 mL)	**olive oil**

Chop the cucumber into fairly small chunks.

Place the cucumber and lemon juice in the blender first, and whiz until they are liquid before adding all the other ingredients.

Now blend the dressing until creamy.

Cucumbers are native to India and have been cultivated there for over 3000 years. Ancient Egyptians ate them with every meal. Columbus brought them westward with him (he must have brought the seeds — cucumbers would never make that voyage!) and 50 years later, they made an appearance in Eastern Canada.

Garam Masala Dressing

Green salads rise to new heights when lavishly coated with this spicy dressing.

Makes at least 2 cups (480 mL).

1 cup	(240 mL)	**olive oil**
4 Tbsp	(60 mL)	**lemon juice**
⅓ cup	(80 mL)	**tomato paste**
1 Tbsp	(15 mL)	**coarsely grated fresh ginger**
½ tsp	(2 mL)	**chili powder**
½ tsp	(2 mL)	**garam masala**
¼ tsp	(1 mL)	**sea salt**
½ Tbsp	(7 mL)	**honey**
¼ lb	(100 g)	**tofu**
½ cup	(120 mL)	**water**

Purée all the ingredients in a blender and chill. What could be easier?

Low Calorie Tomato-Lemon Dressing

An excellent dressing to liven up green salads.

This recipe makes 3 cups (720 mL).

2		**chopped ripe tomatoes**
½ cup	(120 mL)	**fresh lemon juice (2 lemons)**
½ cup	(120 mL)	**orange juice**
½ cup	(120 mL)	**chopped fresh parsley**
¾ cup	(180 mL)	**chopped leeks***
		pinch of salt

Put all the ingredients in a blender and process until the dressing is
  smooth.

*If the leeks are quite strong-tasting, we suggest limiting them to ½ cup
  (120 mL), otherwise the dressing may overpower its green companions.

One-quarter cup (60 mL) has about 16 calories,
if you are concerned about the number you are eating.

Pineapple Dressing

Makes approximately 1½ cups (360 mL).

1 Tbsp	(15 mL)	**arrowroot powder**
1 cup	(240 mL)	**water**
½ cup	(120 mL)	**cashews**
1 Tbsp	(15 mL)	**lemon juice***
½ tsp	(2 mL)	**sea salt**
1 Tbsp	(15 mL)	**chopped leek**
¼ tsp	(1 mL)	**mustard powder**
		pinch of cayenne
¼ cup	(60 mL)	**pineapple juice**
1 Tbsp	(15 mL)	**fresh lime juice** (optional)

Bring ½ cup (120 mL) water to a boil and stir in the arrowroot powder.
Cook until the mixture thickens, then set it aside to cool.
Purée the remaining ingredients in a blender until smooth.
Pour the dressing into a bowl and **gently** stir in the arrowroot mixture. If
  you stir it too much, the arrowroot will lose its thickening properties, and
  you will be left with pineapple cream.

*Add one more tablespoon (15mL) of lemon juice if you like a dressing
  with more tang.

*Pour this dressing over Tropical Coleslaw (page 135),
or use it for a semi-sweet taste on either fruit or green salads.*

*In Europe, lettuce has been known for centuries as a natural sedative
and soporific, which no doubt led to its recommendation by Pliny as a
preventative for both sea-sickness, and storms at sea.*

Raghunath's Ginger Paprika Dressing

This sparky dressing will wake up even the most mundane salad.

Makes 1½ cups (360 mL).

1		piece root ginger (walnut sized)
1 cup	(240 mL)	olive oil
1 tsp	(5 mL)	prepared stone-ground mustard
1½ tsp	(7 mL)	honey
1 tsp	(5 mL)	sea salt
¼ - ½ cup	(60-120 mL)	vinegar
2 Tbsp	(30 mL)	tahini
1½ tsp	(7 mL)	paprika
		freshly ground pepper to taste

Peel and finely grate the piece of ginger.
Blend all the ingredients and chill.

Use a little more salt, if you feel the need.

Shimmering Shakti Dressing

Greener than a green goddess! Parsley is loaded with minerals, and its high chlorophyll content also makes it very soothing to the digestive tract.

		1 bunch fresh parsley
2 cups	(480 mL)	water
½ cup	(120 mL)	tahini
3 Tbsp	(45 mL)	vinegar or lemon juice
2 Tbsp	(30 mL)	miso (preferably white)
4 tsp	(20 mL)	dillweed
		a pinch of oregano
		a pinch of thyme

Coarsely chop the parsley and purée it with the water in a blender.
Add the remaining ingredients, and blend until smooth.

Shakti, as energy, complements her partner Shiva, as principle,
in the Hindu cosmology.
Together they embody the union inside every duality.

Tofu Salad Dressing or Mayonnaise

Makes 4 - 4 ½ cups (about 1 L).

1 lb	(454 g)	**tofu**
1 cup	(240 mL)	**olive oil**
½ cup	(120 mL)	**vinegar or lemon juice**
½ cup	(120 mL)	**water** (use more if you like a thinner salad dressing)
1 tsp	(5 mL)	**Spike or vegetable seasoning**
½ tsp	(2 mL)	**mustard powder**
2 tsp	(10 mL)	**salsa (hot!) sauce — or a pinch of cayenne**
1 tsp	(5 mL)	**dillweed** (optional)

Put everything in a blender or food processor and purée.
You may wish to adjust the Spike or vegetable seasoning by adding an additional half teaspoon.

For Tofu Mayonnaise, just omit the salsa and dillweed.

VARIATIONS:
1 Tbsp (15 mL) **tamari** instead of mustard powder.
Eliminate salsa or cayenne.

Tomato Salad Dressing

Makes 4 cups (960 mL).

1 cup	(240 mL)	**olive oil**
½ cup	(120 mL)	**vinegar**
	1	**large can tomatoes** (26 oz - 796 mL)
1 Tbsp	(15 mL)	**chili powder**
1 tsp	(5 mL)	**dillweed**
1 tsp	(5 mL)	**basil**
¼ tsp	(1 mL)	**celery seed**
2 Tbsp	(30 mL)	**tamari**

Mix all the ingredients in a blender or food processor until smooth for a fabulous dressing!

Savoury Sauces

The right sauce can turn a mediocre dish into a good one but, more importantly, it can help a good dish become an excellent one.

However, as Cervantes said, "There is no sauce in the world like hunger."

In these savoury sauce recipes, you can successfully substitute mild onions for leeks, if you wish. Use slightly less onion than the called-for amount of leek (³/₄ cup [180 mL] mild onions instead of 1 cup [240 mL] chopped leeks), in order to maintain a similar balance of flavours in the sauce.

You can find several other savoury sauces hidden within this book, and here are the clues to locating them:

Berber Sauce

Originally from Ethiopia, this unusual-tasting and spicy relish works best for western palates when spread (gossamer thin or lightly slathered!) over bread, butter and cream cheese, or dabbed onto crackers and hummus, and similar uses. Try adding a teaspoonful or two to a baked bean dish, a spaghetti sauce, a dal of split peas or lentils, and whatever else you might think of....

1 tsp	(5 mL)	ground cardamom
1 tsp	(5 mL)	ground ginger
½ tsp	(2 mL)	ground coriander
½ tsp	(2 mL)	ground fenugreek seed (optional)
¼ tsp	(1 mL)	ground cinnamon
¼ tsp	(1 mL)	ground nutmeg
¼ tsp	(1 mL)	allspice
		fat pinch of ground cloves
¼ cup	(60 mL)	finely chopped leeks
2 tsp	(10 mL)	sea salt
2 Tbsp	(30 mL)	cider vinegar
	1 or 2	cloves garlic, minced (optional)
2 cups	(480 mL)	paprika
2 Tbsp	(30 mL)	chili powder
½ tsp	(2 mL)	black pepper
2½ cups	(600 mL)	water
2 Tbsp	(30 mL)	olive oil

Toast the cardamom, ginger, coriander, fenugreek, cinnamon, nutmeg, allspice and cloves in a heavy pan over low heat for a few minutes. Take care not to burn them. Allow to cool a little.

Put the leeks, salt, vinegar, garlic and toasted spice mixture in a blender, and purée until smooth.

Toast the paprika, chili and pepper over low heat for a few minutes, stirring constantly to ensure they do not burn.

Stir in the water a little at a time, then add the mixture from the blender, and cook for about 10 minutes, stirring over low heat.

Cool the paste to room temperature, then pack it into a wide-mouthed jar, pour the oil over the top, and refrigerate. It will keep well for quite some time.

This sauce teams up very happily with Yewello Ambasha, an Ethiopian spiced bread. You can find the recipe on page 230.

Almost Cheese Sauce

Delicious — serve cold as a dip for raw vegetables, heat it gently in a saucepan to pour over steamed vegetables, or use it as a topping for macaroni and other pasta dishes.

Makes 2 cups (480 mL)

1 cup	(240 mL)	**cashews**
1 cup	(240 mL)	**water**
1 tsp	(5 mL)	**sea salt**
2 oz	(60 mL)	**canned pimento with juice**
1 Tbsp	(15 mL)	**chopped leeks**
		a pinch of thyme
2 tsp	(10 mL)	**fresh lemon juice**
1 Tbsp	(15 mL)	**vegetable oil**

Combine the cashews and water in a blender and whip until creamy. Add the remaining ingredients and blend once again to homogenize everything.

"A BOOK THAT FURNISHES NO QUOTATIONS IS, *ME JUDICE*, NO BOOK — IT IS A PLAYTHING."
T . L.PEACOCK: *THE MISFORTUNES OF ELPHIN*

Creamy Curry Sauce

A sweet but piquant curry sauce that is so tempting that some unconventional friends have served it as a dessert.

Makes 3½ cups (840 mL) of sauce.

1 - 1½ cups (240-360 mL)	**cashews**	(use the larger amount for a thicker sauce)
3 cups (720 mL)	**water**	
2 Tbsp (30 mL)	**butter or oil**	
1 Tbsp (15 mL)	**curry powder,**	OR alternate curry mixture below
2 Tbsp (30 mL)	**whole-wheat flour**	
½ tsp (2 mL)	**sea salt**	

In a blender, purée the cashews in 1 cup (240 mL) of the water until all the nuts are finely ground.

Pour the rest of the water gradually into the blender to make cashew milk.

In a saucepan, melt the butter, stir in the curry powder (or spices), and then the flour. Continue stirring this thick roux for a minute.

Add the cashew milk, a little at a time, as the sauce thickens.

Stir constantly to prevent sticking. Keep the heat high enough for the sauce to thicken, but not high enough to boil.

Add the salt and adjust the cayenne to your taste.

ALTERNATE CURRY MIXTURE:

1 tsp	(5 mL)	**turmeric**
1 tsp	(5 mL)	**ground cumin**
½ tsp	(2 mL)	**ground ginger**
¼ tsp	(1 mL)	**cinnamon**
		a large pinch of ground cloves
		a large pinch of cayenne
		(or more to taste)

As a variation, soy milk or cow's milk can be used in place of cashew milk. If soy milk is used, omit the cashews and the water. If cow's milk is used, omit the cashews and water, and increase the butter and flour to 5 Tbsp (75 mL) each.

At the Salt Spring Centre, we often serve this sauce as an accompaniment to our Shepherd's Pie (recipe page 60).

One last suggestion for this versatile recipe, would be to thin the sauce a little, add a few vegetables, and call it a soup. Et voilà!

*E*den's Ketchup

Avoiding the large amount of sugar found in most commercial ketchup makes this a good sauce for kids and adults alike. Kids around the Salt Spring Centre (the ultimate test) judged it to be very good. If you really want to try fooling your offspring, bottle it up to look like the 58th variety.

Makes 3 cups (720 mL).

1 cup	(240 mL)	finely chopped leeks, packed
2 Tbsp	(30 mL)	butter or ghee
2 cups	(480 mL)	canned tomatoes, crushed
1 tsp	(5 mL)	mustard powder
¹/₄ tsp	(1 mL)	ground cloves
¹/₄ tsp	(1 mL)	allspice
1 - 5¹/₂ oz	(156 mL)	can tomato paste
1¹/₂ tsp	(7 mL)	cider vinegar
5 tsp	(25 mL)	molasses
2		bay leaves
¹/₂ tsp	(2 mL)	sea salt
1 Tbsp	(15 mL)	honey

In a saucepan, sauté the leeks in butter until they are softened.

Blend the tomatoes, spices and leeks in a blender until smooth.

Return the mixture to the saucepan and gently simmer while you add the tomato paste, vinegar, molasses and bay leaves.

Cook the ketchup for only a few minutes more, before removing from the heat and stirring in the salt and honey.

Fish out the bay leaves and discard them, then cool the ketchup and bottle it.

"NOTHING THAT ACTUALLY OCCURS IS OF THE
SMALLEST IMPORTANCE."
OSCAR WILDE (1854-1900)

Golden Sauce

A wonderfully sweet, light sauce that can be used instead of cheese sauces.

Makes close to 2 cups (480 mL).

³/₄ **cup**	(180 mL)	**cubed potato** (one small potato)
¹/₃ **cup**	(80 mL)	**sliced carrot** (half a small carrot)
2 Tbsp	(30 mL)	**cashews**
1¹/₃ cups	(320 mL)	**water**
¹/₂ **tsp**	(2 mL)	**sea salt**
1 Tbsp	(15 mL)	**fresh lemon juice**

Cook potato and carrot in enough water to cover (1¹/₃ cup or 320 mL) until
they are quite tender.
Grind the cashews in a blender with 2 Tbsp (30 mL) of the cooking water.
Add the cooked vegetables, the remainder of the cooking water, and the
remaining ingredients to the blender, and blend until smooth.
Transfer to a saucepan and heat very gently.

Serve hot over vegetables, vegetable pancakes, grains or pasta.

—The Centre—

Middle Eastern Sauce

Ideal served over falafels or steamed vegetables, or use it cold as a salad dressing.

Makes 2 cups (480 mL).

²/₃ **cup**	(160 mL)	**tahini**
¹/₂ **cup**	(120 mL)	**finely chopped leeks**
²/₃ **cup**	(160 mL)	**lemon juice**
1 **cup**	(240 mL)	**water**
1¹/₂ **tsp**	(7 mL)	**cumin**
¹/₂ **tsp plus**	(3 mL)	**salt**
2 **Tbsp**	(30 mL)	**chopped fresh parsley**

Mix all the ingredients in a saucepan, and bring to a gentle simmer.

Cook the sauce, covered, gently for 10 to 15 minutes, adding more lemon juice and salt to taste.

Should the sauce seem too thick, mix in a little more water.

It has been several hundred years since Sauce Guilds thrived in Europe, setting standards of excellence and inventiveness among the brotherhood of sauce chefs who comprised their membership.
To this day, the hand that stirs and seasons, and the delicacy of palate that guides the hand, make the sauce chef one of the most honoured artists, from Maxim's to more humble eateries.

ushroom Sauce

Celebrating the mushroom's finest hour. This sauce makes a great accompaniment for any of our savoury loaves or burgers.

Makes 1¼ cups (300 mL), enough for 2 - 3 people.

¼ cup	(60 mL)	**chopped leeks**
2 cups	(480 mL)	**chopped mushrooms**
2 Tbsp	(30 mL)	**butter**
2 Tbsp	(30 mL)	**whole-wheat flour**
1 tsp	(5 mL)	**engevita yeast**
1 cup	(240 mL)	**milk**
1 tsp	(5 mL)	**lemon juice** (optional)
½ tsp	(2 mL)	**tarragon**
½ tsp	(2 mL)	**dill**
		a pinch of pepper
1 tsp	(5 mL)	**tamari** (optional)

Sauté the leeks in butter for a minute, then add the mushrooms and cook until they are softened.

Add the flour and the engevita yeast, and cook for a minute or two more.

Gradually flow in the milk and then the lemon juice, stirring until the sauce thickens.

Now add the herbs and pepper, and cook briefly on low heat to develop the flavours.

At the end of the cooking time, stir in the tamari, and serve.

Substitute water or stock for the milk, if you prefer a non-dairy sauce.

Mushroom  *Tomato Topping*

This quick and easy sauce is a great way to dress up a plain grain or steamed vegetables.

1½ Tbsp	(22 mL)	**butter**
6 cups	(1.4 L)	**sliced mushrooms**
¼ tsp	(1 mL)	**sea salt**
¼ tsp	(1 mL)	**pepper**
1		**finely chopped tomato**
1 Tbsp	(15 mL)	**tamari**

Melt the butter in a large frying pan.

Add the mushrooms, salt and pepper, and cook gently while stirring, until the mushrooms are almost soft.

Add the tomato and tamari. Stir and cook just long enough to heat the tomato.

It's also a super sandwich filler — see Sid Sandwiches (page 264).
One of our favourite ways is on top of toasted ryebread
and cream cheese. Smashing!

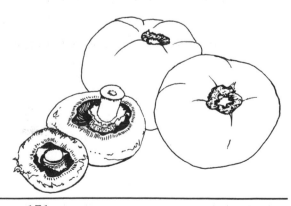

Salsa!

Hot — an absolute necessity with almost any Mexican dish.

Makes about 2½ cups (600 mL) after cooking down.

1-28 oz	(796 mL)	**can crushed tomatoes**
1½ tsp	(7 mL)	**cumin**
1 tsp	(5 mL)	**chili powder**
1 cup	(240 mL)	**chopped leeks**
1 Tbsp	(15 mL)	**honey**
1 tsp	(5 mL)	**crushed red chili peppers**
1		**small green pepper, chopped**

Combine all the ingredients in a saucepan, and simmer the salsa, covered,
for one hour over low heat.
Cool the salsa and store it in a jar, in the refrigerator.

—Fulford Harbour—

High-Protein Spaghetti Sauce

This recipe makes sauce to serve 7 - 10 people.

Only need to serve 4 people? No matter, spaghetti sauce improves if left to sit, tightly covered, for a day or two in the refrigerator. And it will freeze well too.

1 cup	(240 mL)	coarsely chopped leeks
1 cup	(240 mL)	chopped celery
5 Tbsp	(75 mL)	olive oil
1 cup	(240 mL)	chopped green pepper
1 cup	(240 mL)	sliced mushrooms
1 - 28 oz	(796 mL)	can of crushed tomatoes
¹/₂ lb	(227 g)	crumbled tofu
2 - 5¹/₂ oz	(156 mL)	cans of tomato paste
¹/₂ tsp	(2 mL)	black pepper
1 Tbsp	(15 mL)	oregano
4 tsp	(20 mL)	basil
1 tsp	(5 mL)	dillweed
2 Tbsp	(30 mL)	hot Salsa! (opposite) OR
		¹/₂ - 1 tsp (2-5 mL) cayenne
1¹/₂ tsp	(7 mL)	honey
2 Tbsp	(30 mL)	vegetable oil
5 tsp	(25 mL)	lemon juice

In a large skillet or wok, sauté the leeks and celery in the olive oil for a few minutes.

Add the green pepper and mushrooms and cook until soft, but not mushy.

Now add all the other ingredients except the lemon juice.

Simmer for about 1 to 1¹/₂ hours, until the sauce smells irresistibly good.

Add the lemon juice, and serve over noodles, rice or spaghetti squash.

"IT IS A CHEERING THOUGHT TO THINK THAT GOD IS ON THE SIDE OF THE BEST DIGESTION."
D.R.P.MARQUIS: *THE BIG BAD WOLF*

Tamari Cream Sauce

A good savoury sauce to accompany steamed vegetables, grains or the more substantial kinds of entrées, for example Nut Roast, (page 54).

Makes 1 ½ cups (360 mL).

1 Tbsp	(15 mL)	**butter**
1 Tbsp	(15 mL)	**oil**
4 Tbsp	(60 mL)	**whole-wheat flour**
1 cup	(240 mL)	**water**
3 Tbsp	(45 mL)	**light or heavy cream,** to taste
3 Tbsp	(45 mL)	**tamari**
1 Tbsp	(15 mL)	**lemon juice** (optional)

Gently heat the butter and oil in a small saucepan.

Stirring with a wooden spoon, combine the flour little by little with the now-liquid fats, until it forms a smooth paste (known as a roux). Cook the roux for a minute or two over low heat, stirring constantly.

Add a trickle of water and stir to combine it. The consistency will become quite thick, so continue adding the water a little at a time, still stirring. If the water is added too fast, you will find it hard to achieve a smooth and lump-free sauce. (If lumps do appear, show them no mercy —whip them smooth with a whisk.)

In the same way, add the cream, then the tamari and lemon juice, stirring them all into the sauce.

Continue heating the sauce but do not allow it to boil, then serve it in a small jug or gravy-boat.

These basic instructions for a sauce may be varied considerably, omitting the cream, tamari and lemon juice in favour of spices, dried or fresh herbs, cheese or other flavourful ingredients.
Instead of water, you may wish to use milk, or part milk and part water.
For a non-dairy alternative, use nut or seed milks.

"Use it up, wear it out
Make it do, or do without".
New England proverb

Uma's  *arbeque Sauce*

Whenever this sauce is simmering on our stove, a succession of people seem to get drawn into the kitchen to check out what's cooking. Good with the Tofu Cutlets recipe (page 265), on Bean Burgers (page 48), or pour it over rice or tofu wieners.

Makes about 5 cups (1.2 L).

2 cups	(480 mL)	**finely chopped leeks**
1/3 cup	(80 mL)	**olive oil**
3 - 5 1/2 oz	(156 mL)	**cans of tomato paste**
2 cups	(480 mL)	**water**
2 tsp	(10 mL)	**dried parsley**
1 tsp	(5 mL)	**allspice**
1 Tbsp	(15 mL)	**chili powder**
1/2 tsp	(2 mL)	**mustard powder**
1/4 tsp	(1 mL)	**sea salt**
2 Tbsp	(30 mL)	**tamari**
3/4 cup	(180 mL)	**lemon juice**
1/4 cup	(60 mL)	**honey**

In a saucepan, sauté the leeks in olive oil.
Add the tomato paste and water, then mix well.
Add the rest of the ingredients, and simmer gently for a few minutes.

Mmmmmm. Yummy.

Experts disagree as to whether barbeque (or barbecue) derives from 'barbe-à-queue' (French for 'from beard to tail'), or possibly, via Spanish, from the Haitian 'barboka,' meaning 'a framework of sticks.' Quite amazing, really, the things one learns while writing a cookbook.

Dillweed Pesto

A delightful variation on the pesto theme, and one that can be made successfully with dried herbs. For a traditional pesto, <u>fresh</u> basil is a must.

Makes 1²/₃ cups (400 mL).

¹/₂ cup	(120 mL)	**dried dillweed** OR
		1 cup (240 mL) minced fresh dill
2 Tbsp	(30 mL)	**finely ground dried basil** OR
		4 Tbsp (60 mL) minced fresh basil
1 tsp	(5 mL)	**sea salt**
¹/₄ tsp	(1 mL)	**black pepper**
4 tsp	(20 mL)	**parmesan cheese** (optional)
6 Tbsp	(90 mL)	**lemon juice and pulp**
1 tsp	(5 mL)	**Dijon mustard**
6 Tbsp	(90 mL)	**pine nuts** (optional)
³/₄ cup	(180 mL)	**olive oil**

Combine all the ingredients and stir well. You will need to use a blender or food-processor if you include the pine nuts.

Serve over fettucine or spaghetti noodles or with rice, millet, potatoes or any steamed vegetable.

Yeast Gravy

Makes about 3 1/2 cups, (840 mL) enough for 4 - 6 people.

1/2 **cup**	(120 mL)	**wholewheat flour**
1/2 **cup**	(120 mL)	**ghee**
1 1/2 **Tbsp**	(22 mL)	**engevita yeast**
3 1/4 **cups**	(780 mL)	**vegetable stock or water***
1 1/2 **Tbsp**	(22 mL)	**lemon juice**
1 **tsp**	(5 mL)	**Dijon mustard**
1/2 **tsp**	(2 mL)	**tarragon**

* If you use water instead of stock, add **2 Tbsp** (30 mL) **tamar**i.

In a saucepan, blend the flour in the ghee over low heat for 3 - 5 minutes
   until the flour smells "roasted".
Stir in the yeast.
Stir in the vegetable stock, little by little, as the sauce thickens. Continue
   stirring and add lemon juice, mustard and tarragon. As the ingredients
   are thoroughly combined, the sauce will become smooth.

*Serve over plain rice and other grains, or with tofu burgers,
bean burgers, and sunflower millet burgers.*

"This is a serious affair, this existence of ours. It
is important that the real feelings in society,
and the life of the heart, be affirmed."
Leonard Cohen

Dips &
Spreads

Baba Ganouji

*In the Middle East, it seems that just about everyone you meet has their own version of this recipe. Moreover, each one will tell you that their recipe is the original one and by far the best. They are all wrong, however, because **this** is the best Baba Ganouji recipe anywhere.*

Use it as a spread with pita or French bread, or just dip into it with fresh vegetables, (and by the way, you pronounce it ga-noo-ee).

1		**medium eggplant** OR **2 small, thin ones**
1		**clove garlic, pressed or minced**
3 Tbsp	(45 mL)	**tahini**
2 Tbsp	(30 mL)	**fresh lemon juice**
½ tsp	(2 mL)	**sea salt** (to taste)
½ tsp	(2 mL)	**ground cumin**
2 Tbsp	(30 mL)	**olive oil**
2 Tbsp	(30 mL)	**chopped parsley** (optional)

Using a fork, prick the eggplant quite deeply all over its surface. This will help it to cook right through to the centre. Using 2 young, thin eggplants will speed the process considerably and also make for less mess.

If you are cooking over a gas flame, push a skewer right through the eggplant from end to end, or stick a fork in each end. Now cook it directly over the flames. Turn it frequently, until the skin is charred and blistered all over and the eggplant is quite soft, but not so soft that it melts into the gas burner. The charring is what gives this dish its unique flavour. It can be a little messy and smoky, but it's worth it.

An alternative method for charring the eggplant, albeit slower and not quite so tasty, is to prick it all over, place it on a baking tray, and char it directly under the broiler element in your oven, turning it frequently.

Let the eggplant cool a bit, then remove the skin and mash the rest of it in a bowl.

Add the remaining ingredients, mix thoroughly, then let stand for half an hour or so before serving.

Bean Dip

When you find some cooked beans peeking out at you from among the other good things your refrigerator contains, and it's time to prepare a quick snack, then take your "Salt Spring Island Cooking" in hand and turn to that bean dip recipe that you noticed in the Dips and Spreads section a while ago. Welcome those neglected legumes, with a few appropriate companions, into the spinning heart of your blender, and give them a new purpose in life! Great protein, great taste, and a quick snack.

Makes about 2 cups (480 mL) of a satisfying dip.

2 cups	(480 mL)	**cooked pinto beans** (or others)
¾ cup	(180 mL)	**chopped leeks** OR
		½ cup (120 mL) **mild onion**
¼ cup	(60 mL)	**lemon juice**
2 Tbsp	(30 mL)	**tamari**
2 tsp	(10 mL)	**engevita yeast**

Put all the ingredients in a blender and purée them until creamy. Chill before serving with vegetable sticks, crackers, or crusty bread.

"IT IS CLEAR THE FUTURE HOLDS
OPPORTUNITIES — IT ALSO HOLDS PITFALLS.
THE TRICK WILL BE TO SEIZE THE OPPORTUNITIES,
AVOID THE PITFALLS,
AND GET BACK HOME BY 6.00."
WOODY ALLEN

Cheese Balls

Although these elegant and mouth-watering little globes are actually neither dips nor spreads, we include them here since they make such a perfect accompaniment to many of the other recipes in this chapter. Particularly if you enjoy cheeses, you will find many variations and inventive possibilities — use another type of cheese or a blend of several; try different mustards; add a dash of dry red wine, some minced fresh herbs or toasted spices; substitute Eden's Ketchup for the Worcestershire; roll them in buttered breadcrumbs, chopped almonds, finely chopped peanuts, toasted sunflower seeds.......

Makes one dozen 1" (2.5 cm) balls.

1½ cups	(360 mL)	**grated mild cheddar cheese**
2 Tbsp	(30 mL)	**melted butter**
½ tsp	(2 mL)	**Worcestershire sauce***
2 tsp	(10 mL)	**prepared Dijon mustard**
		large pinch paprika (for colour)
		chopped walnuts to coat the balls

Mix all the ingredients until the cheese crumbles and the mixture is well
  blended.
Form the mixture into balls and roll them in the chopped walnuts.
Refrigerate for half an hour before serving.

*French's makes a Worcestershire sauce free of anchovies, which we
  favour, since anchovies much prefer to be in brine.

"JAZZ IS JUST RIFFING ON YOUR MISTAKES."
ORNETTE COLEMAN

Guacamole

Guacamole can be used as a dip for nachos, or as a topping for tacos, enchiladas and burritos. Its mild flavour makes a lovely contrast to the spiciness of salsa and hot pepper. Mayonnaise makes guacamole creamier and is a good way to "stretch" the recipe.

This recipe feeds 4 to 6, or 2 guacamole lovers.

3		**mashed avocados**
2 Tbsp	(30 mL)	**lemon juice**
3 Tbsp	(45 mL)	**Tofu Mayonnaise (page 141)**
1 Tbsp	(15 mL)	**very finely chopped leeks**
¼ tsp	(1 mL)	**sea salt**

Combine all the ingredients, and chill until serving time.

Guacamole always appreciates a siesta,
a few hours just to lie back and mingle flavours somewhere cool,
before all the exertion of being eaten.

.....and also Hot Guacamole

No, it's not straight off the stove-top, but you will quickly know that it's hot! A peppy opener to a party, you might serve it beside any Mexican dish, or as a dip with tortilla chips.

Serves about 8 people.

		8 avocados
		juice of 3 lemons
5 tsp	(25 mL)	**Spike or vegetable seasoning**
½ cup	(120 mL)	**hot salsa sauce**

This is nice and simple: just peel and mash the avocados, mix in all the remaining ingredients and chill.

Rajani's Hummus

Tempting and appetizing, this dip-or-spread has always been a great favourite of both the community and our guests, at the Salt Spring Centre.

Makes about 2½ cups (600 mL).

2 cups	(480 mL)	**cooked garbanzos** (1 cup dry)
⅓ cup	(80 mL)	**diced, well cooked carrots**
⅓ cup	(80 mL)	**carrot-cooking water**
		1-3 minced garlic cloves
		(depending on individual taste)
5 Tbsp	(75 mL)	**lemon juice**
⅓ cup	(80 mL)	**tahini**
¼ tsp	(1 mL)	**cayenne OR hot chili powder**
¼ tsp	(1 mL)	**Spike or vegetable seasoning**
¼ tsp	(1 mL)	**sea salt**
¼ cup	(60 mL)	**olive oil**
1 Tbsp	(15 mL)	**tamari**
1 tsp	(5 mL)	**cumin seeds, toasted and ground**
OR 1 tsp	(5 mL)	**ground cumin,** sautéed in
		1 Tbsp (15 mL) **olive oil**

Purée the cooked garbanzos with the liquids in a blender, in batches if your blender is not a huge one.

Add the remaining ingredients a little at a time, and blend again after each batch until everything is smooth and creamy. Alternatively, you can mash the garbanzos with a potato masher, and combine everything else in with a fork.

If you enjoy wine in cooking, then you might try adding about 2 Tbsp of a dry white to this excellent spread.

Millet Spread

An unusual recipe that creates a useful role for a little extra cooked grain.
At recipe-testing time in the kitchen here, we sometimes referred
to this one as Tissant Cheese.

Makes one cup (240 mL).

½ cup	(120 mL)	water
1 cup	(240 mL)	hot cooked millet
¼ cup	(60 mL)	cashews
1 Tbsp	(15 mL)	lemon juice
1 Tbsp	(15 mL)	finely chopped leek
1½ tsp	(7 mL)	sea salt
1 Tbsp	(15 mL)	finely chopped red pepper
1 tsp	(5 mL)	engevita yeast
1½ tsp	(7 mL)	caraway, dill or celery seed (optional)
¼ cup	(60 mL)	sliced black olives (optional)

Put all of the ingredients into a blender and purée until smooth.
Pour the mixture into a bowl and refrigerate.

Almond Mushroom Pâté

*Amaze and astound your friends with this superb and
incredibly-difficult-to-stop-eating pâté.*

Yields 1½ cups (360 mL).

1 cup	(240 mL)	**toasted almonds**
2 Tbsp	(30 mL)	**finely chopped leeks***
6 cups	(1.4 L)	**chopped mushrooms**
6 Tbsp	(90 mL)	**butter**
1 tsp	(5 mL)	**sea salt**
½ tsp	(2 mL)	**thyme**
		pinch of pepper
1 tsp	(5 mL)	**honey**
1 tsp	(5 mL)	**cider vinegar**
1 Tbsp	(15 mL)	**oil**

Pulverize or finely grind the almonds.

Sauté the leeks and mushrooms in 4 Tbsp (60 mL) butter over high heat,
until the liquid evaporates.

Add the spices, honey and cider vinegar, and simmer until the mushrooms
are almost completely dry.

Purée the mixture in a blender with the ground almonds, then blend in
the remaining 2 Tbsp (30 mL) butter and the oil.

Place your pâté in an attractive bowl, or form it into a loaf shape on a
serving dish.

Cover the pâté tightly and chill to blend the flavours, for at least half an
hour — or better still half a day, if you have the time.

*Optionally, very mild onion will also work in this recipe.

*Adjust the seasonings in this recipe to suit your own personal preference for
saltiness, sharpness and sweetness.*

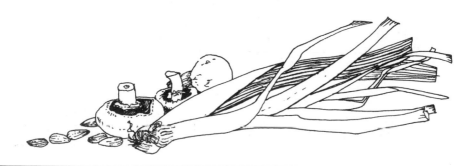

Whether you call it ....

SunSpread

..... or pâté de tournesol, *or* sunseed spread, *or even* vegetarian chopped
liver *(yuck!), as one quizzical but appreciative consumer referred to it, this makes
a satisfying dip for vegetables, crackers, chips and more.*

The recipe yields about 3½ cups (840 mL).

Toss into a blender (in this order), blending each ingredient together
before adding the next:

2 cups	(480 mL)	**sunflower seeds**
3 Tbsp	(45 mL)	**olive oil**
⅓ cup	(80 mL)	**chopped leeks**
1 lb	(454 g)	**tofu**
⅓ cup	(80 mL)	**engevita yeast**
5 Tbsp	(75 mL)	**tamari**
½ tsp	(2 mL)	**pepper**
		enough water to aid blending

We found the blender worked well enough if we chopped the leeks quite
finely first. And don't go overboard with the water — use *just enough* to
facilitate happy blending.

*Serve on rye crackers with lettuce, cucumber slices and
a sprinkle of chopped parsley.*

"IF YOU LOOK TOWARDS THE SUN, YOU'LL SEE NO SHADOWS."

Cashew UnCheese

This tastes quite amazingly like dairy cheese, so much so that your family or guests may not even notice!

Makes 2 cups (480 mL).

3 Tbsp + 1 tsp	(50 mL)	**agar flakes** OR
		1½ **Tbsp** (22 mL) **agar powder**
1½ **cups**	(360 mL)	**cold water**
1½ **cups**	(360 mL)	**raw cashews**
½ **cup**	(120 mL)	**sunflower seeds**
2 **Tbsp**	(30 mL)	**engevita yeast**
1½ **tsp**	(7 mL)	**sea salt**
¼-⅓ **cup**	(60-80 mL)	**freshly squeezed lemon juice**
3 **Tbsp**	(45 mL)	**finely-grated carrot** (well packed)
1 **Tbsp**	(15 mL)	**vegetable oil**

Stir the agar into cold water, then simmer over low heat to soften it.

Pour half of the agar water into a blender and process with half of the cashews and sunflower seeds. Blending half at a time will help make the mixture creamy faster. (Overfilling the blender will result in an uneven texture.)

Add half of each of the remaining ingredients and blend until creamy.

Pour into a mixing bowl.

Process the other half of the ingredients the same way.

Thoroughly mix the two batches together and pour into a mould or bowl. Chill until set.

This non-dairy alternative to cheese may be used as a spread or a grated topping. For a grated topping, freeze the spread before grating.

Vege-Butter

A lovely mellow spread, the combination of flavours reverberates delightfully on the palate. Try a swirl on a slice of fresh crusty bread, and discover new meaning in good old bread-and-butter.

Yields a little over 2 cups (480 mL).

1 lb	(454 g)	butter
5½ oz	(156 mL)	can of tomato paste
3 Tbsp	(45 mL)	very finely chopped leek
		half green pepper, finely chopped
3 Tbsp	(45 mL)	very finely chopped chives OR
		1-2 spring onions, finely chopped
	3	sprigs parsley, finely chopped
1 tsp	(5 mL)	basil
1 tsp	(5 mL)	oregano
		a fat pinch of thyme
		squeeze of lemon juice
		(or dry white wine)
		pinch of salt*

Place all the ingredients in a good-sized bowl, and blend them together with your fingers, until soft and completely mixed. (It's a much quicker way than using a blender or food-processor, and has the advantage of retaining the little variations in colour and texture that give character to the spread.)

Transfer the mixture into an attractive bowl. Smooth and pattern the surface with a fork, and top with a sprig of parsley or wedge of lemon.

Chill the vege-butter for a couple of hours, then remove from the refrigerator and leave at room temperature for about half an hour before serving with crackers, toast or a slab of really wholesome bread.

*Use ¼ - ½ tsp (1-2 mL) more salt if butter is unsalted.

Vegepâté

An excellent and sophisticated pâté that holds its own against all the conventional rivals.

Makes enough pâté for one 8"x 8" cake pan (20 cm x 20 cm), serving about 10 people.

1½ cups	(360 mL)	**ground sunflower seeds**
¾ cup	(180 mL)	**whole-wheat flour**
¾ cup	(180 mL)	**engevita yeast**
1 tsp	(5 mL)	**thyme**
1 tsp	(5 mL)	**basil**
1 tsp	(5 mL)	**sage**
½ tsp	(2 mL)	**cloves** (optional)
1 tsp	(5 mL)	**sea salt**
2 cups	(480 mL)	**grated potatoes**
½ cup	(120 mL)	**vegetable oil or butter**
2 cups	(480 mL)	**warm water**
2 cups	(480 mL)	**chopped leeks***
¼ cup	(60 mL)	**freshly squeezed lemon juice** (2 medium lemons)

In a large bowl, combine the ground seeds with the flour, yeast, herbs and spices.
Add the grated potatoes and the oil or butter, and mix everything well.
Stir in the water, leeks and lemon juice.
Spread the pâté mixture in the ungreased pan.
Bake at 350°F (180°C) for 1¼ hours.

*Or mild onions, if you prefer.

Spinny Dip

This pretty green-and-white spinach dip was sired by the winner of the coveted Salt Spring / Maui Inter-Islands Dip of Dips Award in 1991, held under the umbrellas and palm trees of an exclusive watering-hole. The palm trees were there courtesy of Maui, and the umbrellas, one need hardly say, were Salt Spring's contribution.

1 cup (lightly packed)	(240 mL)	**finely shredded spinach**
8 oz can	(227 mL)	**sliced water chestnuts**
1 cup	(240 mL)	**sour cream**
½ - 1 tsp	(2-5 mL)	**Spike or vegetable seasoning**
¼ tsp	(1 mL)	**engevita yeast**
		fat pinch of salt
		pinch of black pepper
		a round 'cottage' loaf (optional)

After thoroughly washing the spinach, nip off the stalks and discard. Dry it somewhat, either by patting it in a tea-towel or, (and here's the spinny part) by whirling it in a salad spinner. With a sharp knife, finely shred the spinach.

Drain the water chestnuts and chop them into smaller pieces.

Combine all the ingredients in a bowl and mix well.

Chill for an hour or two.

An attractive option for serving the dip is inside a crusty, round, 'cottage' loaf, as follows:

Cut the top off the loaf. Scoop out all the soft inner bread and break it or cut it into chunks. Also cut up the 'lid' of the loaf.

Just before serving, place the crust shell on a big platter, fill it with the dip, and pile all around it the chunks of bread. Garnish with sprigs of parsley.

"THE SHADOW OF THE BAMBOO SWEEPS THE STAIR ALL NIGHT LONG.
YET NOT A MOTE OF DUST IS STIRRED."

CHIKAN

Desserts

"IF THERE BE ANY POETRY AT ALL IN MEALS, OR THE PROCESS OF FEEDING,
THERE IS POETRY IN THE DESSERT."
ISABELLA BEETON : 'THE BOOK OF HOUSEHOLD MANAGEMENT'

Bavarian Apple Flan

To be quite accurate, you would want to call this nutty, fruity, spicy kind of dessert-pizza by its full name of Stettener Apfelkuchen, but that might prove more of a mouthful than the flan itself.

THE PASTRY:

1¹/₂ cups	(360 mL)	**whole-wheat flour**
1¹/₂ tsp	(7 mL)	**egg-replacer**
1 cup	(240 mL)	**butter**
³/₄ cup	(180 mL)	**brown sugar**
1 tsp	(5 mL)	**grated lemon peel** (optional)
7 tsp	(35 mL)	**water**

Sift together the flour and egg-replacer powder, then cut in the butter using two knives or a pastry cutter, until it resembles coarse meal.

Mix in the sugar, lemon peel and lastly the water, combining everything with your fingertips. Pat the dough into a ball, and cool it in the refrigerator for half an hour.

Pat and press the dough into place over a greased baking sheet, and up its sides. Try to make it as even in depth as you can.

THE FILLING:

6 - 10		**green apples** (depending on size)
¹/₂ - ³/₄ cup	(120-180 mL)	**raisins**
		boiling water
¹/₄ cup	(60 mL)	**slivered almonds or walnuts**

Pre-heat the oven to 400°F (205°C). Peel and core the apples (any kind will work; tart cookers are best though). Quarter them, then cut into thinnish slices, about 12 - 20 from each apple. Arrange the slices, overlapping each other, in rows to cover the pastry. Push them gently into the pastry as you lay them out. Now, into the oven for 10 minutes.

While the flan is pre-baking, prepare the nuts and raisins, and then the batter.

Soak the raisins in enough boiling water to cover them, until they are somewhat softened. Tip off the water, squeezing the fruit lightly to remove excess.

When the 10 minutes are up, remove the flan from the oven and scatter the raisins and nuts over the apples.

THE BATTER:

2 Tbsp	(30 mL)	**whole-wheat flour**
1 Tbsp	(15 mL)	**brown sugar**
¹/₂ tsp	(2 mL)	**cinnamon**
¹/₄ tsp	(1 mL)	**ground cloves**
1¹/₂ tsp	(7 mL)	**egg-replacer**
1 tsp	(5 mL)	**vanilla**
		milk

Whisk the above ingredients together with a fork, using enough milk to make the total quantity up to 1¹/₂ cups (360 mL).

Pour the batter over the whole flan, and bake for a further 25 - 30 minutes at 400°F (205°C).

Cool the flan before serving, with or without whipped cream,
or any of the other toppings you may choose.
We enjoyed it unadorned,
and straight out of our fingers.

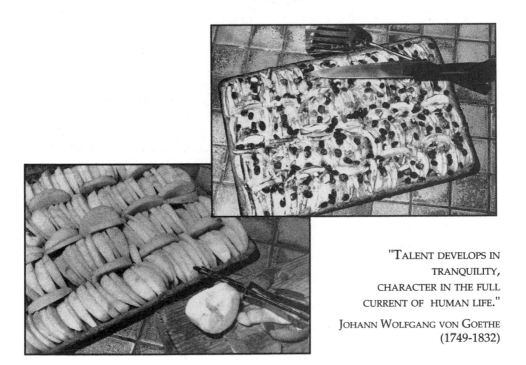

"TALENT DEVELOPS IN
TRANQUILITY,
CHARACTER IN THE FULL
CURRENT OF HUMAN LIFE."

JOHANN WOLFGANG VON GOETHE
(1749-1832)

Apple Walnut Cake

This is a moist, heavily fruited cake with no added sugar.

1½ cups	(360 mL)	dates
1 cup	(240 mL)	raisins
¾ cup	(180 mL)	boiling water
2⅓ cups	(560 mL)	unbleached white flour*
1 tsp	(5 mL)	baking soda
1 tsp	(5 mL)	baking powder
½ tsp	(2 mL)	sea salt
1½ tsp	(7 mL)	cinnamon
½ tsp	(2 mL)	nutmeg
1¼ cup	(300 mL)	apple juice or water
1½ cups	(360 mL)	grated apples (2 medium) OR unpeeled chopped apples
1 cup	(240 mL)	walnuts

Purée carefully the dates, raisins and water in a blender or food processor.
In a medium-sized bowl, mix the dry ingredients and add the purée.
Fold in the juice, apples and walnuts.
Bake in an oiled 8"x 8" (2 L) square pan at 350°F (180°C) for 45 minutes.

* Whole-wheat pastry flour cannot be subsituted for unbleached white
flour in this recipe — it will make the cake gummy.

Baked Pears

Makes 4 to 6 servings.

		3 pears
2 Tbsp	(30 mL)	**raisins**
6 Tbsp	(90 mL)	**chopped almonds**
2 Tbsp	(30 mL)	**maple syrup**
³/₄ tsp	(4 mL)	**cinnamon**

Cut the pears in half lengthwise and scoop out the core.

Lay the pear halves out in a square 8"x 8" (2 L) baking dish.

Heap 1 tsp (5 mL) of raisins and 1 Tbsp (15 mL) of the chopped almonds in the depression of each pear half.

Pour 1 tsp (5 mL) of maple syrup over the filling of each pear and sprinkle each with ¹/₈ tsp (¹/₂ mL) cinnamon.

Cover the bottom of the pan with water, then bake at 350°F (180°C) for 45 minutes.

Some other ideas for fillings:
Chopped raisins with lemon peel
Walnuts

"GO, MARK THE MATCHLESS WORKINGS OF THE POWER
THAT SHUTS WITHIN THE SEED THE FUTURE FLOWER."
WILLIAM COWPER (1731-1800)

Bananas Marrakesh

Serves 4 - 6.

8 cups	(1.9 L)	**pitted dates**
4 cups	(960 mL)	**water**
	3	**large bananas, mashed**
1 tsp	(5 mL)	**grated orange rind**
	4 - 6	**bananas, sliced diagonally**

Simmer the dates and water until quite mushy, about 20 minutes.
  If the dates you use are very dry, it may be necessary to add
  ¹/₂ cup (120 mL) more water.
Add the mashed bananas and the orange rind to the date mixture.
  (Mash the bananas with a fork, a potato masher, or put them in the
  blender if you prefer a smoother look.)
In individual dessert dishes, arrange the banana slices and top them with
  the date sauce.

To serve, garnish with twisted orange slices, a mound of
whipping cream or a sprig of mint.

Janis's Sour Cream Blackberry Pie

Blessed with acres of blackberry bushes in her field above a tiny white-shell beach at Fulford Harbour, Janis and her berry pies gained a well deserved reputation as among Salt Spring's best. Suitable for lazy summer afternoons — as a celebration (or a reward for enduring the brambles in quest of the berries!).

	pastry for a 10" pie plate (see page 186)	
4 cups	(960 mL)	**blackberries**
1 cup	(240 mL)	**sour cream**
½ cup	(120 mL)	**brown sugar**
1 Tbsp	(15 mL)	**flour**
1 tsp	(5 mL)	**lemon juice** (optional)

Line the pie plate with pastry.

Wash the blackberries thoroughly and drain them.

Mix the sour cream, brown sugar and flour.

Place the blackberries and 1 tsp (5 mL) lemon juice (or less if the blackberries are tart, none at all if you prefer) in the piecrust. If the berries are very juicy, sprinkle a little flour on top of the pastry before adding the berries.

Cover the berries with the sour cream mixture.

Bake the pie at 425°F (220°C) for 10 minutes.

Reduce the heat to 325°F (165°C), and continue baking for 30 - 40 minutes until the berries are soft, juicy and bubbling.

VARIATION 1: Combine the berries and the sour cream mixture before placing them in the piecrust.

VARIATION 2: Make enough pastry for a double-crust pie, and cover the berries with a top crust before baking.

*Although the fragrance of freshly baked blackberry pie can drive one to frenzy, **do** try and wait until it has cooled somewhat before cutting.*

"DOUBTLESS GOD COULD HAVE MADE A BETTER BERRY, BUT DOUBTLESS GOD NEVER DID."

WILLIAM BUTLER: *COMPLEAT ANGLER*
(1535-1618)

Carob Chip Cookies

Makes about three dozen good and fattening cookies.

1¼ cups	(300 mL)	**whole-wheat pastry flour**
¼ tsp	(1 mL)	**salt**
½ tsp	(2 mL)	**baking soda**
½ cup	(120 mL)	**rolled oats**
¼ cup	(60 mL)	**shredded or grated coconut**
½ cup	(120 mL)	**butter**
½ cup	(120 mL)	**sugar**
½ tsp	(2mL)	**vanilla**
5 Tbsp	(75 mL)	**water, juice or milk**
¾ cup	(180 mL)	**carob chips** (or more!)

Sift the flour, salt and baking soda together.

Mix in the rolled oats and coconut

Cream the butter and sugar.

Add the vanilla and water to the butter/sugar mixture.

Mix together the dry and liquid ingredients.

Toss in the carob chips.

Drop by teaspoonfuls onto a greased cookie sheet. You won't need to bother mashing them down — they melt.

Bake the cookies at 350°F (180°C) for at least 20 minutes.

*Although terribly decadent already, you can make these cookies yet more so by adding a few raisins and even **more** carob chips. Watch your cooking time, though — they are crumbly if under-cooked.*

Sugarfree Carrot Coconut Cookies

A bright way to enjoy some of the natural sweetness of good foods. The recipe makes four dozen or more fruity cookies.

1½ cups	(360 mL)	**boiling water** OR **very hot apple juice**
1 cup	(240 mL)	**pitted dates**
1 cup	(240 mL)	**raisins**
2 cups	(480 mL)	**finely grated carrots**
1 cup	(240 mL)	**oil**
2 tsp	(10 mL)	**vanilla**
4 cups	(960 mL)	**rolled oats**
2 cups	(480 mL)	**shredded unsweetened coconut**
1 cup	(240 mL)	**whole-wheat pastry flour**
1 tsp	(5 mL)	**grated orange rind**
1 tsp	(5 mL)	**salt**

Pour the boiling water or juice over the dates and raisins and let sit for at least 15 minutes—the longer the better.

Purée them in a food processor or blender. If you don't have a processor or blender, chop them finely by hand before soaking, and then use a potato masher to complete the purée.

Mix the fruit purée, carrots, oil and vanilla until all is well blended.

Mix in the remaining ingredients and drop by the teaspoonful onto greased cookie sheets.

Bake at 350°F (180°C) for 15 minutes. When you remove them from the oven, let them rest on the cookie sheet for 5 minutes or so before sliding them onto a rack. Allow to cool completely before eating.

Cashew Pudding

Makes 6 servings.

1 cup	(240 mL)	**cashews**
3 cups	(720 mL)	**boiling water**
6 Tbsp	(90 mL)	**arrowroot powder**
3 Tbsp	(45 mL)	**honey**
2 tsp	(10 mL)	**vanilla**

Grind the cashews in a blender.
Add the boiling water and blend until creamy. This makes about
  3½ cups (840 mL) of cashew milk.
Pour 1 cup (240 mL) of the cashew milk into a bowl and mix in the
  arrowroot powder until it is quite smooth.
Pour this mixture and the rest of the cashew milk into a saucepan.
Add the honey and vanilla.
Heat over low to medium heat until thickened, stirring all the while so it
  doesn't boil.
Pour into individual serving dishes and allow the dessert to cool before
  serving. It will continue to thicken as it cools.

and a variation that might be known as....

Cashew Rhubarb Pudding

4 cups	(960 mL)	**chopped rhubarb**
½ cup	(120 mL)	**water**
¼ cup	(60 mL)	**honey**

Cook the rhubarb and water in a saucepan over medium heat until the
  rhubarb is quite soft. Keep watching it and stirring — it doesn't take
  long to cook.
Add the honey.
Stir the mixture into the cashew pudding made with the recipe above.
Spoon into individual serving dishes and cool before serving.

Both these recipes make totally far out popsicles!

Chocolate Chip Oatmeal Cookies

*It's difficult to say exactly how many cookies this recipe yields, but if you make 2"
diameter balls, you should end up with about 30 cookies. Now this will also
depend on whether or not someone sneaks in and "tests" the batter or the cooling
cookies while you aren't looking.*

1 cup	(240 mL)	butter
1 cup	(240 mL)	brown sugar, lightly packed
1 tsp	(5 mL)	baking soda
¼ cup	(60 mL)	boiling water
1 tsp	(5 mL)	vanilla
1³/₄ cups	(420 mL)	flour
½ tsp	(2 mL)	salt
2 cups	(480 mL)	quick cooking rolled oats
½ cup	(120 mL)	coconut
2 cups	(480 mL)	semi-sweet chocolate chips

Cream the butter, then blend in the sugar until well mixed.

Dissolve the baking soda in boiling water and add it to the butter/sugar
mixture.

Mix in the vanilla.

Mix together the dry ingredients, then add them slowly to the creamed
mixture. Mix well.

Stir in the chocolate chips.

Chill the dough for half an hour — this will make it easier to handle.

Form cookies as big or as little as you like (but remember to adjust the
cooking time for sizes totally out of the ordinary), and bake them at
350°F (180°C) for 12 - 15 minutes.

"WHAT YOU RESIST, YOU BECOME."
OLD TAOIST SAYING.

.....*And Now For Something Completely Chocolate*

This gâteau serves 16, or 10 without regard for personal safety.

½ lb	(225g)	**butter**
1⅓ cups	(320 mL)	**brown sugar, lightly packed**
½ lb	(225 g)	**unsweetened chocolate**
		(**not** semi-sweet)
1 tsp	(5 mL)	**cornflour**
4 tsp	(20 mL)	**egg-replacer PLUS**
		½ **cup** (120 mL) **water** (or according
		to instructions on the packet**)**

Melt the butter and sugar together in a double-boiler, or in a pan over hot water on low heat.

Add the chocolate and cornflour, and stir until smooth.

In a bowl, measure the egg-replacer and water enough to give the equivalent of 4 eggs; see the instructions on the packet. Blend them together until completely smooth.

Remove the pan from the heat and add the egg-replacer, whisking it in until the mixture is creamy.

Prepare a 7" or 8" (18 - 20 cm) spring form cake pan by brushing the sides with a tasteless vegetable oil, and cutting and fitting a circle of waxed paper in the bottom of the pan. Make sure the paper is trapped by the top part of the spring form.

Pour the mixture into the spring form, place in a pan of warm water, and bake at 350°F (180°C) for one hour.

Allow the cake to cool completely in the pan, then chill for best consistency before turning it out onto a plate.

*This confection is best served in quite small slices with unwhipped, unsweetened heavy cream. It is **very** rich, so eat it slowly, and rarely. You may find a cup of strong coffee fits after this rather particular experience.*

"MORALITY IS SIMPLY THE ATTITUDE WE ADOPT TOWARDS
PEOPLE WHOM WE PERSONALLY DISLIKE."
OSCAR WILDE (1854 -1900)

Old-Fashioned Gingerbread Cake

2 cups	(480 mL)	whole-wheat pastry flour
1 tsp	(5 mL)	baking soda
1 tsp	(5 mL)	baking powder
½ tsp	(2 mL)	sea salt
½ tsp	(2 mL)	cloves
1 tsp	(5 mL)	mustard
1 tsp	(5 mL)	cinnamon
1½ tsp	(7 mL)	ginger
⅓ cup	(80 mL)	oil
1 cup	(240 mL)	molasses
1 cup	(240 mL)	hot water
1 Tbsp	(15 mL)	vinegar

Sift the dry ingredients together.
Stir the liquid ingredients together until homogenous.
Mix the liquids into the dries slowly and thoroughly.
Pour the mixture into a well-greased 8"x 8" (2 L) pan, and bake for
40 - 45 minutes at 350°F (180°C).

*This is bountiful all by itself....but you can try serving it with
unsweetened whipping cream, or slices of kiwi-fruit, or make
a pineapple right-side-up cake by putting pineapple rings on top!
If you place the pineapple rings onto the cake before it goes into the oven,
it will rise around them to give a very pretty effect.*

"I COUNT HIM BRAVER WHO OVERCOMES HIS DESIRES
THAN HIM WHO OVERCOMES HIS ENEMIES."

ARISTOTLE (384-322 BC)

Gormenghast Pie

The story goes that this pie was invented during a three-day marathon reading of a delightful fantasy set in the mythical country of Gormenghast.* We would suggest that you check the first line of the method before proceeding with the recipe, or alternatively buy yourself a copy of the novel to while away the time.

Makes 8 tarts or 1 small pie.

THE FILLING:

½ cup	(120 mL)	**currants**
½ cup	(120 mL)	**raisins**
1 cup	(240 mL)	**chopped dates**
¼ cup	(60 mL)	**sesame seeds**
¼ cup	(60 mL)	**sunflower seeds**
1 cup	(240 mL)	**apple juice**
¼ tsp	(1 mL)	**allspice**
¼ tsp	(1 mL)	**cinnamon**
1 tsp	(5 mL)	**grated lemon rind (or orange)**

THE PIE CRUST:

½ cup	(120 mL)	**hard butter**
1 tsp	(5 mL)	**sea salt**
1 cup	(240 mL)	**whole-wheat pastry flour**
2 Tbsp	(30 mL)	**ice water**

Combine the filling ingredients and let them soak in a cool spot for 2 days. That's all the attention they will need!

For the pastry, cut or rub the butter into the flour and salt until it resembles meal.

Add the ice water and briefly hand mix.

Roll out on a very well-floured board and cut into 8 circles, big enough to fit a tart or muffin tin. Hopefully you can roll it to about ⅛" thick.

Use the leftover pastry to cut decorative tops for the tarts. If not, don't worry — you've just made 8 topless tarts!

For a pie, roll the pastry out evenly and line your pie plate as usual.

Now pour the filling into the tarts/pieshell and bake at 425°F (220°C) for 20 minutes.

If you're a very decadent sort, you might wish to soak the fruit in apple juice combined with a little brandy or sherry.

*The Gormenghast trilogy, by Mervyn Peake, is published by Penguin Books. In the USA, by Overlook Press.

Granola Pie Crust

This recipe makes one bottom crust.

2 cups (480 mL) **granola**
¼ cup (60 mL) **oil or melted butter**

Put the granola in your blender or food processor and blend until it
  resembles fine crumbs. Transfer to a bowl.
Add the oil or butter and mix with your fingers.
Press the mixture into a pie plate and up the sides.
Bake at 350°F (180°C) for 10 minutes.

Cool the crust before pouring in a filling.

*You can also use this mixture as a base
for tasty squares, bars,
diamonds, and so on.
But please,
don't go attempting dodecahedra
or anything rash like that.*

"If you wish to make an apple pie truly from
scratch, you must first invent the universe."
Carl Sagan

Hawaiian Delight

Makes a ten inch pie (25 cm) or an eight inch (20 cm) springform 'cheesecake.'

1 lb	(454 g)	**tofu, drained**
1		**small banana**
1 - 19 oz	(540 mL)	**can crushed pineapple**
¼ cup	(60 mL)	**pineapple juice**
¼ cup	(60 mL)	**orange juice**
2 tsp	(10 mL)	**vanilla**
2 Tbsp	(30 mL)	**honey**
¼ cup	(60 mL)	**maple syrup**
		grated peel from one orange
5 Tbsp	(75 mL)	**unbleached white flour**
¼ cup	(60 mL)	**toasted coconut**
	one	**pre-baked sweet pie shell** (page 174) OR
	one	**graham wafer base** (page 200)

Crumble the tofu into a blender. You may have to do this in two batches if you have a small blender — it gets pretty full when all of the ingredients are added.

Add the banana in pieces and purée until creamy.

Add all of the other ingredients except the peel and coconut.

Purée until well blended and smooth.

Stir in the peel by hand.

Pour the mixture into a prepared pie shell or over a graham crumb base in an 8" springform pan.

Sprinkle with coconut.

Bake at 350°F (180°C) for 30 - 35 minutes, or until the dessert is set and has a golden colour on the top.

"TIME FOR A LITTLE SOMETHING."
A.A. MILNE: *WINNIE THE POOH*

Honey Pie

Bees fly some 35,000 miles (1½ times around the world!) to gather one pound of honey for us, and we rarely even say "thank you". This nut-glazed raisin-pie recipe has so much more than just honey in it, but eat it as a tribute to our little bumbly, busy friends. Thank you, bees everywhere!

10" (25 cm) **pie crust** (as in Jai Pie on page 191)
(see note in method regarding pre-baking)

THE FILLING:			
	1 cup	(240 mL)	**sultanas or seedless raisins**
	1 cup	(240 mL)	**water**
	⅓ cup	(80 mL)	**honey**
	2 Tbsp	(30 mL)	**butter**
	2 Tbsp	(30 mL)	**whole-wheat flour**
	2 tsp	(10 mL)	**egg-replacer**
	2 Tbsp	(30 mL)	**water**
	1 Tbsp	(15 mL)	**grated lemon peel**
	3 Tbsp	(45 mL)	**lemon juice**

THE TOPPING:			
	¼ cup	(60 mL)	**brown sugar**
	3 Tbsp	(45 mL)	**milk or cream**
	¼ cup	(60 mL)	**butter**
	¼ cup	(60 mL)	**honey**
	½ cup	(120 mL)	**crushed walnuts**
	½ cup	(120 mL)	**chopped almonds**

Prepare the pie crust as in Jai Pie, but cover the edges of the crust with foil as well as the bottom before pre-baking.

Pre-bake the crust at 450°F (235°C) for 10 minutes, then reduce heat to 350°F (180°C) for 15 minutes more.

Bring the sultanas and water to a boil over a low flame, remove the pan from the heat and stir in the honey.

Take a half cup of the mixture and cool it. Gently stir in the butter and flour, then return it to the pan.

Cook over low heat, stirring constantly until it thickens.

Mix the egg-replacer and water to a smooth paste, then stir it into the mixture in the pan. Stir in the lemon peel and juice.

The mixture should now be quite thick. Allow it to cool somewhat before placing it in the pie shell, and smoothing the surface.

Stir the sugar, milk, butter, honey and nuts over a low heat until the mixture bubbles, then pour the glaze over the pie filling.

Bake the pie at 400°F (205°C) for about 25 minutes, then chill or cool before serving.

'Love you, honey-pie.

Scrumptious "Ice Cream"

This simple recipe makes an interesting change from the usual ice creams, and it's great for people with milk allergies. You don't have to wait hours before you can eat it, either!

Serves 2 - 4.

1 cup	(240 mL)	**filberts**
2 cups	(480 mL)	**frozen berries**
½ cup	(120 mL)	**pineapple juice**
2 Tbsp	(30 mL)	**maple syrup**

Purée all the ingredients until creamy.
Serve immediately, since it changes its character if left to sit,
  even in the freezer.

"PRACTICE RANDOM ACTS
OF KINDNESS AND SENSELESS BEAUTY"

Jai Pie

Jai, or Jaya, means Victory! in Sanskrit — a kind of Eureka! or Howzat! when you finally reach your goal, so long in the seeking.

We tested quite a few lemon pie recipes in the course of building our desserts section, for some inexplicable reason always the most exhaustively tested chapter of any cookbook. This lemon pie achieved acceptance, disappearing within moments into a horde of humans one brilliant midsummer afternoon, under the flowering black locust tree on the lawns of the Salt Spring Centre. Although this recipe uses a sweetened milk product, there isn't a huge amount more sugar so we felt it worth sharing with you. Jai Jai Lemon Pie!

Makes one 10" (25 cm) pie.

PIE CRUST:	1 cup	(240 mL)	whole-wheat pastry flour
	3 Tbsp	(45 mL)	brown sugar
			a pinch of sea salt
	½ cup	(120 mL)	butter
THE FILLING:	2 cups	(480 mL)	sweetened condensed milk (not evaporated)
	6 Tbsp	(90 mL)	lemon juice
	1½ Tbsp	(22 mL)	grated lemon peel, packed
	¼ tsp	(1 mL)	sea salt

Sift the flour, sugar and salt together into a bowl.

Cut in the butter with a pastry cutter, or two knives, so that it takes on the texture of a coarse meal. Rub it lightly between your fingertips until it can all be shaped into a ball. Chill the pastry for an hour or two.

This kind of shortcrust pastry cannot successfully be rolled out, so, using fingertips and backs of knuckles, press it gently into place in a buttered pie plate, to line it evenly and smoothly. Prick holes all over the bottom of the crust to allow steam to escape as it bakes.

Cover the crust with foil (optional), then fill it with unwanted dry beans or small (washed!) pebbles to weight it down.

Bake the crust at 450°F (235°C) for about 10 minutes, then turn down the heat to 350°F (180°C), and continue baking for another 20 minutes. The crust should be adequately done, but not really dark. If the bottom of the crust seems still damp when you have removed the foil and beans, allow it to dry for a few minutes before filling it with the lemon mixture.

While the crust is baking, stir together the condensed milk, salt, lemon juice and peel, until thickened. Pour the mixture into the pie shell, and chill for several hours.

We have been attempting an eggless meringue to top this pie, but until that unlikely day arrives, Hamsa Cream (page 211) is a suggestion for those who like their Jai Pie dressed up a little.

Kheer

A well-loved East Indian dessert that takes rice pudding two steps beyond.

Makes about 10 cups (2.4 L).

1 cup	(240 mL)	**basmati rice (uncooked)**
¼ cup	(60 mL)	**ghee or butter**
4 cups	(960 mL)	**milk**
2 cups	(480 mL)	**water**
½ cup	(120 mL)	**raisins**
½ cup	(120 mL)	**chopped almonds**
¼ cup	(60 mL)	**brown sugar**
½ Tbsp	(7 mL)	**ground cinnamon**
½ Tbsp	(7 mL)	**ground cardamom**
		pinch of ground cloves
		pinch of ground ginger

Sauté the rice in ghee until it becomes opaque.

Add the milk and water, bring to a boil, then turn the heat down to simmer.

Add the raisins, almonds, sugar and spices.

Cover and cook over low heat, until all the liquid is absorbed and the rice is soft. This will take from 40 to 60 minutes, depending on how mushy you like your rice pudding.

Kheer can be eaten hot or cold, but you may well find you like it best around room-temperature.

"EVERYTHING HAS ITS BEAUTY,
BUT NOT EVERYONE SEES IT."
CONFUCIUS

Lemon Pie

And here is another lemon pie, but this time, we added protein-rich tofu in the hope of seducing those of us who are "nutritionally correct" into eating a dessert.

Makes one 10 inch (25 cm) pie.

		one unbaked pie crust
1 lb	(454 g)	tofu, drained
½ cup	(120 mL)	lemon juice
1 Tbsp	(15 mL)	vegetable oil
½ cup	(120 mL)	honey
¼ cup	(60 mL)	unbleached white flour
		grated rind of one lemon

Crumble the tofu into a blender or food processor.
Add the lemon juice, oil and honey.
Purée until the mixture is smooth and creamy.
Add the flour in two batches, whipping after each addition.
Stir in the lemon rind by hand and pour the filling into your prepared pie
    crust.
Bake at 350°F (180°C) for 30 - 35 minutes, until the filling doesn't jiggle.

"AND SO, WHILE OTHERS MISERABLY PLEDGE THEMSELVES
TO THE INSATIABLE PURSUIT OF AMBITION AND BRIEF POWER,
I WILL BE STRETCHED OUT IN THE SHADE, SINGING."

FRAY LUIS DE LEON

Spicy Nut Diamonds

Makes one 9 x 9 inch (2.5 L) pan of diamonds.

1 cup	(240 mL)	**whole-wheat pastry flour**
¼ cup	(60 mL)	**toasted wheat germ**
1 tsp	(5 mL)	**baking soda**
½ tsp	(2 mL)	**cinnamon**
		a pinch of ground cloves
¼ tsp	(1 mL)	**salt**
⅓ cup	(80 mL)	**oil**
½ cup	(120 mL)	**buttermilk**
1 tsp	(5 mL)	**vinegar**
¾ cup	(180 mL)	**honey**
½ cup	(120 mL)	**dates or raisins**
½ cup	(120 mL)	**chopped walnuts**

Combine the dry ingredients.
Stir together all the liquid ingredients and add them to the dry ones.
Fold in the dates and nuts.
Pour the mixture into a greased and floured 9"x 9" (2.5 L) pan.
Bake at 350°F (180°C) for 35 - 40 minutes — until the middle springs back
   at your touch. Allow to cool after removing from the oven, and slice up
   the cookies into diamonds, or your own choice of size and shape.

Pamela's Applesauce Cake

We've used this wholesome, happy cake for birthdays, the occasional wedding and just-for-nothing days. It simply doesn't let you down!

Makes one 12"x 9" (3.5 L) cake.

4 cups	(960 mL)	whole-wheat pastry flour
2 tsp	(10 mL)	baking powder
2 tsp	(10 mL)	baking soda
2 tsp	(10 mL)	cinnamon
¹/₂ tsp	(2 mL)	allspice
1 tsp	(5 mL)	sea salt
1 cup	(240 mL)	honey
¹/₂ cup	(135 mL)	oil (a generous half cup)
2 Tbsp	(30 mL)	vinegar
2 cups	(480 mL)	unsweetened applesauce
2 Tbsp	(30 mL)	warm water

Sift all the dry ingredients together into a large bowl.
In a separate bowl, mix the liquids well.
Stir the liquids and dry ingredients together.
Pour the mixture into an oiled and floured 12"x 9" (3.5 L) pan.
Bake at 350°F (180°C) for 25 minutes.

THE TOPPING:

1 cup	(240 mL)	chopped dates
		water
1¹/₂ cups	(360 mL)	unsweetened applesauce
2 Tbsp	(30 mL)	maple syrup
¹/₂ cup	(120 mL)	granola or chopped nuts

Simmer the dates for about 10 minutes with just enough water to make a
   thick paste.
Mix the applesauce and maple syrup into the date mixture and spread it on
   the baked and somewhat cooled cake.
Sprinkle granola or chopped nuts over the cake, and serve it with whipped
   cream.

Peanut Butter Parfait

Imagine getting all this protein in a dessert! One might even be tempted to skip the main course.

1 lb	**(454 g)**	**tofu, drained**
½ cup	**(120 mL)**	**fruit juice (orange or apple)**
2 Tbsp	**(30 mL)**	**vegetable oil**
¼ cup	**(60 mL)**	**honey**
¾ cup	**(180 mL)**	**peanut butter**
1 tsp	**(5 mL)**	**vanilla**
1 Tbsp	**(15 mL)**	**flour**
¼ cup	**(60 mL)**	**chopped almonds**

Process the tofu, fruit juice and vegetable oil in a blender until smooth and creamy.

Melt the honey and peanut butter in a saucepan over low heat.

Stir in the vanilla and flour, and cook until slightly thickened. Remove from heat and add the tofu mixture from the blender.

Stir in half of the chopped nuts.

Spoon the mixture into individual serving dishes and sprinkle with the remaining nuts.

Put the dishes into the freezer for a couple of hours, or until the parfait reaches ice cream consistency.

Sharada's Mom's Fresh Pear Cake

A nice moist cake with a delicate flavour.

2 cups	(480 mL)	**unbleached white flour**
1 tsp	(5 mL)	**baking soda**
1 tsp	(5 mL)	**baking powder**
½ tsp	(2 mL)	**Inka (or instant coffee,**
		or coffee substitute)
½ tsp	(2 mL)	**sea salt**
1 tsp	(5 mL)	**ginger** (optional)
		3 medium ripe pears,
		cored and cut into quite small
		pieces
¾ cup	(180 mL)	**butter**
½ cup	(120 mL)	**honey**
1 Tbsp	(15 mL)	**vinegar**
½ cup	(120 mL)	**hot water**

Sift the dry ingredients together.

Add the cut-up pears to the dry mixture, making sure each piece is coated with flour.

Cream the butter and honey in a separate bowl.

Add the vinegar and hot water. (If your butter and honey are hard, you can always add the hot water to them, and then mix well before adding the vinegar.)

Combine the liquid and dry ingredients rather carefully — don't over-mix!

Pour into a greased 8"x 8" (2 L) pan and bake at 350°F (180°C) for 45 minutes, or until an inserted toothpick comes out cleanly.

*P*ie Crust

The Food Processor Way

*I'm one of those people who could never make a decent pie crust. It always sounded so easy, but when I attempted it, I would end up patching bits of pastry together. Then a friend showed me how to make pastry in my food processor. It looked **too** easy — I was sure it wouldn't work.*

But lo and behold — it was perfect! I've made many pies since, and this method has never let me down.

Makes enough pastry for two 9 inch (23 cm) single crust pies.

In a food processor (grinding blade or pastry blade fitted,
   if yours has one), blend:

3 cups	(720 mL)	**whole-wheat pastry flour**
1 tsp	(5 mL)	**sea salt** (optional)
1 cup	(240 mL)	**butter** (cut into bits)

Once these are blended, and while the food processor is still running, pour
   in **10 Tbsp** (150 mL) **cold water**.

Turn the processor off as soon as the pastry is mixed. Over-mixing will
   make the pastry tough.

Turn the pastry out onto a floured board. Pastry should be **slightly** on the
   wet side. Flour your rolling pin, and roll out the dough. Then turn it
   over and repeat. Keep flouring the board and rolling pin and turning the
   dough until you have the right thickness.

Place the pastry in the pie plate and use it for your favourite pie recipe.

Use your leftover bits to make tarts or tiny pies
for your little ones,
your sweetie-pie
and you.

Pumpkin Pie

Don't wait until autumn to make this one.
Surprise your family and friends today!

Makes one 9" (23 cm) pie, or about 18 tarts.

1¹/₂ cups	(360 mL)	**cooked pumpkin purée**
1 cup	(240 mL)	**milk**
¹/₂ cup	(120 mL)	**honey**
¹/₂ tsp	(2 mL)	**cinnamon**
¹/₄ tsp	(1 mL)	**nutmeg**
¹/₄ tsp	(1 mL)	**ginger**
		a fat pinch of ground cloves
¹/₄ cup	(60 mL)	**unbleached white flour**
		one prepared 9" (23 cm) pie crust

Blend all of the ingredients thoroughly.

Pour the filling into a prepared pie shell or a graham wafer crust.

Bake at 350°F (180°C) for one hour or until the pie is just about set in the
middle. It will set completely as it cools.

For tarts, fill the tart shells three-quarters full and bake at 350°F (180°C) for
20 - 25 minutes.

You can also try steaming yellow squash until it's
almost mushy, and then follow the recipe from the top.
If you're one of those people who likes a wee drop, you might wish to
add 2 Tbsp (30 mL) dark rum and cut the milk by 2 Tbsp (30 mL).

Rajani's Graham Crust

This versatile pie-crust recipe works well with all sorts of fillings, and can even be eaten on its own as bars or cookies. Just remember that the correct baking time for cookies will depend on the size and thickness you form them in, so keep an eye on them as they cook.

Makes one 9 inch (23 cm) pie crust.

¹/₂ cup	(120 mL)	**butter**
1 Tbsp	(15 mL)	**honey**
1¹/₂ cups	(360 mL)	**graham wafer crumbs**
¹/₂ tsp	(2 mL)	**cinnamon**
¹/₄ tsp	(1 mL)	**nutmeg**
¹/₃ cup	(80 mL)	**small oat flakes**
¹/₃ cup	(80 mL)	**finely chopped walnuts**

Melt the butter and honey together.

Combine the dry ingredients in a mixing bowl.

Gradually stir in the butter/honey mixture. Keep stirring until all the dry ingredients are moistened.

Save ¹/₄ cup (60 mL) of the crumb mixture to use as topping.

Press the remaining crumbs into a greased, square baking dish, pie plate or springform pan.

A crumb crust does not need pre-baking if you are using a filling that needs to be baked. It **should** be chilled, however, to solidify the butter, or it will dissolve before your very eyes when you fill the pie-shell.

Pour your filling into the chilled crust and sprinkle the saved crumbs over the top. Bake as directed in the filling recipe.

For a pre-cooked filling, bake the crust at 350°F (180°C) for 10 minutes.

Oh, yes. One last reminder. Please don't confuse this *recipe with* Graham's Rajani Crust *— that* will appear in a future edition of this quite remarkable cookbook.

"HAVE NOTHING IN YOUR HOUSES THAT YOU DO NOT KNOW
TO BE USEFUL, OR BELIEVE TO BE BEAUTIFUL."
WILLIAM MORRIS (1834-1896)

Ginger's Mixed Grain and Seed Shortbread

Makes around 30 cookies.

1 cup	(240 mL)	**triticale flour**
1 cup	(240 mL)	**unbleached white flour**
³/₄ cup	(180 mL)	**ghee** (recipe page 79)
¹/₄ cup	(60 mL)	**safflower oil**
¹/₂ cup	(120 mL)	**sunflower seeds**
¹/₄ cup	(60 mL)	**sesame seeds**
¹/₄ cup	(60 mL)	**maple syrup**

Mix the two flours together.

Add the ghee and oil, and mix them into the flour until you have
 a fine texture.

Now add the seeds, and then the maple syrup to moisten.

You'll find the mixture is oily — don't worry. Roll spoonfuls of the
  mixture between your hands and flatten them into cookies.

Bake at 300°F (150°C) for about 20 minutes.

Any combination of flours may be used, as long as the ratio
remains two parts flour to one part ghee/oil.
You can use just oil, though it won't taste as rich. You can also experiment
with the sweeteners. We tried doubling the amount of maple syrup during one rash
kitchen experiment, but it's really not necessary; it just makes the cookies slightly
more addictive.

Sesame Sorbet

"A sorbet...made of sesame...?" I hear you say doubtfully.
No really, please try this one; I think you will be pleasantly surprised.

3 cups	(720 mL)	**sesame milk** (see recipe page 278)
5½ Tbsp	(82 mL)	**honey**
1 tsp	(5 mL)	**liquid lecithin**
1 tsp	(5 mL)	**vanilla flavouring**
¼ tsp	(1 mL)	**sea salt**
4 Tbsp	(60 mL)	**sunflower or safflower oil**
½ cup	(120 mL)	**chopped raisins**

Combine all the ingredients except the oil and raisins in a blender and
process until creamy.

Slowly trickle the oil into the mixture while continuing to blend.

Freeze the mixture in icecube trays or popsicle moulds.

Remove the trays from the freezer an hour or so before serving and blend
the mixture in a food processor or blender until quite smooth.

Now add the raisins and stir them into the sorbet.

Spoon into small bowls or glasses, and return to the freezer.

Serve topped with toasted slivered almonds, if you wish.

Ganges Spiceballs

From the banks of the mighty river to the stalls of our local Ganges village Saturday farmers' market, you won't find a more satisfying treat for your sweet tooth.

Makes 20-some spicy and delectable entertainments.

6 Tbsp	(90 mL)	**tahini**
10 Tbsp	(150 mL)	**finely chopped raisins**
1 Tbsp	(15 mL)	**cocoa or carob powder**
$^1/_2$ - 1 tsp	(2-5 mL)	**cardamom seed, ground very fine***
$^1/_2$ - 1 tsp	(2-5 mL)	**ground ginger***
$^1/_4$ tsp	(1 mL)	**ground cloves**
$^1/_2$ tsp	(2 mL)	**lemon juice**
1 Tbsp	(15 mL)	**honey**
		(solid works better than runny)
		fat pinch nutmeg
		thin pinch salt

Dig down to the bottom of your container of tahini to find the stiffest, least-oily part, and measure it out into a medium-size bowl.

Lightly pack the raisins when measuring them into the bowl.

Sprinkle the remaining ingredients over them.

Using a strong spoon, combine everything to form a stiff mixture, even throughout.

Taking small lumps, shape with your fingertips into 1" balls.

Chill them for an hour or so to help firm them up.

* Use more or less of the cardamom and ginger according to how spicy you are. And remember to measure FIRST, then grind the cardamom.

This recipe is very accepting of variations: substituting peanut butter for tahini is one obvious possibility, almond butter would be another. Or omit the carob and use 2 Tbsp ground filberts instead. Kids really like them with cinnamon instead of cardamom. You could roll the balls in grated coconut, toasted ground almonds or sesame seeds.... the possibilities are as broad as your waist will be if you let yourself get too carried away.

One useful comment, however: These spiceballs have sufficient flavour to make them a good vehicle for anything else less palatable that you (or your child) might want or need to eat — strong-tasting herbs or remedies, and so on.

Sweet Treats Pastry Shell

Makes one single 10" (25 cm) crust.

2 cups	(480 mL)	**unbleached white flour**
¼ tsp	(1 mL)	**sea salt**
1 Tbsp	(15 mL)	**sugar**
2 Tbsp	(30 mL)	**grated coconut** (optional)
½ cup	(120 mL)	**chilled butter**
1 tsp	(5 mL)	**vanilla**
⅓-½ cup	(80-120mL)	**water**

Sift the flour, salt and sugar together.
Stir in the coconut.
Cut the butter into the mixture with two knives or a pastry blender.
Add the vanilla and stir in enough water so the dough will form a ball.
Chill the dough for half an hour.
Roll out the dough and line a 10" (25 cm) pie plate.
Prick the bottom of the crust with a fork to prevent it from bubbling up
   while baking.
Bake at 450°F (235°C) for 8 - 10 minutes, or until lightly browned.

*This pastry recipe works nicely with the Pumpkin Pie recipe on
page 199. Or for something wild, fill it with a Sorbet.
Eat quickly!*

"A MAN CANNOT HAVE A PURE MIND, WHO REFUSES APPLE DUMPLINGS."
SAMUEL TAYLOR COLERIDGE (1772-1834)

Wacky Cake

Just about every Canadian knows this cake, which was often called Depression Cake in the old days. This is our version, revived for a new decade, or a new millenium. Perhaps we can look forward to it becoming just as well known. Elation Cake, do you think?

It's pretty straightforward, whatever you call it, so kids can make this recipe — and bachelors too (of either sex)!

Makes one 8"x 8" (2 L) cake.

1¹/₂ cups	(360 mL)	**whole-wheat pastry flour**
1 tsp	(5 mL)	**baking powder**
1 tsp	(5 mL)	**baking soda**
1 tsp	(5 mL)	**cinnamon**
¹/₂ tsp	(2 mL)	**salt**
¹/₄ cup	(60 mL)	**carob powder**
1 cup	(240 mL)	**raisins**
1 cup	(240 mL)	**warm water**
¹/₂ cup	(120 mL)	**honey**
5 Tbsp	(75 mL)	**oil**
1 Tbsp	(15 mL)	**vinegar**

Thoroughly mix the dry ingredients together in an 8"x 8" (2 L) ungreased pan.*

Mix the wet ingredients until the honey dissolves.

Just pour the liquid over the dry ingredients and mix it in well. (If you wish, you can make three mountains of the dry stuff with three holes in them — "volcanoes" — to receive the liquids.)

Bake yer cake! 350°F (180°C) would be a good sort of temperature, and 30 minutes should be about the right time. Serve it right in the pan.

There! That wasn't too hard now, was it?
And it's moist but not crumbly.

*If you decide you want to get it out of the pan, first you must grease and flour the pan, or line the bottom with waxed paper.

You can practice different spice combinations on this recipe, too.
It's a very forgiving cake.

"I DON'T EVEN KNOW WHAT STREET CANADA IS ON."
ALPHONSE CAPONE (1899-1947)

Cocaroba Everyday Cake

A reliable cake that's simple enough to make any day, and special enough for birthdays, tea-parties and other celebrations.

Makes one 8"x 8" (2 L) cake.

1½ cups	(360 mL)	**brown sugar** (or less, if you wish)
1¾ cups	(420 mL)	**whole-wheat pastry flour**
¾ cup	(180 mL)	**cocoa or carob powder**
		or a combination of both
2 tsp	(10 mL)	**baking soda**
1 tsp	(5 mL)	**baking powder**
½ tsp	(2 mL)	**sea salt**
1 cup	(240 mL)	**buttermilk or sour milk***
1 cup	(240 mL)	**prepared Inka**
		or other coffee substitute
½ cup	(120 mL)	**vegetable oil**
1 tsp	(5 ml)	**vanilla**

Sift together all the dry ingredients in a bowl.

Mix the liquid ingredients together and add them to the dries. Mix them
together just enough to thoroughly combine them, making a thin batter.

Oil and flour a cake pan (8"x 8", or equivalent), and pour in the batter.

Bake at 350°F (180°C) for 40 - 45 minutes, or until the sides of the cake
separate from the pan a little, and a toothpick inserted into the centre
comes out clean.

*If you have neither buttermilk nor sour milk available, you can add a
tablespoon (15 mL) of lemon juice or vinegar to milk to sour it.

Serve the cake as is (once it has cooled, of course),
or top it with any favourite icing — cream cheese, honey and
vanilla blended together is one popular choice.

"I CAME TO THE CONCLUSION MANY YEARS AGO THAT ALMOST ALL CRIME IS DUE TO THE
REPRESSED DESIRE FOR AESTHETIC EXPRESSION."
EVELYN WAUGH (1903-1966)

Sweet Sauces & Toppings

Maple Cashew Cream

1 cup (240 mL) **cashews**
1 cup (240 mL) **boiling water**
2 Tbsp (30 mL) **maple syrup**

Grind the cashews in a blender until fine.
Pour the boiling water CAREFULLY into the blender
 container and add the maple syrup.
Blend until smooth.
Cool, and serve over any dessert that welcomes whipping cream.

Makes enough cream to cover one pie... or forget the pie and just eat the topping.

"AN EXPERT IS A MAN WHO HAS MADE ALL THE MISTAKES WHICH CAN BE MADE
IN A VERY NARROW FIELD."
NIELS HENRIK DAVID BOHR
(1885-1962)

Sweet Peanut Sauce

One for peanut butter aficionados.

¼ cup	(60 mL)	**peanut butter**
2 Tbsp	(30 mL)	**honey**
¼ cup	(60 mL)	**water**
		fat pinch cinnamon

This is what you might call an easy recipe....
Gently heat all of the ingredients in a saucepan, stirring to a homogenous
state.

*Serve with pancakes or banana splits, or use as a dip
with apple and pear slices or celery sticks
for a snack.
You can also use it as a sandwich spread
once it has cooled and thickened.*

Bhavani's Yummy Cake Topping

2½ cups	(600 mL)	**coarsely chopped dates**
		3 - 4 bananas
		juice of one lemon
		pinch of nutmeg

In a saucepan, cover the dates with water and bring them to a boil.
Remove the pan from the heat and let it sit for 30 - 45 minutes.
Blend all the ingredients together in a blender or food processor.

*This makes enough topping for two large cakes
or maybe a filling **and** a topping — decadent!*

*Maybe with ice cream, or yoghurt, or fresh fruit, or granola, on toast.....
where do you draw the line?*

Blueberry Sauce

*A simple and delicious sauce that will happily crown ice cream, yoghurt,
porridge or pancakes.*

Makes 2 cups (480 mL).

2 cups (480 mL) **frozen blueberries**
2 Tbsp (30 mL) **honey**

Cook the blueberries until they are soft and mushy.
Add honey when the cooking is finished.
Don't add water — the sauce will get too runny.

The honey in this recipe allows the sauce to keep, if refrigerated, for
  at least a week.

A variety of other fruit sauces can be made in much the same way,
  using one or a combination of:

strawberries   raspberries
blackberries   blueberries
pineapple   peaches etc.
bananas (with other acid fruits)

When using fresh fruit, you may need to add just a little liquid, either
  water or fruit juice. Add only enough to make it possible to blend
  everything in an electric blender.
If you like a sweeter sauce than this, then add 1 Tbsp (15 mL) more
  melted honey or maple syrup per cup of fruit.
If the sauce is to go over porridge or pancakes, you may wish to re-
  heat it gently in a saucepan (stir!) before serving.

"I VALUE MY GARDEN MORE FOR BEING FULL OF BLACKBIRDS THAN OF CHERRIES,
AND VERY FRANKLY GIVE THEM FRUIT FOR THEIR SONGS."
JOSEPH ADDISON: *SPECTATOR*
(1672-1719)

Carob Sauce

An excellent topping for ice cream or banana splits.

Makes 2 ½ cups (600 mL).

¼ cup	(60 mL)	cashews
¼ cup	(60 mL)	chopped dates
2 cups	(480 mL)	water
½ cup	(120 mL)	carob powder
¼ cup	(60 mL)	unbleached white flour
1½ tsp	(7 mL)	Inka or instant coffee substitute
2 Tbsp	(30 mL)	honey
1 tsp	(5 mL)	vanilla

Purée together the cashews, dates and half of the water.
Combine the carob powder, flour and Inka in a saucepan.
Slowly stir in the remaining water to make a smooth paste.
Stir in the puréed mixture, honey and vanilla.
Cook gently over medium low heat, stirring constantly, until the sauce has
thickened.
Chill and serve.

*This also doubles as a "chocolate milk" base — use 1 tsp (5 mL) of sauce
in each glass of milk.*

"NOTHING IS MISERABLE UNLESS YOU THINK IT SO;
CONVERSELY, EVERY LOT IS HAPPY IF YOU ARE CONTENT WITH IT."
ANICIUS MANILUS SEVERINUS BOETHIUS
(480-525)

Hamsa Cream

Hamsa means "the swan" in Sanskrit. And Hamsa is also the breath of each living thing in the world, inhaling with the sound Ham and exhaling with Sa, a mantra we repeat day in, day out, the soundtrack of our lives.

This cream topping, though apparently somewhat mundane beside the illustrious meanings of its name, shares nevertheless some of the characteristics of the swan. Light, white, and floating over all that stands below, it is the perfect accompaniment to a fresh fruit salad, a pie or similar confection.

1 cup	(240 mL)	**whipping cream**
3 Tbsp	(45 mL)	**light cream**
¹/₂ tsp	(2 mL)	**vanilla**
¹/₂ tsp	(2 mL)	**ground ginger**

Chill the creams, the blender or beater and the bowl, and keep them as cool as possible while beating.

Beat the ingredients until they are thickened, but not fully stiff. Do not overbeat, or the mixture will become granular and start to turn to butter.

If you prefer a stiffer cream topping, you may omit the light cream.

Bread

There is something special about bread. Something magical, something that's warm and nostalgic, too. When you think of bread, you think "staff of life" — the universal food that has sustained our civilizations. To make bread is to be part of that age-old tradition. It also stirs memories from childhood and from holidays past; memories conjured by ghost-like wafts of that unforgettable smell of bread baking in the oven. Everyone swoons over that aroma. It's as if it triggers some primal response. Bread is so much associated with the home and with happy memories, that some realtors will arrange to have a few loaves baking in the oven when showing a house to prospective clients! If when making bread you are connected to the past, you are also joined to the future by creating the memories that will be your children's nostalgia.

Because it is such basic, essential activity, making bread is very grounding and supremely satisfying. Kneading, for example, can be thought of as a tiring chore to be finished as soon as possible, or it can be seen as a chance to put one's life energy into the bread. Feel yourself working with the ingredients and the life force of nature (seen most dramatically in the action of the yeast) in a miraculous process of turning wheat into delicious, life-sustaining bread. The repetitive action of kneading can be a form of meditation, as the mind focusses on each push and turn of the dough. Using a mundane activity in this way helps you to rise above the humdrum busy-ness and demands of life, and to see them in truer perspective. Regular practice of a basic, simple task like breadmaking, wood-cutting, or gardening, can have the same effect. While combining ingredients, and stirring and kneading the dough, you can add your love and energy to the bread. Therefore, make bread in a good state of mind. Focus your attention and energy on what you are doing, for your energy will flow into whatever you make. "What you are, you will eat," so to say. In so doing, what better or more loving gift could you make for your family, your friends, *and* yourself than freshly-baked bread?

GETTING STARTED

Don't be put off by the thought that making bread is just too time-consuming. The amount of time you spend actually making the bread *and* cleaning up is less than forty minutes for most recipes. The rest of the time the bread is working by itself.

UTENSILS

The things needed for easy breadmaking are a reliable oven (one that bakes evenly, without wide fluctuations in temperature), a large ceramic or metal mixing bowl, a non-metallic bowl in which to proof the yeast, a strong wooden spoon, a measuring cup and measuring spoons, and some loaf pans or a baking sheet. Optional tools include: a bread thermometer to test the temperature of the water when activating the yeast, a dough cutter, and a rubber spatula. In addition, you'll need a good surface for kneading the dough: a table or countertop low enough for you to be able to put your weight into the kneading.

YEAST

PURCHASE AND STORAGE

Yeast can be bought fresh, in cakes (mixed with starch), or dried. Yeast is a living organism, a fungus that, when dried, is in a state of suspended animation. The little yeasties come to life and multiply rapidly when given warm water and some form of sugar, on which to feed and grow. It is this population explosion that gives bread its rise.

We use "active dry yeast" in all our recipes. It is easy to use and it's readily available. It can be bought in individual, one-tablespoon packets, or in bulk at most healthfood stores. Buying in bulk is generally cheaper, and you won't have any foil pouches that cannot be recycled. Even though it has been dried, yeast has a limited shelf-life unless it has been frozen. It's a good idea to find a reliable source of "fresh" dried yeast. Yeast can be kept in the freezer in an airtight container, especially if you buy in bulk or if you don't make bread often.

PROOFING

Regardless of how fresh you think the yeast is, it's a good idea to "proof" it, rather than assume that it is going to work. All of our recipes include this step, though some people prefer to mix the yeast directly with the flour. If you do this, use slightly warmer water than is normally called for, because the bulk of the flour and other ingredients will cool it somewhat.

To proof yeast, dissolve it in a non-metallic cupful (yeast can react with metal) of warm, but not hot, water. 105°F (40°C) is optimum. Test the temperature on your wrist or use a thermometer. With experience, you'll come to know what the right

temperature feels like. The yeast will dissolve almost instantly. Now add the amount of sugar indicated by the recipe, and allow the yeast to stand for 10 minutes or so. Cover it with a tea towel to keep it warm and cosy. The yeast will expand and bubble up as though it would like to take over your kitchen. Do not fear. Our research shows that it would take at least 47 cups of yeast, 50 cups of sugar, and 300 gallons of water to seriously threaten an average-sized kitchen. If the yeast doesn't bubble and foam up, start again with fresh yeast, making sure the water is neither too warm nor too cold.

SALT

If you're wanting to cut down on the amount of salt in your diet, it is possible to make bread without it. There is an advantage to using salt, however, apart from the flavour. It controls the rise of the dough, slowing it down so that the flavour is more developed.

SUGAR

Some kind of sweetening is necessary as food for the yeast. Almost any type of sugar can be used: refined white sugar, brown sugar, honey, molasses, maple syrup, etc. White sugar is often used (just about the *only* time it is used) because it dissolves quickly in the warm water, it is easily measured (compared to sticky honey), and such a small amount makes no difference to the taste. Also, as far as we know, yeast is still unconcerned about getting hardening of the arteries, cancer, or even sugar blues, so it doesn't seem to care *what* it gets fed. There is one other option for those who don't wish to use sugar of any kind: dissolve the yeast, then add one or two tablespoons of whole-wheat flour to the water. The yeast will feed on the starches and sugars in the wheat. Be prepared to wait a while for the yeast to bubble up, however.

Used as a sweetener, honey has the advantage of helping to preserve the freshness of the loaf. However, we find that homemade bread rarely sits still long enough to get stale.

LIQUIDS

Breads made with water have a coarser, chewier texture than breads containing milk. One is not better than the other, just different. A classic French loaf, for example, is made with just flour, water, yeast and salt.

If you are boiling potatoes, save the excess water. Or, if you have leftover cooked potatoes, blend them with enough water to make a thin liquid, and use this in place of plain water in the recipe. The starch in the potato will provide food for the yeast.

FLOURS

GLUTEN

It's important to be aware of the gluten content in the flours you want to use. Gluten is a tough, sticky mixture of plant proteins that gives dough its stretchiness, allowing it to rise.

Wheat flour has the highest gluten content. Though white flour will rise faster and higher than whole-wheat flour, it's not because it has more gluten, but because it has had the bran and the germ removed, thus making it less dense (and less nutritious). If you can, buy "bread flour." It is made from hard wheat, which is the highest in gluten.

All-purpose flour comes from a softer wheat, and is not as satisfactory for bread.

Whole-wheat flour, unlike white flour is made from the entire kernel: the germ, the bran and the endosperm. The germ is the innermost part, the part that contains the essential oils and many of the other nutrients in the wheat. The bran is the outer "skin" of the kernel after the husk, or chaff, has been removed. The endosperm forms the bulk of the kernel. White flour has had the bran and the germ removed. "Enriched" white flour has had some, but by no means all, of the nutrients added back that were taken out during the milling process. Without the bran, much of the fibre content (important to good digestion and assimilation of foods) is lost.

Pastry flour, though a fine choice for quickbreads, has very little gluten and will not make a good loaf of bread.

Triticale is a hybrid grain, a cross between wheat and rye. As such, it has more gluten than rye but less than wheat.

Rye flour is dense and heavy. Breads made with rye usually require more kneading and a longer rising time.

All other flours (buckwheat, rice, barley, oat, soy flour etc.) have insignificant amounts of gluten, so they cannot be used in large amounts, unless you want bricks rather than bread.

PURCHASING AND STORAGE

All flour should be kept airtight in a cool, dry place. However, white flour, its germ removed in processing, contains none of the essential oils that can go rancid and spoil; therefore, it will keep for months.

Whole-wheat flour should be used within a few weeks of purchase unless it is kept in the refrigerator. There is little sense in buying in bulk to save money if that means you end up eating rancid wheat. It tends to taste bitter and it may be harmful to health. If you do refrigerate your flour, make sure it stays dry and allow it to return to room temperature before breadmaking starts. Otherwise, it will lower the temperature of the dough and may inhibit the action of the yeast.

If you have a home flour mill, you are guaranteed the freshest wheat. You can then buy wheat berries (the whole, unmilled wheat kernel) which will keep indefinitely because the germ has not been exposed to air and light.

Wheat germ should definitely be stored in the refrigerator. It goes rancid so fast that often the process has already begun by the time it reaches the store shelf. Try to find a reliable source for it fresh. Ask your healthfood store owner when the next shipment is expected. Rancid wheat germ has a decidely bitter taste that does nothing to improve a loaf of bread, a muffin, or a fruit smoothie.

DOUGH ENHANCERS

Commercial bakeries use dough enhancers to make a lighter, fluffier loaf. The main active ingredient of the enhancer is ascorbic acid. You can add your own dough enhancer by using 1 tablespoon (15 mL) of lemon juice per 2½ cups (600 mL) of flour. Denser loaves usually have more flavour, though, so you may trade flavour for texture.

That wraps up all you will be needing for ingredients, so let's begin.

METHODS

THE SPONGE METHOD

For most of our recipes we use the sponge method, which adds to both the flavour and good texture of breads. It involves another rising stage for the dough. After the yeast has been proofed, an amount of

flour is added, usually not exceeding the total amount of liquid, to make a thick batter, or "sponge". If there is more than one type of flour in the recipe, always use the one with the highest gluten content to make the sponge (see "Flours").

Beat the dough with a wooden spoon for about 300 strokes (it doesn't take as long as you think). The idea here is to develop the gluten so essential to a good rise. If you get tired while beating, take a rest; the dough won't mind. The effort you put in at this stage will pay off later. As you beat it, the dough will begin to get sticky and form strands, as if it would turn into spun fibre if you could beat it long enough.

Now cover the dough with a tea towel and let it rise in a warm, draft-free place. When the dough has doubled in size it will look like a puffy sponge. Stir the sponge down, add the remaining ingredients, and proceed with kneading and rising, as in the standard method. A suggestion here — secure the tea towel tightly across the bowl with clothes pegs, thus ensuring the sticky sponge and towel never meet.

THE STANDARD METHOD

After the yeast has been proofed, the liquids are added to all of the flour(s) and dry ingredients to form a stiff dough. The dough is kneaded for 10 - 20 minutes on a lightly floured surface. It's important not to skimp on the kneading because this develops the gluten too. Breads made with heavier, less glutenous flours need more kneading.

RISING

After kneading, place the dough back in the mixing bowl (no need to wash or oil the bowl), cover it with a tea towel or lid, and allow it to rise in a warm place until doubled in size. It is then "punched down," which means pushing one's fist into the centre of the dough perhaps a dozen times, to release the air trapped inside. Now it can be divided and shaped into loaves. The loaves are then left to rise again, this time in loaf tins or on a baking sheet, though this rise will not take as long as the first one. Your loaves should be at least one inch above the top of the loaf pans before they are baked. The standard method has the advantage of being quicker than the sponge method, if you just can't wait!

LONG RISE

Breads that are allowed to rise more slowly develop a fuller, heartier flavour and a harder crust than quickly-risen breads; they will stay fresh longer, too. The results are well worth the extra time it takes. You can use either the sponge or the standard method. For long rise, follow these suggestions:

Cut the amount of yeast by one third. Keep the temperature of the loaf at 65° - 70°F (18°- 21°C). Allow for three risings — two before shaping the dough into loaves and one after. The first rise may take 2 - 3 hours, especially if using the standard method. The second rise should take $1^{1}/_{2}$ - 2 hours, and the third one about 30 - 60 minutes. Total rising time will be about 4 - 6 hours. Add at least 40 minutes for baking, depending on the bread.

If you use the long rise method, cover the bowl in which the dough is rising with plastic or a lid (rather than a tea towel) to keep the dough from drying out and becoming crusty before baking. Use a large enough bowl to allow for expansion. Oiling the top of the dough will keep it from drying, but it will make for a softer crust when baked.

A FINAL NOTE ABOUT RISING

There is no exact time when the bread has risen enough, but over-risen loaves will have big air holes in the middle of the loaf when baked, and under-risen loaves will not be as high as they might be. Never let the dough rise to much more than double its original size during any rising. After the dough has been shaped before the final rise, gently press the top with your finger. The dough will spring back quite fast. Test the dough again when you suspect it has risen enough. This time the dough should spring back much more slowly.

KNEADING

You can hardly knead bread too much, unless you are following a no-knead recipe, of course! Kneading develops the gluten that is so important to a good rise, so don't skimp on this part.

To knead bread, place the dough on a floured board. You may wish to flour your hands as well. Using the heels of the palms of both hands, push down and away from you, thereby flattening and stretching the dough. Now fold the dough in half, turn it on the board one quarter turn, and repeat the downward/forward push. You'll need to add flour occasionally to the board, and possibly to your hands too.

One of the most common mistakes in breadmaking is adding too much flour, thus producing a loaf that is not as moist as it should be. Try to use just enough flour to keep the dough from sticking. An alternative is to oil the board, rather than flour it. While this helps ensure a moist loaf, bear in mind that oil tends to soften the crust.

Depending on the dough, keep kneading for at least ten minutes (preferably longer) until it is smooth and elastic; that is, until it firmly resists the force of your push and springs back after you release the pressure. Experience teaches when the dough feels right. However, there is a simple test you can try. Take a small handful of dough in your hands and slowly stretch it out thinly. Dough that has been kneaded sufficiently will not tear easily when stretched. It will be smooth and very elastic. For a two-loaf recipe, this will take from 10 to 20 minutes.

SHAPING

Divide the dough with a sharp knife, according to the recipe. Take a piece and roll it out with a rolling pin — not thinly, but at least two passes in opposite directions. This also squeezes out excess air. Now take opposing sides of the circle and bring  them to the centre. Take one of the other sides and roll it up, like in the illustration. Pinch the edges together, or, if the loaf is too big for your loaf pan, tuck the edges under the loaf.

Remember though, to thoroughly oil or grease your pans (unless you use non-stick types), and this includes the top edges. Nothing is more frustrating than struggling to release your beautiful loaf from its container once it has stuck.

Or you can take the dough and simply roll the cut edge under, pinch it shut and place it on an oiled baking sheet, (sprinkled with cornmeal if you like).

BAKING

Need we say how important it is to preheat your oven? Otherwise, especially with electric ovens, the intense heat generated by the top element as it brings the oven up to temperature, will kill the yeast prematurely, overcook the top crust, and undercook the middle.

CRUSTY LOAVES

Putting a pan of water on the bottom rack of your oven, and brushing the top crust with water two or three times during baking, will yield a lovely hard crust. Milk and oil both have a softening effect, so the hardest crusts (on long French loaves, for example) are achieved on loaves made without these ingredients.

IS IT DONE YET?

Just because the bread has been in the oven for the given length of time, doesn't necessarily mean that it's done. Your oven could be slow (cool) or fast (hot). Take the bread out of the oven and remove it from the loaf pan. It should come out quite easily if the pan was oiled. The sides should be firm and dry, and the crust should be golden brown. Pick up the loaf and give it a firm slap on the bottom. It should sound resoundingly hollow. If all these tests are passed, the bread should be ready. If you are using glass pans, your loaves will probably cook somewhat faster than in metal pans.

Take the bread out of the pans and place them on a rack to cool. If they are left in the pans or flat on the counter, the moisture in the loaf will create condensation and might make the bottom of your loaf soft and soggy.

For the sake of your whole family's digestion (this means you too, dear bread-maker) please allow your bread to cool before cutting it for the first reverent slice. Otherwise, you will gulp it down, appreciatively no doubt but far too hot, and will feel it turn back into big doughy cannonballs in your dismayed digestion. Be patient.... just a little while..... it's going to taste great....

219

Multigrain Bread

Makes 4 big loaves.

6 cups	(1.4 L)	**warm water**
2 Tbsp	(30 mL)	**yeast**
2 Tbsp	(30 mL)	**sugar**
9½ cups	(2.3 L)	**whole-wheat flour**
½ cup	(120 mL)	**oil**
½ cup	(120 mL)	**buckwheat flour**
2 cups	(480 mL)	**barley flour**
2 cups	(480 mL)	**rye flour**
2 Tbsp	(30 mL)	**sea salt**
1 cup	(240 mL)	**rolled oat flakes**
1 cup	(240 mL)	**sunflower seeds**
1 cup	(240 mL)	**flax seeds**
1 cup	(240 mL)	**sesame seeds**
		additional whole-wheat flour as necessary

In your largest bowl, dissolve the yeast in warm water, then add the sugar, and let stand for 10 minutes until the yeast bubbles up.

Add 6 cups (1.4 L) of the whole-wheat flour to the liquid. Beat quickly and strongly, until the mixture forms "threads" (like spun fibres). This will take about 300 strokes — but it's not as long a job as you might think.

Let this sponge rise for at least 1 hour, then add the oil and beat it in.

Mix the salt with the remaining flours, oat flakes and seeds, then work them into the sponge thoroughly.

Knead for at least 10 minutes, working in up to 1½ cups (360 mL) of additional whole-wheat flour as you go. Try not to add more than this. Instead, if the dough is still wet and sticky, oil your hands and the kneading board and keep at it.

When the dough is smooth and elastic, place it back in the bowl, cover it with a tea towel and let it rise in a warm place until doubled in bulk (about 1 hour). In the meantime, go read a book, weed the garden, or pet the dog.

Punch down the dough and divide it into 4 pieces. Shape each piece into a loaf, place in well-greased, regular loaf pans and let rise again until the dough is an inch or more above the top of the pans. Go finish the last chapter of that Agatha Christie novel.

Bake the loaves at 350°F (180°C) for 35 - 40 minutes.

Vegetable Bread

(Sponge Method)

Makes 4 big loaves.

1 cup	(240 mL)	**chopped fresh parsley**
	1	**medium carrot**
	2	**medium celery sticks**
	1	**medium leek**
	1	**medium potato**
3 cups	(720 mL)	**water**
4 cups	(960 mL)	**milk**
2 Tbsp	(30 mL)	**yeast**
½ cup	(120 mL)	**oil**
½ cup	(120 mL)	**honey**
4 cups	(960 mL)	**unbleached white flour**
14 - 16 cups	(3.3-3.8 L)	**whole-wheat flour**

Purée the first five ingredients plus 1 cup (240 mL) of the water in your food processor or blender.

Mix the milk, remaining water, yeast, oil, honey and 6 cups (1.4 L) flour together in a very large bowl. Beat until the gluten develops — this means the batter will have "strands" (see page 216). Let sit covered, in a nice warm place for an hour.

Now add the vegetable purée and stir in as much of the remaining flour as you can, until you have to knead by hand (see page 217).

Knead for at least 10 minutes (why not knead to music?) adding additional flour to keep the dough pliable but not stiff.

Transfer to a large slightly oiled bowl and let rise 2 hours, and then punch down and work the air out of the dough.

Cut into four portions and shape into loaves.

Let rise a second time, for about 1 hour.

Bake at 350°F (180°C) for 35 minutes.

"EAT SLOWLY; ONLY MEN IN RAGS
AND GLUTTONS OLD IN SIN
MISTAKE THEMSELVES FOR CARPET BAGS
AND TUMBLE VICTUALS IN."
SIR WALTER RALEIGH (1552-1618)

Cheese Bread

An easy, cheesy, rich (and squeezy!) fine-textured bread.

Makes 2 loaves.

1 Tbsp	(15 mL)	yeast
¼ cup	(60 mL)	warm water
1 Tbsp	(15 mL)	melted honey
1 cup	(240 mL)	milk
1 Tbsp	(15 mL)	oil
2 tsp	(10 mL)	salt
1 cup	(240 mL)	toasted wheat germ
4½ cups	(1.1 L)	whole-wheat flour
½ cup	(120 mL)	poppy seeds
2 cups	(480 mL)	grated cheese*
1 cup	(240 mL)	warm water
1 Tbsp	(15 mL)	milk
¼ cup	(60 mL)	finely chopped walnuts

Dissolve the yeast in ¼ cup (60 mL) warm water, then stir in the melted
   honey and let the yeast sit for about 10 minutes, until it foams up.
In a large bowl mix the milk, oil, salt and wheat germ.
Add the yeast mixture and 1 cup (240 mL) of the flour. Beat until the gluten
   develops.
Stir in the cheese, ¼ cup (60 mL) of the poppy seeds and 1 cup (240 mL)
   warm water, then blend thoroughly.
Keep adding flour until the dough is fairly stiff, but not dry.
Knead on an oiled surface until the dough is smooth and elastic, about 15
   minutes.
Let rise in a covered bowl until doubled in size, about 1 hour.
Punch it down and shape into 2 loaves.
Place the dough in oiled loaf tins, cover, and let rise to about 1 inch or so
   above the top of the tins, about 30 minutes in a nice, warm place.
Brush the top with milk and sprinkle remaining poppy seeds and walnuts
   on top.
Bake at 400°F (205°C) for 25 to 30 minutes.
Remove from the tins immediately and let the loaves cool on racks.

   * *When using a mild cheese such as farmers, increase the amount to 2½
   cups (600 mL). When using a strong cheese such as blue, reduce the
   amount to about 1 cup (240 mL).*

Rye Bread

A simple, tasty, sandwich rye loaf. When making a toasted rye sandwich, slice the bread thinly so that the toasting fully enhances the rye flavour.

Makes two good-sized loaves.

3 cups	(720 mL)	**warm water or warm potato water**
1 Tbsp	(15 mL)	**active dry yeast**
1 Tbsp	(15 mL)	**sugar or honey**
1 Tbsp	(15 mL)	**Inka (or other coffee substitute)**
¼ cup	(60 mL)	**molasses**
4 cups	(960 mL)	**whole-wheat flour**
3½ cups	(840 mL)	**rye flour**
1 Tbsp	(15 mL)	**salt**

Optional:

		grated rind from one orange
1 Tbsp	(15 mL)	**fennel seeds** OR
		1 Tbsp (15 mL) caraway seeds

Dissolve the yeast and sugar in the warm water and allow it to stand for 10 minutes or so until the yeast foams up.

Add the Inka, molasses and the 3 cups (720 mL) of wheat flour.

Make a "sponge" by beating this mixture at least 300 strokes, until the gluten forms in strands.

Allow the sponge to stand in a warm, draught-free place for one hour or more. The sponge needs to double in size.

In another bowl, combine the rye flour with the salt and any optional ingredients you want.

Stir down the sponge and add the rye flour mixture.

Knead this dough for 10 - 20 minutes, adding as little additional whole-wheat flour as possible to keep it from sticking to the kneading surface. The dough should become smooth and elastic.

Divide the dough into two pieces and form them into oblong loaves.

Place on a greased baking sheet, cover with a tea towel and allow to rise in a warm place for an hour or so. The loaves should double in size.

Bake at 350°F (180°C) for 35 - 40 minutes.

*With fennel or caraway seeds added, this bread makes
a fine 'wry' comment of its own!*

"WITHOUT BREAD, EVEN A PALACE IS SAD, BUT WITH IT, A PINE TREE IS PARADISE."
SLAVIC PROVERB

Rye Sourdough Starter

Making a starter for a rye sourdough recipe is quite straightforward:

Use a non-metallic container because sourdough is acidic and will corrode metals, doing nothing to improve the flavour.

Stir one cup of rye flour into one cup of warm water (105°F, 40°C). Or, instead of water, use whey, buttermilk or sour milk.

Leave it loosely covered for a few days to a week in a draught-free place that ensures a snug room temperature: 70°-80°F (21°-27°C). Stir it well each day. You will see it become bubbly and fermented.

The smell of the starter should be sour but not acrid — a fresh and pleasant note that may have a hint of sharpness to it. If it smells **strongly** of vinegar, it has probably been too warm, or has sat for too long, and you need to start again.

Some people recommend adding a few drops of milk and a tiny pinch of yeast to the water when the starter is first mixed. Rye flour has such a great talent for fermentation that it usually has no problem getting started without help, since yeast spores float by the billion on every breath of wind. If you do have difficulty though, in getting a starter to bubble up and smell the way you would like it to, then perhaps these two small additions will just make all the difference to your endeavours.

Once the starter is bubbly and smells right, it is ready to be fed for making bread, or may be refrigerated for later use. Store sourdough starter loosely covered when it is active (i.e. at room temperature), so that carbon dioxide does not build up and crack the container. While refrigerated, the starter is still alive though dormant, and only a few bubbles of gas are formed, so it can be covered more tightly.

Sometimes some blackness appears in the liquid, but this is no cause for alarm, just a sign of oxidation, similar to a cut potato turning black; stir the starter thoroughly before using it.

Starter may be kept unused in the refrigerator for a surprisingly long time, though it is best if you make bread with it every week or ten days. You may store it almost indefinitely, by remembering to feed it two tablespoons (30 mL) of flour and two tablespoons (15 mL) warm water each week, then let it bubble up. Keep it always the consistency of pancake batter.

If at any time you are uncertain whether your starter is still healthy and thriving, just feed it a couple of tablespoons of flour, leave it in a warm place for a few hours, and see whether it bubbles up once again.

Whole-wheat Sourdough Starter

Amazingly hardy little things, yeast! All of the above applies equally to the preparation of a whole-wheat sourdough starter, with the following differences:

Scald your non-metallic container briefly before starting.

Whole-wheat flour requires yeast to be added to make a starter, so use 1 packet of active dried yeast (about 2 tsp, 10 mL) dissolved in 2 cups (480 mL) of warm water (about 110°F, 43°C), then beat in 2 cups (480 mL) of whole-wheat flour, or faster-acting whole-wheat pastry flour.

Store the starter at room temperature and stir it daily. The starter will be ready to use after several days, when it is bubbly and has reached a degree of sourness that smells right to you. If the smell is pleasing, then it will taste right in bread. The longer it ferments, the stronger it will taste.

Salt Spring Whole-Wheat Sourdough

A century ago, they flooded through here on their way to the goldfields. In the seasons that followed, many of them passed by once again, sometimes dampened in their fervour, or just with a changed notion of where the gold might really be found. Some among them stayed here, to find a life and a future surrounded by these fields, these forests and mountains. Some finally found their gold, in the drying stooks of wheat, the sun setting behind Mount Maxwell, and the light in their children's eyes. This recipe comes full circle, uniting the prospectors who first baked sourdough around their campfires, with a new generation of Salt Spring islanders, prospecting for a brighter gold in these times.

The recipe makes 2 loaves.

1 cup	(240 mL)	**whole-wheat sourdough starter** (see page 224)
2 cups	(480 mL)	**warm water** (105°F, 40°C)
3 Tbsp	(45 mL)	**honey**
2 tsp	(10 mL)	**sea salt**
scant ½ cup	(105 mL)	**oil**
6 cups	(1.4 L)	**whole-wheat flour**

Feed your starter the night before, and let it get bubbly, active and all ready to jump into bread.

Warm your bread bowl (ceramic, earthenware, even plastic, but not metal), and beat together all the ingredients above, save the flour.

Now add the flour, and mix well, kneading lightly to make a smooth elastic dough. Try to avoid adding more flour, unless the dough is too sticky.

Cover the bowl with a tea-towel and set it somewhere warm, not hot, to double in size. This may take 3 or 4 hours, maybe even longer, depending on how energetic your sourdough is feeling, and the ambient temperature.

Give the dough a punch, then knead it for twenty or thirty strokes. Cut it into two pieces.

Shape the dough into 2 loaves by flattening each piece, then rolling it up and pinching the seams together. Place each, seam side down, into an oiled loaf pan.

Let rise until doubled once again, 1 or 2 hours, then bake at 350°F (180°C) for 30 to 40 minutes.

Turn your loaves out onto a rack to cool.

The amount of honey and salt in this recipe may be adjusted according to how sour your starter is.

eatrix's No-Knead Sourdough Rye

For those among you who love a loaf that really has texture, crust, flavour, depth. Slice this one not too thickly with a sharp knife, and chew it slowly. Grown-up bread.
Makes 3 or 4 loaves.

1 cup	(240 mL)	**rye sourstarter** (instructions on page 224)
1 cup	(240 mL)	**water**
1 cup	(240 mL)	**rye flour**

In a large non-metallic bowl, stir together these ingredients to make a smooth batter (a 'sponge'). Cover with a cloth, and leave overnight in a warm, draught-free place. Some suggestions for a suitable spot would include: in an oven with just the light on; on a shelf near the woodstove; near the pilot-light on a gas stove. Only a little supplemental heat is needed to keep the temperature close to its ideal level of 85° - 95°F (29°- 35°C).

Next morning, add **1 cup** (240 mL) **water** and **1 cup** (240 mL) **rye flour**, then beat smooth.

The sourdough will change in consistency as it ferments, becoming sometimes more, sometimes less dense. The aim is to keep it similar to thick pea soup in consistency, while building up the volume of mixture. Sometimes you will need to add only a half cup of water and more flour; at other times, the mixture will seem thick and will need more water and less flour — it's a question of judgement that you will soon gain. Allow the sourdough 8 - 12 hours between "feeds" to become bubbly once again.

During the approximately 3 days after starting the "sponge", add a total of, say, **4 cups** (960 mL) **of rye flour** and **3½ - 4 cups** (840-960 mL) **water**, maintaining the thick-soupy consistency that sourdough likes best for its development.

At the end of this stage, remove 1 cup (240 mL) to keep refrigerated as starter for future baking sessions.

On the morning of baking day, add **4 cups** (960 mL) **rye flour** and **3 cups** (720 mL) **warm water,** then beat smooth and leave for an hour or two. Now add all the following ingredients:

4 cups	(960 mL)	**bran or bran flour**
1 cup	(240 mL)	**7-grain cereal, soaked in a little boiling water**
1 cup	(240 mL)	**oatmeal**
1 cup	(240 mL)	**wheatgerm**
2 cups	(480 mL)	**whole-wheat flour**
1½ cups	(360 mL)	**sunflower seeds**
1 cup	(240 mL)	**flax seeds**
1 Tbsp	(15 mL)	**crushed caraway seeds**
1 tsp	(5 mL)	**crushed coriander seeds**
2 tsp	(10 mL)	**sea salt**
½ tsp	(2 mL)	**cardamom seeds** (optional)

Stir your mixture to combine it all. It will be like very thick porridge once you have done so. The consistency (and the total quantity of mixture) will be affected by how much cooked cereal has been added, and by the proportions of water and dry ingredients used. If you find it too solid to be stirred, you may add a very little warm water. If you find it too soft and liquid, then add more flour, aiming to end up with a mixture that will just fall heavily from the stirring spoon, breaking as it falls.

Oil your loaf pans thoroughly, or grease them with a little butter, and scatter some oat flakes over the bottoms and sides of the pans before placing the dough in them. Fill each pan about two-thirds to three-quarters full, then sprinkle oat flakes over the top. Let the loaves rise for about 45 minutes.

Finally, baking time is here! Bake the loaves at 450°F (235°C) for 20 minutes with a shallow pan of water in the bottom of the oven.

Remove the pan of water and reduce the heat to 350°F (180°C) for a further 90 minutes. When you reduce the heat, spray the crust of the loaves with a plant-mister, and also spray around the inside of the oven; repeat this every half hour. The crust should be somewhat dark and firm when done. When taking the bread out of the oven, spray the crust immediately, then leave the loaves to cool thoroughly before cutting your first slice.

These loaves improve greatly by being given a day or two to sit before being consumed, if you are able to restrain yourself.

A final note: variations on the added grains and flours are acceptable, as long as one remembers to limit the quantity to less than the total volume of the "sponge."

inder's Sourdough Muffins

Makes 20 or so chewy little numbers.

2 Tbsp	(30 mL)	**dry yeast**
2 cups	(480 mL)	**warm water**
1 Tbsp	(15 mL)	**sugar or melted honey**
¼ cup	(60 mL)	**oil**
4 tsp	(20 mL)	**salt**
½ cup	(120 mL)	**powdered milk** (optional)
5½ cups	(1.3 L)	**whole-wheat pastry flour and/or unbleached white flour**
1 cup	(240 mL)	**whole-wheat sourdough starter** (see page 224) **cornmeal, for coating**

Dissolve the yeast in the warm water, then add the sugar or honey. No need to wait, this time.

Add the oil, salt, powdered milk and 3 cups (720 mL) of the flour.

Beat the mixture vigorously for 300 strokes to develop the gluten.

Gently add the sourdough starter and blend it in thoroughly.

Add the rest of the flour, stirring to form a stiff dough. Knead the dough for at least 10 minutes.

Now roll it out to ¼" (6 mm) thickness on a floured surface, and cut it into large circles (3" or 75 mm wide).

Sprinkle cornmeal on a cookie-sheet, and leave the circles of dough on it to rise for about an hour.

Heat a cast-iron frying-pan over a high flame, or set your electric frying-pan to 375°F (190°C).

Lower the heat to medium if using an iron pan, then lift the circles onto the ungreased surface with a flat spatula.

Cook for about 5 minutes each side, until nicely browned.

Let them cool a little before eating, otherwise the insides will be rather doughy.

Bagels

These bagels are the result of a challenge issued by one of our members:
"Make me a bagel as good as Sophie's bagels, but without the eggs."
We did.

Makes one dozen wonderful bagels.

2 Tbsp	(30 mL)	**active dry yeast**
4¹/₂ cups	(1.1 L)	**unbleached flour**
1¹/₂ cups	(360 mL)	**lukewarm water**
3 Tbsp	(45 mL)	**honey**
2 tsp	(10 mL)	**salt**

Combine the yeast and 2¹/₂ cups (600 mL) of the flour in a large bowl.
Dissolve the honey in water and add to the yeast mixture.
Beat until the gluten forms.
Add the salt and enough of the remaining flour to make a moderately stiff
dough.
Turn out onto a floured surface and knead till smooth and elastic to the
touch (about 12 - 15 minutes).
Cover with a tea towel and let rest in a warm place for 15 minutes.
Cut into 12 equal portions. Shape each portion into
a ball, punch a hole in the centre with a
floured finger. Use a finger of the other
hand to poke through from the
opposite side and circle fingers around
each other, gently pulling the bagel as
you turn it, until the opening is
approximately 1¹/₂" in diameter.

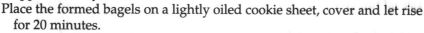

Place the formed bagels on a lightly oiled cookie sheet, cover and let rise
for 20 minutes.
In a large pot, heat 1 gallon (4 L) of water to which 1 Tbsp (15 mL) honey
and 1 Tbsp (15 mL) salt have been added. The water should be hot but
not boiling — water that is too hot will kill the action of the yeast.
Drop the bagels into the hot water a few at a time. Don't crowd them as
they will increase in size as they cook. Cook for a total of 7 minutes,
turning them over halfway through.
Drain them and place on a lightly oiled baking sheet.
Bake at 375°F (190°C) for 25 - 30 minutes.

"The optimist sees the bagel, the pessimist sees the hole."
Anon.

Yewello Ambasha (Ethiopian spiced bread)

This bread is so unique, so delicious, and so beautiful that it's worth the extra effort to make it. Try it plain, with butter, or with cream cheese. The very piquant Berber Sauce is great not only on this bread, but on almost any bread or cracker. Or use it to make an African or Indian curried dish.

First prepare spiced ghee (niter kibbeh) as follows:

½ cup	(120 mL)	**ghee** (see page 79)
1 tsp	(5 mL)	**cinnamon**
2 tsp	(10 mL)	**minced root ginger**
¼ tsp	1 mL)	**nutmeg**
2 Tbsp	(30 mL)	**cumin**
1 tsp	(5 mL)	**ground fenugreek**
1 tsp	(5 mL)	**ground cardamom**
1 tsp	(5 mL)	**black pepper**

Gently simmer all the ingredients for 20 minutes in a heavy saucepan or skillet, then strain the liquid through a sieve lined with something like a thin linen tea towel. Set aside.

Now prepare the dough:

3 Tbsp	(45 mL)	**active dry yeast**
4 cups	(960 mL)	**warm water**
3 Tbsp	(45 mL)	**sugar**
½ cup	(120 mL)	**niter kibbeh**
2 Tbsp	(30 mL)	**ground coriander**
1 Tbsp	(15 mL)	**ground cumin**
1 tsp	(5 mL)	**ground fenugreek**
1 tsp	(5 mL)	**ground cardamom**
1 tsp	(5 mL)	**black pepper**
1 Tbsp	(15 mL)	**sea salt**
8 cups	(1.9 L)	**whole-wheat flour**
3 Tbsp	(45 mL)	**Berber Sauce** (page 144)

In a large bowl, dissolve the yeast in warm water, then add the sugar and let stand for 10 minutes until the yeast bubbles up. Add the niter kibbeh, spices, salt and 4 cups (960 mL) of flour and combine these ingredients thoroughly.

After setting the sponge to rise, you can turn your attention to making the
Berber Sauce (see page 144).

When the sponge has risen, stir it down, then stir in the remaining 4 cups
(960 mL) flour. Turn the dough out on to a floured board and knead for
10 - 15 minutes, until it is smooth and elastic.

Make two 1 inch (2.5 cm) diameter balls of dough, then form the rest into
two round loaves and place them on oiled cookie sheets.

Using a sharp knife, make two shallow slices through each loaf as if
dividing them into quarters.

Make short, shallow cuts across each axis line to make a pattern
resembling railway tracks on a map:

Now make 8 to 12 shallow cuts on each loaf in a sunburst pattern.

Finally, place one of the little balls of dough on the centre of each loaf.

Allow to rise in a warm place until doubled in bulk (about 1 hour), then
bake at 350°F (180°C) for 50 - 55 minutes.

Brush with Berber Sauce while the loaf is still hot, then leave to cool.

Among the Wodaabe people of the southern Sahara,
the tradition is to share three glasses of tea:
the first "strong like life";
the second "sweet like love";
the third "subtle like friendship."[1]

Quickbreads & Muffins

When time is too short for the pleasures of freshly-baked yeast bread, or when you feel like a change from the usual, there is at least the happy alternative of quickbreads and muffins. Whether fruity, nutty, seedy or even corny, they all have something a little tempting to offer to the taste, along with their ease of preparation.

Since these eggless recipes rely on the action of baking powder, baking soda and vinegar for their rise, we feel it is important to note that over-mixing will turn your quickbread into wallpaper paste. Please don't overmix!

Some quickbreads may be made by using two or three times the usual quantity of yeast, to give a very quick leavening. Most quickbreads, however, derive their rise and consistency from baking powder, baking soda or a combination of the two. Both of these ingredients contain large amounts of sodium, which can destroy the body's store of thiamine (vitamin B1); clearly this would also be a matter of concern to those for whom a low-sodium diet is recommended. Baking powder also contains aluminum salts that many people choose to avoid for the sake of their health.

For these reasons, you may wish to substitute a potassium bicarbonate baking powder for the regular leavening agents — you will most likely find one at the health food store, and in some supermarkets.

Alternatively, you can make up your own as follows: mix together well two parts each of cream of tartar and arrowroot powder, and one part of potassium bicarbonate. (Most pharmacies will either have the latter in stock, or be able to order it for you quite easily.) Store the powder in an airtight jar, and use in the same quantities as normal baking powder or soda, usually about one teaspoon per cup of flour. Since this baking powder is, to some tastes, a little more bitter than the usual, you may find it works best in the sweeter and more flavour-filled quickbreads.

anana Bread

Believe it or not, this recipe presented us with one of our toughest challenges: how to achieve an eggless banana bread that doesn't come out of the oven looking like a soggy mass? Well, after repeated trials we can say, this is how you do it.

Makes one dozen muffins or one loaf.

1 cup	(240 mL)	chopped dates
½ cup	(120 mL)	boiling water
⅓ cup	(80 mL)	oil
1 cup	(240 mL)	mashed banana
2 tsp	(10 mL)	vinegar
½ cup	(120 mL)	honey
1 tsp	(5 mL)	grated orange rind
2 cups	(480 mL)	whole-wheat pastry flour
1 tsp	(5 mL)	baking soda
1 tsp	(5 mL)	baking powder
½ tsp	(2 mL)	sea salt
½ cup	(120 mL)	chopped nuts

Soak the dates in the boiling water for 10 minutes, then purée them.

Combine the oil, mashed bananas, vinegar, honey and orange rind with the date purée.

Sift the dry ingredients into a separate bowl and add the nuts.

Make a well in the centre of the flour mixture, and pour in the liquids.

Stir just enough to blend — the batter should still be lumpy.

Fill the muffin cups two-thirds full, then bake them at 350°F (180°C) for 30 minutes.

If you are making the recipe as a loaf, then fill a regular size, oiled and floured loaf pan, and bake at 350°F (180°C) for one hour.

"ALL SORROWS ARE LESS WITHOUT BREAD."
SPANISH PROVERB

Blueberry Muffins

Although we have specified blueberries, you can have fun integrating some different kinds of berries into this recipe: blackberries, raspberries, salal berries — but, please, not gooseberries. Since this recipe relies on the berries for sweetness, you may wish to add more of them if you have a sweet tooth — perhaps an extra half cup.

Makes one dozen muffins.

1³/₄ **cups**	(420 mL)	**whole-wheat pastry flour***
¹/₂ **tsp**	(2 mL)	**salt**
1 **tsp**	(5 mL)	**baking powder**
1 **tsp**	(5 mL)	**baking soda**
¹/₄ **cup**	(60 mL)	**butter**
¹/₂ **cup**	(120 mL)	**honey**
1 **Tbsp**	(15 mL)	**vinegar**
³/₄ **cup**	(180 mL)	**milk**
1 **cup**	(240 mL)	**blueberries**

*Half whole-wheat flour & half unbleached white flour works, too.

Carefully sift the dry ingredients.

Melt the butter and honey in a small pan, and allow to cool a little.

Add the vinegar and milk to the honey mixture and stir them together until homogenous.

Combine the liquid ingredients into the dry ones and mix until just well blended. It is important not to overmix.

If you are using canned or frozen berries, dredge them in 2 Tbsp (30 mL) flour — this will help to keep them afloat in the batter. Don't bother to thaw frozen berries — they'll be too soggy.

Now lightly stir in the berries.

Fill a well-oiled muffin tin two-thirds full of batter, and bake at 400°F (205°C) for 20 minutes or until an inserted toothpick comes out clean.

One tsp (5 mL) or more grated lemon or lime rind added to the dry ingredients turns on the tastebuds just a little more!

Basic Bran Muffins

This is, as it says, a basic bran muffin recipe, so you can play with it at will. You might, for instance, try a little orange rind, chopped nuts, or use half honey, half molasses for sweetener.

As another option, whip up a batch of "Bran Muffins for the Sluggish." Cut out the wheat germ, substitute molasses for honey, and add an extra half cup of bran.

Makes one dozen muffins.

1 cup	(240 mL)	bran
½ cup	(120 mL)	wheat germ
1½ cups	(360 mL)	whole-wheat pastry flour
1 tsp	(5 mL)	baking soda
1 tsp	(5 mL)	baking powder
1 tsp	(5 mL)	salt (optional)
1 cup	(240 mL)	warm water
½ cup	(120 mL)	honey
1 Tbsp	(15 mL)	vinegar
5 Tbsp	(75 mL)	oil
½ cup	(120 mL)	chopped dates
½ cup	(120 mL)	raisins

Combine all the dry ingredients, making sure the soda is well mixed in.
Now mix all the liquid ingredients together until the honey is dissolved.
Toss the dates and raisins into the dry mix.
Combine the liquid and dry ingredients until they are just mixed.
Drop spoonfuls of the batter into a greased 12-hole muffin tin.
Bake at 350°F (180°C) for 22 minutes precisely.

"OH, DO YOU KNOW THE MUFFIN MAN, THAT LIVES IN DRURY LANE?"
ANON.

Coconut Orange Muffins

Makes one dozen fruity muffins.

2 cups	(480 mL)	**whole-wheat pastry flour**
1 tsp	(5 mL)	**baking powder**
1 tsp	(5 mL)	**baking soda**
1 tsp	(5 mL)	**sea salt**
1½ cups	(360 mL)	**unsweetened grated coconut**
		grated rind of one orange
½ cup	(120 mL)	**honey**
		juice of one orange plus enough
		hot water to make 1 cup (240 mL)
1 Tbsp	(15 mL)	**vinegar**
5 Tbsp	(75 mL)	**oil**
		toasted coconut for topping
		(optional)

Sift together the dry ingredients. (Baking soda has a bitter taste if you bite
   into a lump of it in a muffin! Make sure you sift thoroughly.)
Stir in the coconut and orange rind.
If it's hard, melt the honey in the hot water and orange juice mixture.
   Otherwise just mix all those ingredients together.
Add the vinegar and oil to the liquid ingredients.
Combine the wet ingredients with the dry ingredients, until just mixed.
Pour the batter into greased and floured muffin tins.
Sprinkle the toasted coconut over the top if desired.
Bake for 20 - 25 minutes at 350°F (180°C).

Sky Valley Cornbread

Many of our friends around here have a favourite cornbread recipe. This one, a savoury, cheesy version rounded out by the sweetness of corn kernels, first emerged from a wood cookstove high on Sky Valley Ridge, overlooking the peaceful countryside around the Salt Spring Centre.

1 cup	(240 mL)	**stone-ground corn meal**
½ cup	(120 mL)	**whole-wheat flour**
2 tsp	(10 mL)	**baking powder**
½ tsp	(2 mL)	**sea salt**
1 cup	(240 mL)	**grated sharp cheese**
1 cup	(240 mL)	**fresh or frozen corn kernels**
1 Tbsp	(15 mL)	**egg-replacer plus**
¼ cup	(60 mL)	**water** (or see package instructions for equivalent of 2 eggs)
1 cup	(240 mL)	**milk**
2 tsp	(10 mL)	**molasses or honey**
¼ cup	(60 mL)	**oil**

Sift together all the dry ingredients but the corn, then mix in the cheese.

If you are using frozen corn, pour boiling water over it to cover, and let stand for a few minutes. Drain the corn and combine with the liquid ingredients, then combine them into the dry ingredients.

Pour the mixture into a hot, oiled 8"x 8" (2 L) pan, and bake at 375°F (190°C) for about 40 - 45 minutes, until the cornbread is browned and crispy on top. A toothpick inserted under the crust will come out clean when the cornbread is adequately cooked.

Enjoy hot, cold or in-between.

"ALL RISING TO GREAT PLACE IS BY A WINDING STAIR."
FRANCIS BACON: *OF GREAT PLACE*
1561-1626

Julie's Date Loaf

A delicious and magical loaf, guaranteed to disappear within moments of being presented to your audience.

1 cup	(240 mL)	boiling water
1 cup	(240 mL)	chopped dates
1 tsp	(5 mL)	vanilla
1 tsp	(5 mL)	baking soda
2 Tbsp	(30 mL)	melted butter
1 cup	(240 mL)	brown sugar
1½ cups	(360 mL)	whole-wheat pastry flour
1 tsp	(5 mL)	baking powder
		pinch of salt

Pour boiling water over the dates, vanilla and baking soda and let this stand for a few minutes.

In another bowl, cream together the butter and sugar.

Mix all the dry ingredients in yet another bowl.

Add the dry ingredients to the sugar and butter alternately with the date mixture. Stir just enough to moisten the dry ingredients.

Pour into an oiled and floured regular-sized loaf tin.

Bake at 350°F (180°C) for 45 - 50 minutes.

....and a variation of the recipe that gives you enough delicious date/nut squares for a (small) sweet-toothed army.

Substitute ³/₄ cup (180 mL) **finely ground walnuts** for the wheat flour.

Use **2 cups** (480 mL) **chopped dates.** Grind 1 cup (240 mL) of the dates before soaking them. Reduce the sugar to ¹/₂ cup (120 mL).

Instead of a loaf tin, use a greased and floured 8"x 8" (2 L) baking pan, and bake the squares at 350°F (180°C) for about 40 - 50 minutes. The top will be fairly firm when done, and the inside still quite soft and moist.

Cool and cut into squares, before removing from the pan.

Various garnishes and toppings are options to be used on these squares,
either after baking (thin, thin slices of a whole peeled orange or thinly sliced
candied fruits, such as pineapple, papaya, ginger etc);
or ones that are sprinkled over the mixture partway through baking
(such as flour, cinnamon, brown sugar and butter,
as for an apple crumble topping,
pressed gently into the date mixture).

Lemon Muffins

Makes a dozen very lemony muffins.

2¹/₂ cups	(600 mL)	**whole-wheat pastry flour***
1 tsp	(5 mL)	**baking powder**
1 tsp	(5 mL)	**baking soda**
3 Tbsp	(45 mL)	**lemon rind (almost 3 lemons)**
1 cup	(240 mL)	**currants**
¹/₄ cup	(60 mL)	**honey**
1 cup	(240 mL)	**hot water**
¹/₄ cup	(60 mL)	**lemon juice** (about 1 large lemon)
¹/₄ cup	(60 mL)	**oil**
1 Tbsp	(15 mL)	**vinegar**

*Half whole-wheat flour & half unbleached white works well, too.

Oil a 12-hole muffin pan.

Sift all the dry ingredients together.

Toss in the currants, and mix until they are well covered with the flour mixture.

Now mix the honey and hot water, stirring until the honey is dissolved.

Add the remaining liquid ingredients to the honey mixture.

Blend the wet and dry ingredients, stirring just until the dry ingredients are moistened.

Fill each muffin cup nearly full.

Bake at 350°F (180°C) for 20 - 25 minutes.

"TELL ME WHAT YOU EAT, AND I WILL TELL YOU WHAT YOU ARE."
ANTHELME BRILLAT-SAVARIN: *PHYSIOLIE DU GOÛT*
(1755-1826)

Poppyseed Muffins

Makes 12 chewy muffins with a Jackson Pollock look.

¹/₂ cup	(120 mL)	raisins
¹/₄ cup	(60 mL)	boiling water
2¹/₂ cups	(600 mL)	whole-wheat flour
		(or unbleached white flour)
1 tsp	(5 mL)	baking soda
¹/₂ tsp	(2 mL)	sea salt
¹/₄ tsp	(1 mL)	nutmeg
3 Tbsp	(45 mL)	oil
2 tsp	(10 mL)	vinegar
¹/₂ cup	(120 mL)	honey
³/₄ cup	(180 mL)	milk
		juice of 1 lemon
2 Tbsp	(30 mL)	poppyseeds
2 tsp	(10 mL)	grated lemon peel

Oil a 12-hole muffin pan.

Soak the raisins in the boiling water for 5 minutes, then purée.

Sift together the dry ingredients.

Beat together the wet ingredients.

Add the wet mixture to the dry mixture, along with the raisin mixture,
poppyseeds and peel.

Stir just enough to coarsely mingle.

Spoon the mixture into the muffin cups, and bake at 350°F (180°C)
for 20 - 25 minutes. The muffins should be sunny yellow on the top and
tawny brown on the bottom, to be fully done.

If you are allergic to citrus, eliminate the lemon peel and juice;
the results will be almost as good.

"UNITED METROPOLITAN IMPROVED HOT MUFFIN &
CRUMPET BAKING & PUNCTUAL DELIVERY COMPANY, LIMITED."
NICHOLAS NICKLEBY, CH. II
CHARLES DICKENS (1812 - 70)

Scarborough  *Fair*

Biscuits

A quick, if not musical, savoury dinner biscuit to accompany soups and salads.

Makes about 12 or so 2" (5 cm) square biscuits.

1 cup	(240 mL)	**unbleached white flour**
1 cup	(240 mL)	**whole-wheat flour**
½ tsp	(2 mL)	**sea salt**
1½ tsp	(7 mL)	**baking powder**
¼ tsp	(1 mL)	**dried sage** OR
		1 tsp (5 mL) minced fresh sage
½ tsp	(2 mL)	**dried parsley** OR
		1½ Tbsp (22 mL) minced parsley
1 tsp	(5 mL)	**dried, crumbled rosemary**
¼ tsp	(1 mL)	**dried thyme** OR
		1½ tsp (7 mL) fresh minced thyme
⅓ cup	(80 mL)	**oil or butter**
½ cup plus	(135 mL)	**milk, millet milk or soymilk**

Sift together the flours, salt and baking powder.

Add the dried (or fresh) herbs, and mix well.

Incorporate the oil into the flour by rubbing the mixture between your fingers until the flour is in lumps no larger than small peas. If you are using butter, a pastry-cutter or two knives will work well to cut it into the flour.

Add the milk, stirring just enough to moisten everything.

Turn the dough onto a floured board, and roll it out about ½" (12 mm) thick.

Fold the dough in half and repeat the process of rolling and folding twice more. (This procedure will make a light, fluffy, appealing biscuit that pulls apart easily for buttering — though they are terrific even without butter.)

Cut into squares or rounds, brush with milk, and bake on an ungreased cookie sheet at 400°F (205°C) until they are lightly browned, about 12 - 15 minutes.

Seed Tea Cake

This is an unpretentious loaf to enjoy with a really good, hot cup of tea, preferably around 4 pm.

Makes one loaf.

1¼ cups	(300 mL)	raisins
⅓ cup	(80 mL)	boiling water
1½ cups	(360 mL)	unbleached white flour
½ cup	(120 mL)	whole-wheat pastry flour
1 tsp	(5 mL)	baking powder
1 tsp	(5 mL)	baking soda
½ tsp	(2 mL)	sea salt
½ cup	(120 mL)	chopped walnuts
¼ cup	(60 mL)	sesame seeds
¼ cup	(60 mL)	oil
1 Tbsp	(15 mL)	vinegar
1½ cups	(360 mL)	milk

Soak the raisins in the boiling water while you combine the dry ingredients.

Purée the raisins and liquids in a blender.

Stir the puréed liquid into the dry ingredients.

Pour the batter into a regular-sized oiled loaf pan.

Bake at 350°F (180°C) for 50 - 60 minutes.

Sesame Crackers

It's probably best for us to confess right from the outset that these excellent crackers actually began life as a piecrust that closely resembled plywood; only proving once again, that there are no failures in the kitchen, only opportunities for creative improvement.

¼ cup	(60 mL)	millet
¼ cup	(60 mL)	sesame seeds
⅓ cup	(80 mL)	cashews
1½ cups	(360 mL)	whole-wheat flour
1 tsp	(5 mL)	sea salt
½-¾ cup	(120-180 mL)	water

Grind the millet, 3 Tbsp (45 mL) sesame seeds and cashews until they
 resemble coarse meal. (You may prefer mincing the cashews and using
 the sesame seeds whole.)
Now add the meal mixture to the flour and salt.
Add enough water to make a stiff dough.
Roll out on a floured surface to about ⅛" (3 mm) thick.
Sprinkle the remaining 1 Tbsp (15 mL) sesame seeds over the dough, and
 roll over them once to set the seeds into the dough.
Cut the dough into squares, diamonds, rhomboids or whatever you like.
Bake the crackers on a lightly-oiled cookie sheet for 12 - 15 minutes
 at 375°F (190°C).

In India, sesame seeds are an integral part of many Hindu rituals and ceremonies.
At the sraddha ceremony held after the death of a family member, little round
honey-sesame cakes are offered to the spirits of the dead.
It is believed the dead relative may then by-pass as many hells as the number of
cakes that were offered. The little cakes also provide the elements of the new body
that the individual takes at rebirth.

Zucchini Bread

Non-dairy, sweetened only with raisins, and absolutely delicious!

Makes 2 loaves.

2 cups	(480 mL)	raisins
2 cups	(480 mL)	whole-wheat pastry flour
2½ tsp	(12 mL)	baking powder
2 tsp	(10 mL)	baking soda
1 Tbsp	(15 mL)	cinnamon
½ tsp	(2 mL)	sea salt
½ cup	(120 mL)	chopped walnuts
2 cups	(480 mL)	grated zucchini
1 cup	(240 mL)	oil
1 Tbsp	(15 mL)	vinegar
2 tsp	(10 mL)	vanilla
½ cup	(120 mL)	raisin water

Soak 1½ cups (480 mL) of the raisins for 30 minutes in enough boiling water to cover.

Pour off most, but not all of the water into a bowl and set aside. In a blender, grind the raisins with just enough of the liquid to keep them moving.

Mix all the dry ingredients in a large bowl, and add the remaining ½ cup (120 mL) raisins.

Add the grated zucchini and mix until the zucchini is well coated.

In another bowl, combine the wet ingredients, then add them to the dry mixture, stirring just enough to coat everything.

Pour into two oiled and floured regular-sized loaf pans and bake at 350°F (180°C) for 40 minutes.

"So munch on, crunch on, take your nuncheon,
Breakfast, supper, dinner, luncheon."

Robert Browning (1812-1889)

Kids' Food

We asked twenty-six kids around the Salt Spring Centre School and environs what they felt about being called kids, children, youngsters, young people and so on.

Their preference, twenty-four to two, was for "kids." Who are we to argue? Kids' Food became the name of the chapter.

We should make it clear right off, that it would not be a wise proposition to feed your kids *entirely* from the range of recipes that follow. It's not that they aren't good food, of course — we know some adults who aren't averse to Pita Pizza from time to time — but see that they get a taste for brown rice and steamed greens along with all the rest, won't you? If nothing else, you will be grateful for the ability that they *may* develop, to put some adult food on the table to feed you in your old age. Consider the alternative: are you really ready for a long retirement filled with Face Sandwiches and Carob Banana Popsicles?

A Healthy Banana Split!

Serve your little people this one as an unusual breakfast, and their expectations on awakening will never be the same again. Or when they walk in ravenous at the end of school.... as a surprise dessert when all their greens are cleaned away.... you can be sure that, after the first time, they will find some good reason why they deserve it. And, oh yes, it's a great way to make use of a little leftover grain.

For a single serving:

½ cup	(120 mL)	**cooked millet (or rice)**
1		**medium-sized banana**
½ cup	(120 mL)	**any fruit sauce**
		(maybe Blueberry Sauce page 209)
¼ cup	(60 mL)	**fresh fruit or berries**
¼ cup	(60 mL)	**Maple Cashew Cream** (page 207),
		OR **Carob Sauce** (page 210),
		OR **yoghurt**
1 Tbsp	(15 mL)	**chopped nuts**
2 Tbsp	(30 mL)	**grated coconut**

Using an ice cream scoop, dish up a couple of scoops of millet and arrange them in a cereal bowl or banana-split dish.

Split the banana in half lengthwise and lay the halves alongside the mounds of millet.

Pour your choice of fruit sauce over the bananas and millet.

Arrange the fresh fruit around the edge of the dish.

Drizzle the Maple Cashew Cream over the fruit.

Sprinkle the entire dish with the chopped nuts and coconut.

Serve this splendid confection with large spoons — and napkins for all.

This is a good build-it-yourself meal for children.
Serve up the millet and bananas yourself,
and set out the toppings so the kids can create
their own combinations.

"AND HE WHO GIVES A CHILD A TREAT
MAKES JOY-BELLS RING IN HEAVEN'S STREET."
JOHN MASEFIELD: *THE EVERLASTING MERCY*

Bliss Balls

Goodness Gracious! Great balls of..... Why not teach your kidlets the Jerry Lee Lewis original while you roll the Bliss Balls up together?

Makes about thirty 1" (2.5 cm) balls.

½ **cup**	(120 mL)	**almonds**
½ **cup**	(120 mL)	**granola**
½ **cup**	(120 mL)	**sunflower seeds**
1 **cup**	(240 mL)	**raisins**
1 **cup**	(240 mL)	**tahini**
½ **cup**	(120 mL)	**honey**
		grated coconut (to roll the balls in)

Grind the nuts, granola, sunflower seeds and raisins together in a grinder or blender.

Transfer to a bowl, add tahini and honey, and mix well with your hands.

Form the mixture into balls and roll them in coconut.

Chilling the balls for a short while will help to firm them up.

Lunch Box

Send them off tomorrow morning with this super sandwich substitute.
For each filled tortilla:

tortillas
grated cheese
grated carrots
chopped tomatoes
Guacamole (recipe page 163)
mild salsa sauce

Fold each tortilla around the cheese and carrots.

Put the tomatoes, guacamole and sauce into separate sealed containers for your child to add to the tortilla at lunchtime. Here's an opportunity to recycle those small snap-top yoghurt pots, and an empty 35mm film can will do just fine for the salsa!

This way the tortillas won't be mushy by lunch time.

Breakfast Pizza

An easy though unconventional breakfast.

Sourdough Muffins (page 228)
tomato sauce
avocado slices
tomato slices
green pepper slices
mushroom slices
shredded cheese

Split the muffin and spread each half with tomato sauce and toppings, with
the cheese going on the top.
Pop into a 400°F (205°C) oven for 10 minutes.

or alternatively.....

Split the muffin and toast the halves in a toaster.
Now spread them quickly with sauce, and add the cheese, with the
toppings going on last. The cheese will melt from the heat of the muffin.
Serve to the smallest member of the family first.

Carob Banana Pops

If your kids usually say YUCK to carob, then try out this recipe without letting them know. We think it might just change their minds.

4 Tbsp	(60 mL)	**carob powder**
³/₄ cup	(180 mL)	**water**
¹/₂ - ³/₄ cup	(120-180 mL)	**dates**
¹/₂ cup	(120 mL)	**tahini**
1 - 1¹/₂ tsp	(5-7 mL)	**vanilla**
		pinch of salt
6		**bananas**
		chopped or crushed peanuts
		grated coconut
		12 - 18 sticks*

Purée together the first six ingredients for the sauce, then heat them to
   boiling in a saucepan, then simmer for 5 minutes.
Chill.
Peel the bananas and cut them crosswise into two or three chunks. Insert
   one stick into each banana chunk.
Dip the banana pieces in the sauce, then roll the pieces in the chopped nuts
   and coconut to coat them.
Chill them for a while to use as a quick dessert, or freeze them for at least
   30 minutes to use as a frosty treat.

* Use popsicle sticks, chopsticks or even clean peeled twigs.

Celery Stuffers

Just a few variations on an eternal theme to help make those celery sticks disappear down tiny throats.

peanut butter and raisins
peanut butter and crushed pineapple
peanut butter and dates
mashed bananas and raisins
cream cheese and raisins
nut butters

Cut the celery into manageable 4" lengths.
Smooth the chosen filling into the groove and serve.

Let the kids invent their own wonderful combinations — set out a variety of toppings in separate dishes and they can serve themselves.

Face Sandwiches

These artistic concoctions are usually a big hit with kids. You can try all sorts of variations — below are just a few suggestions. Do let the kids make their own though, 'cuz they're willing to eat almost anything they prepare themselves!

rice cakes (just so long as they're round, OK?)

Spread **cream cheese, sunflower seed spread or mashed raw tofu** on the rice cake, then follow on with....

HAIR	**alfalfa sprouts or lettuce**
MOUTH	**tomato or red pepper**, cut to a mouth shape
NOSE	**chunk of carrot, celery or cheese**
EYES	**rounds or half rounds of olive, carrot or cucumber**
EYEBROWS	**slices of green pepper, celery or cheese**
EARS	**sections of celery stalk**

ranola Squares

Makes one 8"x 8" (2 L) panful.

½ cup	(120 mL)	**peanut butter**
½ cup	(120 mL)	**honey**
4 cups	(960 mL)	**granola**
½ cup	(120 mL)	**grated coconut**

Melt the peanut butter and honey together over low heat.

Mix the granola and coconut in a large bowl.

Pour the melted honey mixture over the granola and coconut and stir
    until well blended.

Press firmly into a greased 8"x 8" (2 L) baking pan.

Chill and cut into squares.

*If your peanut butter is rather dry or stiff, add ½ - 1 tsp (2 - 5 mL) oil to the
mixture to prevent it crumbling when cooled.*

Kids' Kebabs

SUPPER KEBABS

cheese	**cherry tomatoes**
avocado	**carrots**
potatoes	**yams**
broccoli florets	**cauliflower florets**
cucumber	

Cube the cheese into large-sized cubes.

Cube the vegetables likewise and steam or parboil them until they are tendercrisp and brightly coloured.

Peel and cube the avocado and cucumber. Remove the stems from the tomatoes.

You can assemble the vegetables on blunt skewers or chopsticks, or you can set the pieces out in muffin tins (to separate the types of vegetables) and have the kids assemble their own. More mess perhaps, but our research shows that kids are more likely to eat vegetables when they help to make them, and when they are fun to eat.

FRUIT KEBABS

pineapple chunks	**apples (fresh or dried)**
banana chunks	**pears (fresh or dried)**
strawberries	**cantaloupe balls or cubes**
melon balls or chunks	**peach cubes**
dried figs	**dried apricots**

Set out a selection of fresh and dried fruits for the kids to skewer their own snacks or desserts.

"....HE MAKES THE FIGS OUR MOUTHS TO MEET
AND THROWS THE MELONS AT OUR FEET."
ANDREW MARVELL: *BERMUDAS*
(1621-1678)

Fruit Leather

A great tasting, natural alternative to sugared treats.

Use any one or a combination of fruits.
The following have all worked well for us:

apples	**pears**
apricots	**peaches**
strawberries	**plums**
oranges	**pineapples**

You will need 6 large apples or pears to make enough to cover a cookie sheet.
Prepare your chosen fruit by washing, coring, removing stones or pith.
Cut your fruit into chunks, put them in a pot and add just enough water to
cover the bottom — about a quarter cup (60 mL) in a medium-sized pot.
Cover the pot and cook until tender, then mash.
Continue cooking over low heat in an open pot until all the liquid has cooked
away, leaving a thick purée.
Let the fruit cool slightly.
Line a baking sheet with plastic film or a cut-open plastic bag.
Spread the cooked fruit in a thin layer over the surface.
Place the sheet in a very warm spot, or in a 150°F (65°C) oven, and let it stand
overnight or until all of the moisture has evaporated, leaving a leather-like
base.
Cut the fruit with the plastic into squares, and roll or stack for storage.

"CHILDREN BEGIN BY LOVING THEIR PARENTS. AFTER A TIME, THEY JUDGE THEM.
RARELY, IF EVER, DO THEY FORGIVE THEM."
OSCAR WILDE (1854-1900)

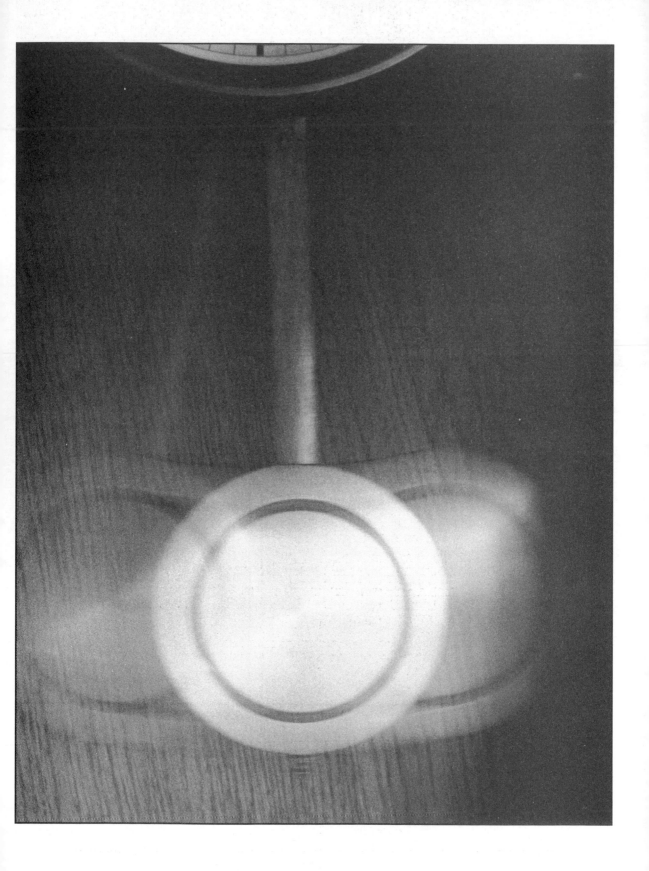

ast Food

While taking time for tasks and pleasures like cooking is a healthy and balanced way to live one's life, there are nevertheless occasions when the aim is simply to get some wholesome and nutritious food into yourself or your family quickly and without having to give it too much thought. The majority of us lead lives where we must constantly balance the demands of society, our work and our play, with the intention to feed ourselves in a way that will promote health, energy and clarity. Sometimes, circumstances demand fast food.

Many of the recipes in this book can be prepared within about half an hour from scratch, particularly once you are already familiar with the recipe. Below we have indicated some of them that you can refer to as examples, and on the next few pages are a selection of others.

A couple of tips that certainly help, when it comes to preparing a quick meal that will give the necessary carbohydrate, protein, vitamins and so on:— cooked beans, particularly, save time, as they can be incorporated into a dish in many appealing ways; cooked grains, and lentils too, are useful for making burgers and patties. Apart from their use in recipes requiring cooked grain though, try to avoid re-heating grains where possible, since they have so much more when freshly cooked. Rather, use fast-cooking grains like basmati rice, millet, quinoa, buckwheat, bulgur and cous-cous, all of which can be ready within half an hour. Most vegetables cook inside 30 minutes, so just minimize the time taken to prepare them, by scrubbing briefly instead of peeling. Stir-frying, then steaming till tendercrisp makes a good technique. Several recipes in the Savoury Sauces section make a tasty accompaniment to grains and vegetables prepared this way.

One of the most widely encountered misconceptions about vegetarian food seems to be that it *always* takes ages and ages to prepare. You may find though, as your interest grows in the variety and possibilities of food, that cooking becomes an art and a pleasure, such that spending several hours making your own bread, creating a supper dish you haven't tried before, or arranging the parts of an ambitious and fanciful dessert, is a delight rather than a chore. Cooking *anything*, be it a vegetarian dish or otherwise, will take time if that is how you approach it.

So now for some recipes that can be used when you have around half an hour to make a dish. Those marked with an asterisk are ones that require a pre-cooked ingredient, such as beans, kasha or panir.

continued overleaf....

more quick recipes...

Many of the dips and spreads, desserts, drinks, and other recipes can also be made very quickly of course, but this list will give you some suggestions to start with.

Pita Pizza

Even if they delivered wholefood pizzas through the telephone, you couldn't sink your teeth into the first bite any quicker than with this one.
Grateful compliments are due to the youngest chef on our staff.

Makes pizza for one, but you may want two, three....

1 pita bread		(sometimes sold as pocket bread)
2 Tbsp	(30 mL)	**tomato sauce**
⅓ cup plus	(100 mL)	**grated cheese**
2 Tbsp	(30 mL)	**grated parmesan cheese**

any or all of the following options:
> **dried or fresh herbs (oregano, garlic, basil, thyme, fennel etc)**
> **green and red pepper strips**
> **sliced olives**
> **sliced mushrooms**
> **sliced pineapple**
> **sliced tomatoes**

Spread the tomato sauce over the pita bread.
Sprinkle the grated cheese over the sauce.
Arrange the toppings over the pizza, beginning with the herbs.
Scatter the parmesan over the toppings, then broil under the grill for about 5 minutes, until the cheese is abubble.
Serve hot hot!

Cauliflower Cheese

Most members of the household over twelve years old can not only enjoy eating, but can also enjoy preparing this easy standby for lunch or dinner. If there is enough time to bake potatoes and prepare some salad as well, then you will have a really complete meal, but that takes a little longer than thirty minutes.

Serves 4.

		head of cauliflower
2 Tbsp	(30 mL)	**butter or oil**
¼ cup	(60 mL)	**whole-wheat flour**
1 - 1½ cups	(240 - 360 mL)	**milk, or milk and water**
1 tsp	(5 ml)	**tamari**
1 - 2 cups	(240 - 480 mL)	**grated cheese**
		black pepper
1 - 2 cups	(240 - 480 mL)	**cooked beans**
		(or medium can baked beans)
2 Tbsp	(30 mL)	**sesame seeds**

Divide the cauliflower into florets, cut the stalk and little leaves in pieces, and steam until tendercrisp; alternatively, simmer it in a little boiling water, and save the water.

THE SAUCE:

Stir together the butter or oil and the flour over low heat, to make a roux. Cook it briefly, stirring constantly, then combine into it, a little at a time, the milk, (or milk and water) then the tamari and the pepper, to form a smooth white sauce.
As it thickens, stir in half the amount of grated cheese you intend to use.

ASSEMBLY:

Put alternating layers of beans, then cauliflower pieces in an oven-proof bowl or baking-dish, pour the cheese sauce on to cover it all, and top with the remaining grated cheese and sesame seeds.
Broil it in the oven until the cheese is bubbly, and browned in places. Timing depends on the type of cheese chosen, so keep an eye on it.

My children like this dish very saucy, so I sometimes increase the sauce ingredients by half, particularly if the beans have less juice.

Speedy Burritos

A burro is a donkey, a burrito is an affectionate name for a little donkey, and Speedy I think we all understand. When the hordes descend on the kitchen and demand "What are we having for dinner?" just pat them on the head and reply very calmly, "I thought we might have small, fast donkeys that are friendly." It will probably keep them busy discussing your sanity until the first burrito comes out of the pan, and after that they will have their mouths full and you will be, so to speak, out of the woods.

The recipe makes a good way of getting real food into small people (and bigger people who are in a hurry), without having to resort to coercion.

Feeds a family of 4 (with large appetites).

THE BEANS:

4 cups	(960 mL)	**black turtle beans**
8 cups	(1.9 L)	**water**
1 Tbsp	(15 mL)	**ground cumin**
up to 3 tsp	(15 mL)	**chili powder**
		minced clove garlic (optional)
		tamari or salt, and pepper (to taste)

THE REST:

tortillas (prepared, or see page 89)
grated cheddar cheese
sour cream
salsa (prepared, or see page 152)
shredded lettuce, chopped tomato

Wash the beans, and pick them over to remove any tiny twigs or stones. Soak overnight in cold water. Place them in a pan with the spices and garlic, and cook until quite soft, about 1 hour.

Alternatively, if you have an electric crockpot, cook the beans while you are away, as follows: put in the soaked beans, the measured amount of water and spices, and turn to HIGH when you get up in the morning. Turn to LOW before you leave for the day. When you return in the evening, the beans should be cooked just right. Stir in the seasonings.

If your beans are pre-cooked but cold, heat them till just bubbling, and stir in the seasonings. The beans should neither be runny nor thick.

Place a tortilla in a heavy skillet over moderate heat, (no need to add oil) and scatter as much grated cheese as you wish (maybe 2 or 3 Tbsp - 45 mL) over the area between the centre and the top: see illustration.

As it starts to melt, put a small ladle-full of the beans over the cheese, then a blob of sour cream, a dab-to-a-spoonful of salsa, and the shredded salad ingredients. Fold the bottom of the tortilla up over the contents, fold each side over and slide the burrito onto a plate (see illustration).

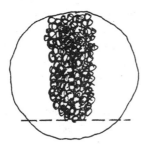 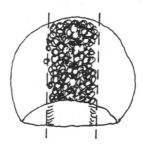 

The whole process takes about half as long to do, as it took to describe!
If you find the salad makes the burrito too fat to roll up successfully,
just serve it separately on the plate instead.

"THE ONLY THING THAT DISTINGUISHES MAN FROM THE ANIMALS IS
THAT HE EATS WHEN HE IS NOT HUNGRY, DRINKS WHEN HE IS NOT THIRSTY —
FREE WILL."
FLAUBERT

Sid Sandwiches

There is little basis in fact to the rumour that these sandwiches were originally designated Standard and Indispensable Dining. Though an excellent way to pass the day, and quite possibly a total diet by themselves, we would recommend following the example of the real-life Sid and serving them for breakfast, lunch and in-between times rather than reserving them just for dining. No-one knows better than Sid about rye toast, and what goes on it.

On a piece of thinly sliced, toasted rye bread, try any combination of the following:

> **mayonnaise**
> **hot mustard**
> **avocado**
> **cream cheese**
> **mashed raw tofu**
> **Scrambled Tofu** (recipe page 25)
> **tomato slices**
> **cucumber slices**
> **Mushroom Tomato Topping**
>   (recipe page 151)
> **grated feta cheese**
> **salt or Spike (or any vegetable**
>   **seasoning) and pepper**

Sid's recommendations: The hot mustard goes well with avocado and tofu variations; Mushroom Tomato Topping is great with cream cheese and/ or avocado.

*If your immediate reaction to the idea of eating raw tofu in a sandwich is a
downward curl of the corners of the mouth in disbelief, please
give it a chance to pleasantly surprise you — buttered toast, then
plenty of Dijon mustard, slices of raw tofu,
topped with mayonnaise and seasonings.*

Tofu Cutlets

This is a quick, nutritious, delicious snack whether eaten plain, with ketchup or other savoury sauce, or served as the protein complement to a meal of steamed vegetables, rice and salad.

1 lb	(454 g)	**tofu**
¼ cup	(60 mL)	**tamari**
¼ cup	(60 mL)	**engevita or torula yeast***
4-6 Tbsp	(60-90 mL)	**olive oil, vegetable oil or ghee**

*Optional: replace half the yeast with whole-wheat flour.

Slice the tofu into approximately ¼ inch (6 mm) slices (about 7 or 8 slices per block of tofu).

Pour the tamari onto a plate or pan, wide enough to accomodate the slices of tofu, and marinate them in the tamari for a few minutes. Make sure both sides are moistened with the tamari.

Put the yeast in a bowl and dip each slice of tofu into it, turning it to coat it well on both sides.

In a heavy skillet, fry the cutlets in oil or ghee over medium heat until the bottom is browned and a little crispy. Repeat the process for the other side.

Get the kids to help with this simple meal.
It's a good way to get them interested in tofu.
If the flavour is too strong for them,
cut the yeast with an equal amount of flour.

Drinks

It would be hard to start any discussion of drinks without at least a reference to the most essential drink of all, namely water. Indeed, it would be hard to start any **drink** without water — even milk, where of course the cows and the grass take care of delivering it to us without all the complicated intervention of taps, reservoirs and pumps.

Worth considering, though, is the fact that we cannot last more than a day or two without drink, while most of us could fast from food for a week at least, without ill effect. We could live a long and healthy life with no recourse to any other drink than water — perhaps it might even be a longer or healthier life. So with this in mind, it seems that drinks must actually be the opportunity we take to fly from necessity to indulgence. That must be O.K., I guess, since I don't actually *know* anyone who drinks only water.

We indulge ourselves and our taste for other tastes — sweet ones particularly; our taste for stimulants and mood elevators, whether tea, coffee or cola drinks; depressants — beer, wine and spirits; even our taste for unusual sensations in the mouth, as with fizzy drinks. Our taste for the bizarre is evident in the glasses of bright green fluid (it's not *really* anti-freeze is it?), with a tiny umbrella floating in it, so popular among the totally smart and sophisticated.

The drinks you will find in the following chapter, however, while unashamedly still indulging you in wild taste sensations and oral excitement (bring me chai!), at least can still demurely pose as respectable and sober concoctions that health-conscious folk could afford to be seen with. Almonds, bananas, carob, cashews, coconut, millet, pineapple, yoghurt....why, they almost sound like food, decent food, not decadent **drinks** at all.

Almond Milk

A delightful and refreshing alternative to moo-milk.

		30 almonds
		boiling water
1½ tsp	(7 mL)	ground cardamom
1½ tsp	(7 mL)	ground cinnamon
¼ tsp	(1 mL)	black pepper
1 Tbsp	(15 mL)	honey
3 cups	(720 mL)	boiling water

Cover the almonds with boiling water in a bowl, and let them sit overnight.
   Drain and peel the almonds, then grind them in your blender.
Add the spices and honey to the blender.
Pour one cup (240 mL) of boiling water over the contents of the blender.
Blend once again till smooth.
Add two cups (480 mL) of boiling water and blend again.
Strain any solids out of the almond milk, if you wish, or drink it thick!

VARIATION: Try replacing the water with soy milk or cow's milk, and leave
   out the black pepper.

We used almond milk as a dairy substitute in many of our recipes,
but most of what we made, we drank by the glassful.

Banana Carob Smoothie

Makes about 3 cups (720 mL) of a rich and delightful drink-dessert.

2 cups	(480 mL)	**soymilk (or milk)**
3		**bananas**
3 Tbsp	(45 mL)	**carob powder**
2 Tbsp	(30 mL)	**honey**
1 Tbsp	(15 mL)	**lecithin** (optional)

Blend all the ingredients and serve.

A fat pinch of ground cardamom, cloves or cinnamon all make tasty
   additions to this basic smoothie recipe.

Kids love this smoothie — and you can make popsicles with it too!

Cashew

Milk

Makes about 2 cups (480 mL) of nut-milk, creamy and rich.

½ **cup**	(120 mL)	**raw cashews**
½ **cup**	(120 mL)	**boiling water**
1 cup	(240 mL)	**cold water**

In the blender, grind the cashews, then slowly pour the boiling water
over them while you continue blending.
Add the cold water and blend it all until smooth.

Cashew milk can be used as a dairy substitute in gravies,
savoury and sweet sauces.

"WHAT SORRY MAN DRINKS FOR PLEASURE?
NIGHT AND DAY I RAISE OBLIVION'S GLASS.

LET ME BE CLEAR: HOWEVER THE WORLD'S GOBLET TURNS,
THOSE WHO KNOW ARE ALWAYS DRUNK ON THE WINE OF THE SELF."

GHALIB (1797-1869)

Chai

"Chai" in Hindi just means tea, though here we are referring to a sweet and aromatic spiced tea with milk. In India, there are many grades of chai, depending on the resources available. The best is "Bhatt Chai" or royal chai, made with pure cows' milk, best leaf tea, cardamom and sugar. The bottom end is "Chello Chai," sold cheaply to the poor in little tea stalls all over North India. It is made from tea dust with only a trace of milk, but lots of sugar.

Everyone has their own way of making chai, and some Babaji's and Mataji's produce such heavenly, bliss-bestowing brews that one comes to believe the most important ingredients to be invisible. This is one chai-drinker's method...
(Please brew with love and attention.)
Makes a spicy chai for 3.

		walnut-size piece fresh ginger
1 or 2 -		2" pieces cinnamon stick*
2 cups	(480 mL)	water
		little pinch black pepper
1/4 - 1/2 tsp	(1-2 mL)	ground cardamom*
1/8 - 1/4 tsp	(1/2-1 mL)	ground cloves*
1 Tbsp	(15 mL)	loose leaf black tea (not herb tea)
2 cups	(480 mL)	milk
2 Tbsp	(30 mL)	honey

*The larger amount gives an "espresso-strength" chai, rather than your everyday cuppa. If you are sensitive to spices, use the smaller amount.

Finely grate the ginger and crush the cinnamon sticks into small pieces.
Add them to the water in a pan, and bring to a boil. Turn the heat very low and simmer, do not boil, for 5 minutes.
Add the pepper, cardamom and cloves, and increase the heat to bring back to a boil.
Turn off the heat, add the tea, stir once and leave for about 3 minutes to brew.
Pour in the milk, and heat, but do not allow to boil.
Strain through a sieve, add the honey and serve hot in big mugs.
Try it a little more or less sweet, until it really hits the spot for you.

Hints: ground cinnamon, though quicker, makes chai rather gloopy.
A trace of cayenne adds zest, and a truly wonderful chai can be made using saffron. Enough spice should be used to create some heat and fragrance in the brew, so do experiment. Each spice subtly alters the overall experience, and after the first hundred cups or so, you will start to find some favourite personal combinations. Chai is great before, during and after meditation, yoga, chanting, work, play or anything else.

"I AM GLAD I WAS NOT BORN BEFORE TEA."
SYDNEY SMITH: *LADY HOLLAND'S MEMOIR, RECIPE FOR A SALAD.*

oconut Milk

A refreshing and rather unusual cold drink.

Makes about 1 ½ cups (360 mL).

> **1 cup** (240 mL) **grated coconut**
> **2 cups** (480 mL) **water**

Blend the coconut and water together at high speed until fairly smooth.
Strain twice through a sieve (or through a coarse sieve and then through a
  fine one).
Press the pulp gently with the back of a spoon to help extract most of the
  liquid during the first pass through the strainer.
Chill for an hour or so before serving.

> *The coconut milk you make can be enjoyed as it is, or used in*
> *a number of different recipes including CocoPine Juice,*
> *which you will find on the next page.*

"......FROM SILVER SPOUTS THE GRATEFUL LIQUORS GLIDE."
ALEXANDER POPE (1688-1744) *THE RAPE OF THE LOCK*

CocoPine Juice

A lively blend of the cream and the tang!

Makes 4 servings.

1¹/₂ cups	(360 mL)	**Coconut Milk** (opposite)
6		**rings of pineapple** OR
³/₄ cup	(180 mL)	**crushed pineapple**
1¹/₂ cups	(360 mL)	**pineapple juice**
1 Tbsp	(15 mL)	**honey**
³/₄ tsp	(4 mL)	**lemon juice**
2 tsp	(10 mL)	**agar flakes** (optional*)
²/₃ cup	(160 mL)	**water** (optional*)

Pour the coconut milk from the preceding recipe back into the blender and
   add the other ingredients.
Blend them all together until smooth, then chill.
Shake or stir the juice before serving.

** If you would prefer the juice creamier, boil the agar and water together
for 3 minutes and add it to the juice. It will thicken as it cools.
You may wish to adjust the proportions of lemon juice
and honey after this.*

"WORK IS THE CURSE OF THE DRINKING CLASSES."
OSCAR WILDE (1854-1900)

Inkocoa

*A great many different beverages are drunk at the Salt Spring Centre — each of us has a personal favourite, be it herb tea, black tea, fruit juice, coffee, milk, soy milk, almond milk, even **water**, would you believe? For many people here, the cup of choice, however, is Inka, a grain-and-root extract that certainly deserves a better name than coffee substitute.*

Inka lends itself well to additions that yield quite new tastes. When one of our Centre members gave up a long-standing black tea habit some time ago, he really missed a drink that had similar zip; from the ensuing experiments came Inkocoa.

Makes one cup (240 mL).

1 - 2 tsp	(5 - 10 mL)	**Inka or other coffee substitute**
½ - 1 tsp	(2 - 5 mL)	**cocoa**
1 cup	(240 mL)	**boiling water**
1 tsp	(5 mL)	**honey**, or to taste
		cream or milk to taste

For easy mixing, pour just a dash of boiling water onto the Inka and cocoa powder in a mug or cup, stir well, then fill 'er up.

Other variations that you may enjoy:

Omit the cocoa, and add either...

1 tsp	(5 mL)	**carob**
¼ - ½ tsp	(1 - 2 mL)	**ground ginger**
	OR	
¼ - ½ tsp	(1 - 2 mL)	**finely-ground cardamom**
	OR	
¼ - ¾ tsp	(1 - 4 mL)	**cinnamon**

Ginginka? Inkcardamom? Cinnamonka?
Well...... maybe it's best you find your own names for these.

Kalpana's **S**alt **S**pring Punch

A refreshing cooler for summer days, or maybe between dances at an energetic Winter Solstice celebration.

Makes about 11 cups.

8 cups	(1.9 L)	**boiling water**
	2	**peppermint teabags** OR
		2 tsp (10 mL) **loose peppermint tea**
	2	**hibiscus teabags** OR
		2 tsp (10 mL) **loose hibiscus tea**
1½ cups	(360 mL)	**pineapple juice**
1½ cups	(360 mL)	**apple juice**
		juice of one lemon
2 - 3 Tbsp	(15-30 mL)	**honey** (to taste)

Pour boiling water over the loose tea or teabags, and leave to steep for
   about 5 minutes.
If you are using loose herb teas, strain off the liquid; otherwise just remove
   the teabags.
Add the pineapple and apple juices.
Add the lemon juice, and stir in the honey.
Chill and serve.

*In Africa, the zing that comes from the dried petals of the hibiscus has made them
so popular for flavouring soft drinks, both home-made and commercial, that they
are now widely used throughout the entire continent.*

Lassi

A variation on the traditional Indian cold drink that you will find particularly refreshing when served after a good curry.

Makes 4 cups (960 mL).

1 cup	(240 mL)	**yoghurt**
3 cups	(720 mL)	**ice-cold water***
3 Tbsp	(45 mL)	**honey**
¼ - ½ tsp	(1-2 mL)	**cardamom, ground very fine**

Blend all the ingredients briefly in a blender, or with a hand whisk.
Serve immediately, or chill, covered, for an hour then stir and pour into
   glasses.

*If you are using a blender, you will find that a combination of 3 cups (720 mL) water and ice cubes is an easy way to make it really cold.

(We decided that any references to lassi being a heart-warming story of one boy and his yoghurt would only confuse things. It's OK on a slow morning in a communal kitchen, but the people who buy the book shouldn't have to put up with all these distractions when they're just trying to make a drink.)

Millet Milk

This milk is excellent for cooking, and for topping cereals or desserts.

Makes 6 cups (1.4 L).

1 cup	(240 mL)	**cooked millet** OR
		cooked brown rice
½ cup	(120 mL)	**cashews or peeled almonds**
4 cups	(960 mL)	**water**
¼ tsp	(1 mL)	**sea salt** (optional)
	2 - 6	**pitted dates**
		(optional, for sweetness)

Process the cooked millet, nuts, 2 cups (480 mL) water, salt and dates (if using) in a blender until smooth. This works best when the millet is still warm.

Pour the mixture into a 1½ quart (1.5 L) jug and stir in the remaining 2 cups (480 mL) water. If necessary, add more water to get the proper consistency.

Refrigerate, and stir before using.

"I WAS THIRSTY, AND YE GAVE ME DRINK...."
THE BIBLE: MATTHEW v 25

Sesame Milk

One of our oldest foods, sesame is rich in protein, fats, complex carbohydrates, minerals and other nutrients. Here's a way to enjoy all of that in a glass, too.

Makes about 5 cups (1.2 L).

½ cup	(120 mL)	**hulled sesame seed**
4 cups	(960 mL)	**water**
2 Tbsp	(30 mL)	**honey**
¼ tsp	(1 mL)	**salt**

Use whole, white sesame seeds for this recipe.
Place the seed in a blender and grind it to a fine meal.
Add the other ingredients and blend until smooth.
Strain the sesame milk through a sieve, and chill.

*If you are using the sesame milk in a recipe, rather than as a drink,
you may wish to increase the amount of sesame by a quarter or a half
to give a richer milk.*

"TEA! THOU SOFT, SOBER, SAGE AND VENERABLE LIQUID;
THOU HEART-OPENING, WINK-TIPPLING CORDIAL,
TO WHOSE GLORIOUS INSIPIDITY I OWE THE
HAPPIEST MOMENTS OF MY LIFE,
LET ME FALL PROSTRATE."

COLLEY CIBBER (1671-1757)

Soymilk

Soymilk is becoming more widely available these days, in healthfood stores, delicatessens and even regular grocery stores. Increasing numbers of people find it a good alternative to cows' milk, and a solution to the health problems that sometimes afflict us when foods produce excessive mucus in the body. Here's how to make soymilk in your kitchen.

3 cups (720 mL) **soybeans**
20 cups (4.8 L) **boiling water**

Soak the soybeans in lots of cold water in a cool place, preferably overnight. The minimum soaking-time should be 4 hours, but 8 - 10 hours is better. Soybeans will turn sour quite quickly in warm temperatures, so don't leave them for too long.

After soaking, drain the beans and rinse them in warm water.

Pre-heat the blender with a couple of cups of boiling water. (If your blender-jug is glass, add the water slowly and swirl it around, to avoid cracks.)

Now coarsely blend the beans, one cup (240 mL) at a time to two cups (480 mL) of boiling water.

Pour the mixture into a large pan and simmer over low heat for 20 minutes. Watch it while it cooks to make sure that it neither foams over nor burns on the bottom, which it does rather easily.

Strain the mixture through a tea-towel laid over a colander atop a large bowl or pan. Gather the edges of the tea-towel together to make a bag, and twist to squeeze out the milk. Use a wooden spatula to squeeze out more milk from the remaining solids.

Sweeten the soymilk with a little honey or rice-syrup, and add salt to taste.

It is important to store soymilk in the refrigerator soon after it has been strained, since it will sour quite easily.

The pulp that remains is called okara and can be used to make Okara Loaf (see page 55), or it may be added to cookies, muffins, soups and stews. To use the okara, steam it for an hour and a half, and continue with the recipe.

Appendix A:
Imperial/ Metric Conversion

Because very few imperial measures convert accurately to whole numbers in metric measure, a certain degree of rounding-up or rounding-down to the nearest whole number is inevitable, in converting from one system to the other.

We had all gone to great pains to bring you recipes that were as fine-tuned as possible, testing and re-testing them until we were satisfied, so we could not in good conscience then use a system of conversion from the imperial amounts into metric that involved wide disparities between one conversion and another. The food industry, for instance, is usually content to replace 2 Tbsp with 25 mL, but then switches to 50 mL as a replacement for 3 Tbsp. The error in proportions that this kind of inconsistency introduces, was liable to lead to some less-than-successful recipe results, we discovered.

For this reason, we settled on a set of conversions that remain as close as can be managed to accuracy, while still making it possible to cook your recipe with the kind of success you deserve. It also ensures that if you should need to size a recipe up, or down, for a party perhaps, or because you are eating alone this evening, then the results will still conform pretty closely to what we tasted in the kitchen at the Centre, when our final test was approved. A little more or less of certain ingredients can make a drastic difference to some dishes, and we wanted you to have the best possible opportunity of coming out a winner first time.

Naturally, you will find that some recipes receive your own modifications to quantities, cooking times and so on, once you have seen how the basic recipe turns out from the amounts that we specify. Using your sensitivity and skill to suit a recipe to the tastes and preferences of those who will actually eat it, is just part of the joy of cooking.

VOLUME		TEMPERATURE	
¼ tsp	1 mL	250°F	120°C
½ tsp	2 mL	300°F	150°C
1 tsp	5 mL	325°F	165°C
1 Tbsp	15 mL	350°F	180°C
2 Tbsp	30 mL	375°F	190°C
3 Tbsp	45 mL	400°F	205°C
¼ cup	60 mL	425°F	220°C
½ cup	120 mL	450°F	235°C
¾ cup	180 mL		
1 cup	240 mL		
2 cups	480 mL		
3 cups	720 mL		
4 cups	960 mL		
5 cups	1.2 L		
6 cups	1.4 L		
7 cups	1.6 L		
8 cups	1.9 L		

Food Allergies

Over the past few years, an increasing number of friends and visitors to the Salt Spring Centre have told us about their physical reactions to a variety of different foods. The accompanying symptoms are mostly just a nuisance, but occasionally become distressing or even overwhelming. By and large, these conditions are referred to as "food allergies," by those who suffer from them.

A true food allergy, however, differs from the more common food sensitivity in two important regards. The first lies in the fact that a food sensitivity is reversible, while an allergy is not — a piece of information that will either cheer or depress you, depending on what you think you've got.

The other difference is found in the severity and nature of the body's reaction to a particular food. In a clinical sense, a true food allergy produces a reaction that provokes various responses, including skin rashes and life-threatening anaphylactic shock. Food sensitivity, on the other hand, is a reaction to a particular substance that is experienced as digestive discomfort, sore joints, sinus discharge, depression, fatigue, and a wide variety of systemic reactions.

The cause of many of these problems can be found in the health and efficiency of the digestive system: "Food sensitivity means weak digestion," in the words of one naturopath we interviewed. Over the years, this causes chronic disease.

When one's ability to digest foods properly is impaired by reduced secretion of the necessary enzymes, several results occur.

There is incomplete breakdown of the proteins in the food, the carbohydrates ferment in the digestive tract, and fats are not absorbed into the system. If this situation is allowed to persist over a long period of time, and the gastrointestinal tract is exposed to an "altered" environment because of it, then allergy reactions and symptoms will manifest themselves in the body.

It is important to understand that this is just a *symptom* of the body's condition, rather than a disease.

Food, therefore, is medicine.

To cure the condition, it is necessary first to find the cause and remove it. Chew your food slowly and thoroughly — chew each mouthful thirty times and live a hundred years, as the saying goes.

Other ways to support digestion include herbs and enzyme supplements, advice on which you will be able to find from qualified practitioners, and from the extensive literature that is available on the subject. (Papaya, for example, is an excellent source of digestive enzymes. A few fennel seeds after a meal is another aid to proper assimilation that you may find helpful, and tasty).

If you are experiencing reactions that seem to be food-related, try cutting out (for several days or weeks, depending on the severity of the reaction), the Big Seven known food allergens, as they are called by naturopaths, namely:

Wheat	Dairy foods
Chocolate	Soy foods
Oranges	Peanuts
Eggs	

If the symptoms of allergy or food sensitivity disappear after a short time, then you may wish to re-introduce to your diet the foods you have dropped, one at a time. Should symptoms then reappear, you have probably identified the culprit (or one of them).

Rotating grains is also advisable, so that you eat a variety of different cereals, one each day. Eat plenty of cooked or raw vegetables, particularly dark leafy greens.

If you experience problems related to dairy foods, try dropping milk, butter and cheese from your diet and using only yoghurt — because the fats and proteins are already partially broken down by the action of the bacteria, it is much easier for the body to assimilate. (This substitution works fine on granola, less well in a morning cup of tea, though.)

Eat small amounts of food more frequently, rather than a big meal once a day when you are already tired, and hurrying because of time and hunger. This will aid complete digestion.

Regular exercise should not be ignored — apart from all its other benefits, it has a wonderful toning effect on appetite, digestion and elimination. Bowel motility is essential.

Avoid sugar: a common allergen, it exhausts the pancreas, depresses the immune system, and encourages the pathogenic growth of normally innocuous micro-flora — candida, staphylococcus, streptococcus etc.

Teach your taste buds, instead, to enjoy the natural sweetness of fruit, dried fruit, even grains. As the craving dies out for that sharp-edged sweetness that is peculiar to sugar, so you will discover that sweetness itself is much more than the accustomed one-dimensional candy taste. Appreciation of subtle and complex flavours will blossom again on your palate.

Salt, too, if used to excess day after day, tends to cramp one's ability to experience the full flavour of food. Unless one finds health problems from their use, however, both salt and sugar in modest amounts have their place in cooking, and consequently in this book.

Warming spices, such as black pepper, cayenne, cinnamon, cloves, cumin and root ginger will be helpful in strengthening your digestion. Khichari, recipe on page 108, is a very suitable dish too, since it contains the ideal balance of protein, carbohydrate and spices.

Summing up, then, a diet to minimize problems with food allergy and sensitivity should emphasize these features:

> whole grains
> plenty of vegetables
> low in oil
> low in sugar
> moderate to low in protein.

If you really like and enjoy food, then do it justice, and be kind to yourself as well: regard mealtimes as an opportunity to slow down from life's otherwise hectic pace. If you eat alone, you can allow yourself a little more time; if you eat with a family, then understand that your children will adopt many of your own eating habits, and show them how to approach food in an appreciative and relaxed fashion. Encourage them to put their knife, fork or chopsticks down on the plate once in a while, and finish chewing a mouthful, rather than bolt-it-and-run. This more relaxed pace provides an opportunity to enjoy family mealtime conversation. For your kids, it can be an unpressured opening to share some of their daily experience and comment. For you, it can be a chance to welcome them step by step through the stages of their formative years, broadening their minds to the whole of human culture and understanding, that is their real heritage.

Perhaps you are feeling that this is going too far, making too much of a thing out of the ordinary, everyday lunch or dinner. Yet it is precisely because it is an everyday experience for every (fortunate) person on the planet, that it deserves this attention to what happens here. Subtract the hours you are working, sleeping or away, the hours they are schooling, sleeping or away, and you may discover that mealtimes *are* your life with your kids. Eight and a half thousand meals together, from cradle to adulthood, certainly deserve some thought about how they happen.

Food is so much more than protein, vitamins and so on — more than anywhere else, it is the part of our lives where we as humans have come together, over the course of thousands and thousands of years. Mealtimes are the meeting place of civilisation.

At the Salt Spring Centre, dinner each evening starts with "circle time": blowing the conch from the porch outside the kitchen door calls our guests and staff from the gardens, the lake or the offices. Sometimes we join hands in a circle for a moment of silence, then a food prayer, before filling our plates to eat. It has become, over the years together here, a little ritual that allows us all to pause from the sometimes hurried moments before dinner — preparing food on time for a large community can have some "hurried moments," believe me — and then focus ourselves on eating in a peaceful and convivial atmosphere. We certainly like it, and our guests seem to pick it up very quickly as a natural beginning to a meal.

You may or may not find that "saying grace" or "giving thanks" works with your family situation, or for you as an individual. Perhaps remembering to eat and savour your first mouthful of food in a quiet and focussed moment of awareness will feel more comfortable, as Aldous Huxley describes in his visionary novel "Island." For sure, finding some way of slowing your revs from frenzied to freewheeling before starting to eat will help your digestion, and thus your health.

ॐ अत्रं ब्रह्या रसो विष्णुः
भोक्ता देवो महश्वरः
एवं ञात्वा तु यो भुत्वे
अन्न दोषेर्ण लिप्यते

Om annam Brahma raso Vishnu
Bhokta devo Mahéshvarah
Evam jñatva tu yo bhunktve
Anna doshern lipyate - Om

"Food is Brahma, the creator.
Its juice is Vishnu, the preserver.
The one who eats the food is Shiva, the destroyer.
One who eats with this thought in mind will not be harmed by any
negativity involved in the food."

A free translation from the Sanskrit of the food prayer that
we use at the Centre

Bibliography

We have owned and borrowed, shared, studied and browsed our way through so many fine (and awful) cookbooks over the course of the years, that it is very hard now to single out just a few as "Suggested Reading." Let's just say that the following are some good friends, who seem to be walking a similar path. Our sincere thanks to cooks and authors everywhere.

Boxer, A., & Back, P. *The Herb Book*. London: Octopus Books, 1980.

Brown, Edward Espe. *Tassajara Cooking*. Boston and London: Shambhala Publications, 1986.

_____. *The Tassajara Bread Book*. Shambhala Publications, 1970.

Ford, M.W., Hillyard, S., & Koock, M.F. *The Deaf Smith Country Cookbook*. New York: Macmillan Publishing, 1973.

Hagler, Louise. *Tofu Cookery*. Summertown, Tennessee: The Book Publishing Co., 1982.

Hurd, Frank J. & Rosalie. *A Good Cook...Ten Talents*. Chisholm, Minnesota: Dr. & Mrs. Frank J. Hurd, 1968.

Jaffrey, Madhur. *World-of-the-East Vegetarian Cooking*. New York: Alfred A. Knopf, 1981.

Levitt, J., Smith, L. & Warren, C. *Kripalu Kitchen*. Summit Station, Penn.: Kripalu Publications, 1980.

McClure, J., & Layne, K. *Cooking for Consciousness*. Denver, Col.: Ananda Marga Publications, 1976.

Moosewood Collective. *New Recipes from Moosewood Restaurant*. Berkeley, Ca.: Ten Speed Press, 1987.

Roberts, L., Flinders., C., & Ruppenthal, B. *The New Laurel's Kitchen*. Berkeley, Ca.: Ten Speed Press, 1986.

Rombauer, I., & Rombauer Becker, M. *Joy of Cooking*. New York: Bobbs-Merrill Company, 1975.

Rosenthal, S., & Shinagel, F. *How Cooking Works*. New York: Macmillan Publishing, 1981.

Rupp, R. *Blue Corn and Square Tomatoes*. Pownal, Vermont: Stovey Communications, 1987.

Santa Maria, Jack. *Indian Vegetarian Cookery*. New York: Samuel Weiser, 1977.

Stuart, M., ed. *The Encyclopedia of Herbs and Herbalism*. London: Orbis Publishing, 1979.

Thomas, Anna. *Vegetarian Epicure*. New York: Vintage Books, 1972.

Uprisings Publishing Company. *Uprisings - The Whole Grain Bakers' Book*. Hendersonville, N.C.: The Mother Earth News, 1984.

Index

Footnotes

Chapter IX: Vegetables
1. Barth, John *The Sotweed Factor*. Garden City, N.Y.: Doubleday & Co. p. 734

Chapter XIV: Bread
1. Beckwith, Carol. "Niger's Wodaabe: People of the Taboo" *National Geographic Magazine* 164:4. National Geographic Society, Washington, D.C.